LIBRARY OF
MONEY AND BANKING HISTORY

THE INDEPENDENT TREASURY
OF THE UNITED STATES

Also by DAVID KINLEY

In REPRINTS OF ECONOMIC CLASSICS

THE USE OF CREDIT INSTRUMENTS IN
PAYMENTS IN THE UNITED STATES [1910]

NATIONAL MONETARY COMMISSION

THE
INDEPENDENT
TREASURY
OF THE UNITED STATES
AND ITS RELATIONS TO
THE BANKS OF THE COUNTRY

BY

DAVID KINLEY

[1910]

REPRINTS OF ECONOMIC CLASSICS

Augustus M. Kelley · Publishers
NEW YORK 1970

First Edition 1910

(Washington: Government Printing Office, 1910)

REPRINTED 1970 BY
AUGUSTUS M. KELLEY · PUBLISHERS
REPRINTS OF ECONOMIC CLASSICS
New York New York 10001

. . . .

I S B N 0 - 678 - 00545 - 1

L C N 74 - 81508

. . . .

PRINTED IN THE UNITED STATES OF AMERICA
by SENTRY PRESS, NEW YORK, N. Y. 10019

| 61ST CONGRESS | SENATE | DOCUMENT |
| 2d Session | | No. 587 |

NATIONAL MONETARY COMMISSION

The Independent Treasury of the United States and Its Relations to the Banks of the Country

BY

DAVID KINLEY, Ph. D., LL. D.

University of Illinois

Washington : Government Printing Office : 1910

NATIONAL MONETARY COMMISSION.

NELSON W. ALDRICH, Rhode Island, *Chairman.*

EDWARD B. VREELAND, New York, *Vice-Chairman.*

JULIUS C. BURROWS, Michigan.	JOHN W. WEEKS, Massachusetts.
EUGENE HALE, Maine.	ROBERT W. BONYNGE, Colorado.
PHILANDER C. KNOX, Pennsylvania.	SYLVESTER C. SMITH, California.
THEODORE E. BURTON, Ohio.	LEMUEL P. PADGETT, Tennessee.
HENRY M. TELLER, Colorado.	GEORGE F. BURGESS, Texas.
HERNANDO D. MONEY, Mississippi.	ARSÈNE P. PUJO, Louisiana.
JOSEPH W. BAILEY, Texas.	ARTHUR B. SHELTON, *Secretary.*

A. PIATT ANDREW, *Special Assistant to Commission.*

G.|t 2|04

NOTE.

This monograph is a revision and continuation of the work of the present writer, published by Crowell & Co., New York, in 1893, under the title "The Independent Treasury of the United States." The main purpose of the essay, when first written, was not so much to trace the history of the United States Treasury in great detail as to state its influence as a receiver and disburser of money upon the money market and business interests of the country. That purpose has been held in view in the revision, although a few details have been added to the historical part.

For kindly help in furnishing materials necessary for bringing the discussion down to date I am indebted to the First Assistant Secretary of the Treasury, the Treasurer of the United States, and the assistant treasurers in New York and Chicago.

DAVID KINLEY.

CONTENTS.

5

APPENDICES.

THE INDEPENDENT TREASURY OF THE UNITED STATES AND ITS RELATIONS TO THE BANKS OF THE COUNTRY.

CHAPTER I.—THE BANKS AND THE TREASURY TO 1833.

PROCEDURE PREVIOUS TO THE ESTABLISHMENT OF THE SECOND UNITED STATES BANK.

The policy of the Federal Government with reference to keeping public money and dealing with banks has not been consistent. It shows alternate attempts at the use of banks and independent management. Roughly speaking, our practice in this matter, since the adoption of the Constitution, may be divided into six periods. During the first two years—that is, until the establishment of the First United States Bank—the officers of the Government followed the practice pursued under the confederation, of utilizing the banks and also leaving public money in the hands of collectors until it was needed. From 1791 to 1811 the First United States Bank and its branches were the principal depositaries.[a] The third period, from 1811 to 1817, was the first era of the use of state banks as the term is commonly understood. From 1817 to 1833 the Second United States Bank was the principal agency of the Treasury. From 1833 to 1846 was the second era

---

[a] This word is spelled both depositories and depositaries. The latter is preferable, and is used in this monograph, except in quotations. Of late years the reports of the Treasury Department use it almost uniformly.

of the state banks as government depositaries and agents. There was, indeed, a year within this period, from June, 1840, to August, 1841, the period of the first establishment of the independent treasury, during which the Government was supposed to keep its own money. From 1846 to the present time the so-called independent treasury, or the subtreasury system, has been in operation.

Under the terms of the law establishing the independent treasury the Government was expected to keep its own money and to have no connection with the banking institutions of the country. But the sixty years during which the law has been in operation show the same attitude of inconsistency as to the use of banks found in the preceding sixty years. That is to say, there are times within this period when the treasury officers, interpreting the law strictly, have kept away from the supposed evil influence of the banks; while there are other times in which the opposite spirit has been shown, and the use of banks has been resorted to so far as the law would allow, if not, indeed, beyond what, in the opinion of many, was legally proper.

For example, from the time of its establishment down to the civil war the law was pretty strictly interpreted. The fiscal necessities of the Government in the civil war forced a closer connection between the banks and the Treasury, and the law establishing our present national banking system recognized the necessity of this by making these banks government depositaries of internal revenue. Since the civil war the pressure of business interests and the differing policies of successive Secretaries of the Treasury have given us varying periods of large and small use

of the banks by the Treasury, until of late our policy has
seemed to be to have a Treasury as little independent of
the banks as possible under the law.

The first attempts at independent holding and management of the public money were due to circumstances not
connected with either public or official hostility to banks.
This feeling came later. During the confederation, and
for a short time afterwards, circumstances did not make
a large use of banks by the Government necessary. The
attention of the people had been occupied with other matters. The West was very young, commercial development was not great, and it is was customary for other governments to handle their fiscal affairs through the banks.
Our officers, therefore, had followed the traditional methods, and no public opinion had been formulated to influence them on the matter.

But the feeling against banks, the popular distrust of the
"money power," showed itself early in our history, and
has continued with varying intensity until the present
time. There is in this country a widespread feeling of
dislike of banks of issue. Many people think that the
privilege of issue is a government function and yields such
large returns that private individuals and corporations
should not be permitted to enjoy it. Our agricultural
classes, especially, seem to think that our national banks
deprive the people at large of something that rightly
belongs to them. At various times farmers' alliances and
other agricultural associations have adopted resolutions
in favor of the abolition of national banks, or of depriving
them of the privilege of note issue. This feeling of prejudice is part and parcel of the general antipathy to monop-

oly and the fear that the interests of the people will be subjected to the control of wealth.

Previous to the adoption of the Constitution no place was provided by law for the keeping of public money. It was left in charge of a committee of Congress, and they used the Bank of North America at Philadelphia as a depositary and fiscal agent, sometimes left the money with the collectors and sometimes made use of the loan offices. The Treasury was established by act of Congress September 2, 1789. This act gave it a legal but not a physical existence. The law made it the duty of the Treasurer to receive, keep, and disburse the money of the United States. As a matter of fact, the collectors of customs, commissioners of revenue, and selected banks became the custodians of the government money. The collectors kept the money until they could deposit it in some bank designated by the Treasurer, or until it was drawn on or called for by the Treasury Department. At this time the banks used as depositaries were the Bank of North America, which had been in use from the time of the Confederation, and the banks of Massachusetts, New York, and Maryland. This practice was continued for the next two years, until, under the influence of Alexander Hamilton, a charter was granted to the First United States Bank.

It was in the third session of the First Congress that events began so to shape themselves as to point to a national bank as a part of our governmental machinery. In this session provision was made for the payment of the debts of the States which had been assumed by the General Government. The hostility of the antifederalists toward the adoption of the Constitution was turned largely against the assumption of these debts and, later, against the measures of the Government to provide for their payment. In his report on a national bank, Hamilton emphasized the utility of such an institution. He expressed the opinion that "a national bank is an institution of primary importance to prosperous administration of the finances, and would be of the greatest utility in the operations connected with the support of the public credit." Provisions for the establishment of the bank were finally approved substantially as proposed by Hamilton, and a charter was granted in 1791 to run for twenty years. Although the law did not so specify, Hamilton apparently thought its intent was that the bank should be used as a depositary of public money and as a fiscal agent of the Government. [a] Indeed, there was no legislation giving directions to the Treasurer concerning the keeping of public money before the time of the charter of the Second Bank of the United States. Undoubtedly it was one of his purposes, in seeking the establishment of the bank, to promote his own plans for strengthening the credit of the Federal Government. Moreover, as we know, Hamilton's ideas were colored largely by European experience and a central bank was in his mind a normal part of the fiscal machinery.

Accordingly, Hamilton used the United States Bank and its branches from the start. The branches were at Boston, New York, Washington, Newport, Charleston, Savannah, and New Orleans. He was not able to break away from the use of the state banks at once, and con-

---

[a] See his letter to an officer of the Bank of New York. Hamilton's Works [Ed. by Hamilton, J. C.], V: 486.

tinued to use them until 1794, gradually reducing the number. In 1794 only one state bank was in use.[a]

The United States Bank and its branches were utilized until the expiration of its charter in 1811. Hamilton was successful in eliminating the state banks as the principal custodians of the public money, and the people of the country seem to have acquiesced. This may mean that the people shared his views as to the desirability of utilizing the United States Bank; more likely, however, it means simply that there was no public interest in the matter. At any rate, there was no public agitation of the subject. "This method of keeping the public money evidently worked satisfactorily, since for a number of years no Member of Congress seems to have thought it necessary to inquire by resolution in regard to the safe-keeping of the public funds. In 1801 a committee of the House, appointed to examine the state of the Treasury, dismissed the whole subject of keeping the money in a single sentence, by saying: 'All moneys received by the Treasurer are deposited by him in the Bank of the United States and other banks.' It is evident from this that the system gave general satisfaction."[b]

Gradually, however, the use of the state banks again increased, very likely because the branches of the Bank of the United States were not sufficiently numerous or not located in all places where government collections and disbursements were necessary. Possibly the cause may have been the political character of the state banks; for

a American State Papers, Finance, I: 283.

b Phillips, J. B.: Methods of Keeping the Public Money of the United States, Publ. Mich. Pol. Sci. Assoc., IV: 3: 6.

we know that attempts were made to establish banks, not for legitimate banking, but for political influence. Even as late as 1859, the bank commissioners of Maine, in their annual report, say that the history of banking legislation in that State shows that charters were not always, if generally, granted on evidence of public need or the legitimate business wants of the place in which they were to be located.[a] Whatever the cause, the use of state banks gradually extended. In 1806 Gallatin reported that, besides the Bank of the United States and its branches, five state banks were used as depositaries.[b] In 1811 twenty-two such banks were used and, in 1816, ninety-four.[c] In 1809 Congress passed a law requiring disbursing officers of the Government to keep the public money in their charge in banks selected by the President.

There was no loss of public money through the use of state banks as depositaries during this period, but some embarrassment was caused by the use of state-bank notes. As is well known, these were not accepted at par in places remote from the bank of issue; and, indeed, were not accepted without discount among the banks themselves. The experience of the public at large in this respect seems not to have shown them the difficulties of an alliance with the banks, even though the latter discharged their services as mere depositaries without defalcation.

While things were running smoothly, during the period of active operation of the United States Bank, people

---

[a] See Report of the Bank Commissioners of the State of Maine, 1859. Also Sumner, W. G.. Andrew Jackson, 228; and Gallatin's Writings [Ed. by Henry Adams], I:129.

[b] American State Papers Finance, II.216.

[c] Ibid., II:517 and 131.

forgot, as they usually do, the real causes of the smooth working of the fiscal machinery. The notion that the Government can do things as well as private corporations, especially in banking matters, and the belief that many things should be done through direct Government agency, gradually created a prejudice against the use of the bank and its branches by the Government.

The question of rechartering the bank came up in Congress in 1810, and was supported by Secretary Gallatin. His reasons for supporting the proposal were that the bank had kept the public money safely, transferred it to the various centers of disbursement, and had been a successful fiscal agent of the Government in placing loans and in collecting the revenues. On account of the lateness of the session, no action was taken and application for a renewal of the charter was made again in the following year. But the state banks had become relatively numerous and powerful. The policy of giving bank charters to representatives of the dominant party in order to tie them to the administration, so eloquently urged by Jefferson, was too successful. They became masters of the situation, so that under pressure from them a renewal of the charter was refused, in spite of the fact that the bank "so far as we can judge from the information we have in regard to it, was soberly managed, successful, and beneficial in restraining the issues of smaller banks." [a] Undoubtedly it was this restraining influence that produced hostility sufficient to prevent the passage of the law.

The First United States Bank, therefore, rapidly wound up its affairs and the Government was confronted with

[a] Sumner, W. G.: History of American Currency, 63.

the necessity of finding other agents to do its fiscal business. For, as we have remarked, the United States Treasury, by the law creating it, had a legal, but no physical existence. Consequently it became necessary again to use state, or local, banks. This necessity came upon the Government at a time when smoothness in financial administration was to be of greater importance than at any previous time since the adoption of the Constitution. For the country was on the verge of war. The experience of the next four years taught the opponents of the United States Bank that, whatever demerits characterized the old system, the state banks with their political pull and selfish interests were by no means able to render the public service required.

From 1811 to 1817, then, the Government perforce used state banks as its depositaries and fiscal agents. There was a boom in the establishment of state banks immediately after the United States Bank wound up its affairs. No security was required by the Government for its deposits, but the banks submitted weekly and monthly statements of accounts to the Secretary of the Treasury. Under the agreement entered into between the banks and the Treasurer, the banks were required to receive to the credit of the Government such payments as individuals offered them for the Treasury. Drafts on the banks which did not have sufficient funds to make the necessary payments were met by a supply of bills on the principal cities. Banks were required to pay treasury, war, and navy warrants, or drafts by the United States Treasurer, and to make their payments in specie if so demanded by the holder.[a] The difficulties of administration, however, especially in transferring money, were very great. It sometimes took months for banks to get the money required by a draft from one city to another. Consequently it was necessary for the Government to give notice of its drafts for considerable periods in advance of making them.

As already remarked, a "bank boom" followed the dissolution of the United States Bank, which led to a large increase in the number of state banks.[b] From 1811 to 1814, 120 banks were established. These banks were established in places where they were not needed and every effort was made to circulate their notes at a sufficient distance from home to prevent their early return. The usual results followed. Specie disappeared from circulation, and suspensions became numerous, especially in the West and South. In the fall of 1814 all the banks south of New England suspended payments. Nearly 100 of these had been fiduciaries of the Government and carried down with them about $9,000,000 of government funds. In order to meet its expenses, the Treasury contracted loans which were placed at between 80 and 90 and paid for in bank notes depreciated from 10 to 20 per cent. The confidence of the people in this method of keeping of its money received a rude shock.

THE SECOND UNITED STATES BANK.

The lesson of the four years of the war period was heeded and when application was made for a charter for a second

---

[a] American State Papers, Finance, II: 520.
[b] Crawford in American State Papers, Finance, III: 494.

United States bank, the request met with but little opposition. Even Henry Clay, who in 1811 had opposed the bank, now supported the measure as necessary under existing conditions. Accordingly, on April 10, 1816, the bank act was passed.

The capital was $35,000,000, one-fifth of which was to be subscribed by the Government in coin or "stock;" one-fifth was to be in specie, and the other three-fifths in specie or government stock. The bank was to pay the Government a bonus of $1,500,000; it was to be the depositary of public moneys, and was required to disburse them, free of charge, in any part of the country. Five of the 25 directors were to be appointed by the President. The charter was, as before, for twenty years.

The bank was to begin business January 1, 1817. The conditions under which it started, however, were unfavorable. Specie payments were suspended, the country had just gone through a great commercial crisis, the state banks were hostile because they were to be deprived of the use of United States deposits, and the field of operation of the bank was as yet untried.

At the time of the opening of the Second United States Bank 89 state banks were used as depositaries, and the Treasurer had many bank notes on special deposit which were uncurrent and irredeemable.

The Secretary of the Treasury did not transfer the public deposits immediately from the state banks to the new bank of the United States. Indeed, Secretary Crawford had definitely promised not to withdraw any part of the public money before July 1, 1817, provided the banks would resume specie payments by the last week of the preceding February. Although the proposition was not accepted by the banks, the Secretary was not able to withdraw the deposits. Later, the banks agreed to resume payments toward the end of February on condition that the government deposits would not be transferred before July, and on condition also that the United States Bank would not draw on its balances in the state banks until it had discounts aggregating something like six millions in the principal cities of the country.[a] The favorable condition of foreign trade in the winter of 1816–17 helped the banks in their efforts to bring about resumption.

Instead of establishing independent offices of discount and deposit in different parts of the country, although under the charter they were authorized to do so if they saw fit, the officers of the bank, in conjunction with the Secretary of the Treasury, arranged a plan to conduct the treasury business through the bank, its branches, and state banks selected by the United States Bank for the purpose and approved by the Secretary. After the arrangements were perfected, the direct relationship of the Treasury with the state banks holding public deposits ceased, and the relationship continued only through the United States Bank.

Under the new arrangements, receipts for public money must show the source of the money, and weekly statements of each depositary bank must be made which would correspond strictly with these receipts. All receipts must give the amounts, which must be entered by the banks to the credit of the United States Bank for the use of the Treasurer, and all treasury drafts were to be

[a] American State Papers, Finance, III: 231.

drawn on the United States Bank. The treasury drafts, however, had to show the office of discount or deposit, or the state bank at which they were to be paid. Monthly reports were required from all depositaries.

It was obvious from this arrangement that, although the law establishing the United States Bank aimed to separate the Treasury from the state banks, it did not succeed. Treasury operations made depositaries necessary in all parts of the country, and as it was impossible to establish independent offices, state banks had to be used. During the first two years of its existence, the management of the bank was far from satisfactory. It aggravated the troubles of the financial situation instead of relieving them. Specie payments were nominally resumed in 1817, but the insidious canker of inflation had eaten its way into the arteries of business, and in the crisis of 1819 came another suspension, that lasted for two years. "In the first two years of its existence the great bank was carried to the verge of bankruptcy by as bad banking as was ever known. Instead of checking the other banks in their improper proceedings, it led and surpassed them all. A clique inside the bank was jobbing in its shares, and robbing it to provide the margins. Instead of rectifying the currency, it made the currency worse. Instead of helping the currency out of the distress produced by the war, it plunged the country into the commercial crisis of 1819, which caused a general liquidation, lasting four or five years. * * * It is almost incredible that the legislation of any civilized country could have opened the chance for such abuses of credit, banking, and currency as then existed."[a]   On April 1, 1819, just fifteen months after the bank began its career for the purpose of restoring financial health to the country, the history of its operations was told in the following statement of its condition:

Specie...	$26,745.28
Notes..	6,000,000.00
Due other banks......................................	79,125.99
Due Government.......................................	500,000.00
Due Barings..	900,000.00

The New York and Boston branches were in worse condition.   The Baltimore branch had given $3,000,000 discounts, of which the parent bank had no knowledge, apparently from corrupt motives, and $1,671,221 were lost there.   The total losses to date were $3,500,000. Dividends for $4,410,000 had been paid, of which $1,348,553 had been gained by interest on public securities.   Net loss over $500,000.   "The bank now took the most energetic measures to save itself, and in seventy days was once more solvent, but it had ruined the community.   The 'golden age' was now far in the past, and was seen to be only a gilt paper age after all.   The ruin was almost universal."[b]

After the recovery a period of several years of prosperity followed, and the management of the bank was thoroughly reorganized and sound.   From this time on until the great "bank war" its affairs seem to have been conducted with a view to performing its duty to the Government as well as to its individual stockholders, and it rendered such aid to the public, directly and in-

---

[a] Sumner, W. G.; Andrew Jackson, American Statesmen Series, 233.

[b] Sumner, W. G.: History of American Currency, 78.

directly, as entitled it to respect and fair treatment on the part of the servants of the people.

The events of what is known as the "bank war" are familiar to all students of American history, so that a detailed account of it is not necessary.[a] But it will be well for our present purpose, to recall its main features, because it was really the first step in the immediate sequence of events that led to the establishment of the independent treasury.

As already said, the ten years following the revulsion of 1819–1825 were years of almost unbroken prosperity. The bank management was sound, government credit was excellent, the public debt was rapidly reduced, and the industrial and commercial situation was healthy. Matters between the Treasury and the banks seem to have gone very smoothly. State banks in larger or smaller number were used throughout the period, as many as 15 being employed between 1830 and 1833. There had been some loss,[b] indeed, during the period of action of the United States Bank, but not through the transactions of that institution. The question of the continuance of the bank was not under discussion. In fact, scarcely any mention of the subject was made until President Jackson referred to it in his message of December, 1829. In this message he reopened the question of the

---

[a] For a general survey of the whole matter see von Holst, H.: Constitutional History of the United States, II; Schurz, Carl: Henry Clay (American Statesmen Series); Sumner, W. G.: Andrew Jackson (*Ibid*); Benton, Thos. H.: Thirty Years' View; Bolles, A. S.: Financial History of the United States; Young, A. W.: American Statesman; Story, J.. Commentaries on the Constitution, III: xxv; Lalor, J. J.: Cyclopedia of Political Science, bibliography and article on Bank Controversy.

[b] Executive Documents, No. 10, 26th Cong., 1st sess.

constitutionality of the bank, but the committee to which this portion of the message was referred in the House of Representatives made a report favorable to the institution.

Foiled in this line of attack, General Jackson turned his attention to securing evidences of mismanagement and illegal procedure, and it was on the basis of alleged unsoundness that he justified the removal of the deposits from the bank in 1833. Although his effort to prove mismanagement was a failure, yet certain occurrences lent color to his charges. The principal of these were the disagreement that arose between Secretary Ingham of the Treasury and Mr. Biddle, president of the bank, concerning the management of the branch bank at Portsmouth, N. H.; the delay of three months in paying $5,000,000 of 3 per cent government stock which fell due in July, 1832; the refusal to pay drafts on the branch banks except at the branches themselves; and the alleged interference of the bank in the presidential campaign of 1832.

Moreover, there were many points of bad management, but they were mistakes to be corrected, not to be made reasons for destruction. The usurpation of the important business of the bank by the exchange committee was wrong; the discretion allowed President Biddle in the struggle was too great; the policy of temporarily loaning the cash in the drawer on collateral securities, without interest, was exceedingly bad business policy. These and similar administrative mistakes were the first steps in the career of the bank that led to its downfall and ruin. It was guilty of great financial erorrs, but they were not beyond remedy, and that they formed a reasonable ground for such hostility as was displayed is untrue. Speaking merely from the point of view of sound bank management, in the list of charges made since Jackson first attacked the bank in 1829, "we can find nothing but frivolous complaints and ignorant criticism, successfully refuted except when we touch the branch drafts." [a] And it may fairly be questioned, even though we deny the legitimacy of the point, whether the President's hostility was not a powerful force in driving the institution into the road that led to ruin. It is not proven that the funds of the bank, acknowledged to have been used in legitimate methods of self-defense, were ever devoted to the uses of political partisanship. It is hardly correct to say that the bank made a panic in 1834, for the tangible grounds of a panic were absent; and the crisis that came, real and distressing as indeed it was, may be fairly attributed less to contraction by the bank than to the fears engendered as to the possible consequences of the enmity of the Executive.

In the struggle with the President, however, the bank forgot that it was more than a private institution; that one of the purposes of its existence was the service of the Government, and that in its capacity of fiscal agent it owed the country a duty and a service with which its private interests should not have been allowed to interfere. Yet even here, while it can not be justified, it might claim to be excused, on the ground that the Government itself, whose interests it had in charge, was seeking to cripple its power to conserve these interests.

---

[a] Sumner, W. G.: Andrew Jackson (American Statesmen Series), 267.

Through most of the years of its existence the bank gave the country a more uniform currency than existed at its creation; it facilitated the fiscal operations of the Government; it collected its revenues; it equalized exchanges; and it gave a healthy tone to the business of the country. But neither its principles nor its acts were perfect. It was not a panacea for industrial distress, nor a preventive of its occurrence. It may justly be charged with sins of commission and omission, and the path it finally trod, whatever the force that impelled it thereto, can but make us rejoice that its custody of the people's money ceased before it leaped over the precipice of ruin on which it for a long time stood, and over which it finally plunged. In its management there were forces at work that, if it had been let alone, would probably have finally brought its ruin. But they could have been checked if the Government had been friendly instead of hostile, and if the bank had kept its policy up to the high-water mark of business integrity. As it was, the course of the administration aided in hastening the end.

In 1835 the "bank war" may be said to have come to a close, so far as actual conflict was concerned, and the President had won. The remaining acts of the bank were only the making of arrangements for surrender. When the time came, however, for the charter to expire the bank did not give up its corporate existence. It obtained a charter from the State of Pennsylvania by means that would not bear a critical examination according to the standards of either business or political integrity. Instead of winding up its·affairs and paying the Government the money it owed, it transferred all its effects to the new corporation and continued business as before. It even put into circulation again the notes which it had issued as Bank of the United States.

It may be easily believed that an institution that could do such things had sunk far below the plane of strict business honor. In fact, the affairs of the bank were at this time very dishonestly managed. No means now seemed too corrupt for it to use in the accomplishment of its purposes, and if it had now been in control of the government resources there probably would be a sad story to tell of their loss. The inevitable end came in the crash of 1837. The bank at this time was engaged in operations for which it merits the severest condemnation, and against the results of which it was not able to sustain itself. It closed its doors in October, 1839, opened them for a short period afterwards, and finally suspended in February, 1841. It managed to pay its debts, but its whole capital was lost. President Biddle was sued for over $1,000,000 paid out during his administration, for which no vouchers could be found. He and several directors were indicted by the grand jury, but were discharged.

The removal of the deposits to state banks by President Jackson in 1833 was the voluntary use of a system which would necessarily have come into operation at the expiration of the bank charter. For a few years, as we have seen, the system was used without legislative sanction, and its compulsory employment, caused by the downfall of the United States Bank, was the next step toward the policy of an independent treasury. To trace the history of this step and its influence in the evolution of the sub-treasury will be our effort in the next chapter.

Chapter II.—The State Banks as Depositaries.

The Removal of the Public Deposits and the Specie Circular.

There appeared to be no reason for thinking that the local banks would be more faithful to their trust if given another trial than they had been before. In fact, if we may trust Benton, such was, perhaps, President Jackson's opinion; for Benton seems to intimate [a] that he regarded the plan of using the banks as depositaries as a temporary expedient, and looked to the ultimate separation of the Government from all banks. But if the President contemplated this separation, he must have seen that its accomplishment was impossible.

In September, 1833, Mr. Roger B. Taney, who had been appointed Secretary of the Treasury to carry out the President's policy with reference to the bank, ordered the collectors of revenue to cease depositing in the bank of the United States and to employ designated state banks for that purpose.[b] Secretary Taney's alleged reasons for this action were, briefly, that public opinion was against the bank; that it would be better to withdraw the deposits gradually than to do it suddenly when the bank charter expired; that the bank had brought about a bad condition of the market and oppressed the state banks by taking away their specie. Strictly speaking, the government

[a] Cf. Thirty Years' View, I: 553.
[b] Ex. Docs. 23d Cong., 1st sess., No. 2: 33.

deposits were not "removed" from the United States Bank. The Government simply ceased depositing its receipts there; and the withdrawal of what was already in the bank took place in the ordinary course of government business.

The use of the state banks as depositaries began again in October, 1833. There was no law regulating the use of these banks, and therefore the public moneys were for a time practically under the control of the President and the Secretary of the Treasury. It fell to them to select the banks to be intrusted with the public deposits and to name the conditions on which they should be received and kept. Contracts were made by the Secretary with selected banks, according to which the banks were to give security for the government money whenever the deposits should exceed one-half the bank capital paid in. In addition, the Government reserved the right to demand security whenever it was though advisable, even if the deposits did not exceed the sum mentioned. The banks further agreed to perform for the Government all the services formerly rendered by the bank of the United States, to render weekly reports, and to submit to examinations when the Secretary thought necessary.

The banks also undertook by mutual agreement to honor one another's notes and drafts, thus seeking to provide a "general currency at least as sound as that of the bank of the United States." They were forbidden to issue small notes and were required to keep one-third of their reserve in specie. The problem before the Government was to make regulations which should secure the safety of its deposits and to provide a circulation of state bank notes to replace the $35,000,000 [a] soon to be withdrawn by the national bank.

In his report, submitted in December, 1834, Secretary Taney urged on Congress the necessity for an act regulating the deposits, but nothing was done about the matter. A bill for the purpose did, indeed, pass the House, but met its death in the Senate on the report of the Finance Committee that it ought not to pass, mainly because its passage would indicate acquiescence on the part of the Senate in the course pursued by the Executive. The provisions of the bill were also regarded as inadequate for safety.

The use of the state banks selected by Secretary Taney continued, therefore, until the middle of 1836, when Congress passed an act embodying the recommendations made by Mr. Taney two or three years before, authorizing the Secretary of the Treasury to select state banks as depositaries. He was required to find one in each State and Territory. Certain stipulations were made as to the conditions of receipt and disbursement of the public money and concerning the redemption of the banks' own currency, together with proper requirements as to regular statements of the condition of the banks.[b] The banks which could not pay specie were to be dropped from the list of depositaries. The bill finally passed was identical with that which had been defeated in the Senate two years before.

In consequence of this act the number of depositaries increased steadily. Political influence in currency mat-

---

a Young, A. W.: American Statesman, 666.
b U. S. Revised Statutes, V: 52

ters was at that time so powerful that the Secretary was not able to adhere strictly to the provisions of the law. More money was left on deposit in some banks than the law permitted, there was delay in honoring drafts, the provision forbidding the use of banks which had in circulation notes below $5 was not strictly enforced, and in other matters the law was departed from.

A circular letter of the Treasury Department to the deposit banks, September 26, 1833, said: "The deposits of public money will enable you to afford increased facilities to commerce and to extend your accommodations to individuals." It also recommended "merchants engaged in foreign trade" as the most deserving recipients of extended credit. The invitation of the Secretary of the Treasury to the banks to use the public money as a basis for enlarging their discounts is interesting, in view of the fact that, in the minds of the supporters of the administration, such use of them by the national bank had constituted one of the chief grievances against it. The hint was not needed, however. New banks came into existence every day, and all increased their discounts rapidly. In the eight years between 1830 and 1838 the bank capital of the country increased from $145,192,268 to $290,772,091, deposits rose from $55,559,928 to $127,397,185, and discounts and loans from $200,451,214 to $525,115,702.[a] There was a large surplus in the Treasury, and the deposits in the banks were therefore excessive. They were tacitly assured that the Government would not draw on its balances, and

---

[a] Sumner, W. G.: History of American Currency, 123. Bolles, A. S.: Financial History of the United States, II: 346.

these were therefore left for their use in speculation. Previous to the issue of the specie circular in 1836 bank notes were received by the land office, and being deposited in the banks became again the basis of discounts to land speculators.

Signs of a coming storm had been gathering for a considerable time. Imports had swollen from $101,030,000 in 1832 to $189,980,000 in 1836, an increase of 87 per cent. The customs receipts of 1836 exceeded by 44 per cent those of the year 1834, and the sales of the public lands for 1836 were for the only time in the history of the country in excess of the customs receipts. The large importations were in this case an indication of rising prices, of which foreign manufacturers were hastening to take advantage. The upward trend of prices came from the inflation of the currency by excessive issues of bank notes. The increased sales of public lands were another sign of inflation. It was by means of these increased sales that the Government was enabled to get rid of its debt and found itself the possessor of the surplus of millions that were distributed, or "deposited," among the States in 1837.

But, as usual, these signs of a coming storm were unheeded by all save a few. In 1836 came the inevitable results—a marked rise of prices and rife speculation. The inflation bubble grew rapidly greater until, in 1837, it burst, scattering ruin in all directions. Nearly all the banks failed.

The catastrophe was probably hastened by several acts of the Executive, which received severe condemnation at the time, but must in our better light meet with approval and commendation in spite of their immediate effects. By order of the Secretary of the Treasury the receipt, after September 30, 1835, of bank notes of a denomination less than $5 had been prohibited. In the following year their payment to public officers or creditors was prohibited, and no notes less than $10 were to be received or paid by the Government after July 4, 1836. Moreover, the deposit banks were ordered to make one-fifth of every payment which did not exceed $500 in gold, if so desired by the creditor. They were also requested to cease issuing notes below the denomination of $5 by July 4, 1836, and below $10 by March 3, 1837. The purpose of these regulations was "to render the currency of the country more safe, sound, and uniform." Of course the immediate result intended to be produced was the displacement of small notes by coin. The orders were an effort to create a specie circulation. And within the limits of denominations chosen there is no more efficacious method of replacing specie with paper, or vice versa, than the prohibition of such coins or notes of the assigned denominations as are in common use.

These orders of the Treasury Department were supplemented with the famous "specie circular" issued July 11, 1836, which raised public excitement to a higher pitch probably than any incident in the bank war, unless we except the removal of the deposits. The object of this circular was to prevent the absorption of the public lands by speculators and to check the accumulation in the Treasury of bank notes, many of which would doubtless prove inconvertible. It required payments for public lands to be made in gold and silver. "The best justification of this measure was that $10,000,000 of paper on its way to the land office was arrested by this circular." Between August 16 and December 15 exceptions were to be made in cases of purchases not greater than 320 acres. After the 15th of December the operation of the order was unconditional.

This famous "circular" pricked the bubble of inflation. It is unfair to say that the responsibility for the panic that followed must be laid at the door of these orders. The panic was the result of the tremendous inflation, and would have come in any case. The specie circular simply aided in hastening the explosion, thereby probably making its evils less than they would have been had credit been allowed to be inflated to its self-bursting point. Moreover, the circular had the good effect of saving the public lands from the grasp of speculative monopoly and of making the losses of the Government less than they would have been had it gone on receiving worthless notes. The measure had a beneficial effect from the social standpoint also in saving "the new States from a non-resident proprietorship, one of the greatest obstacles to the advancement of a new country, and the prosperity of an old one." [a]

Another measure that had a large influence in precipitating the crisis was the law for the deposit of the surplus revenue among the States.[b] Speaking of this, Schurz says:[c]

"The effect of the law was to hurry on a crisis. The distribution of the public deposits among the 'pet banks' had served to place capital arbitrarily in different parts of

---

[a] Jackson's Message, 24th Cong., 2d sess.
[b] Bourne, E. G.: The Distribution of the Surplus Revenue in 1837.
[c] Henry Clay, II:121.

the country, without much regard to the requirements of legitimate business. The regulations imposed upon the deposit banks by the new law, especially the provision that the public deposits in no one bank should exceed three-fourths of its paid-up capital, led in some cases to an equally arbitrary dislocation of funds from banks which had an excess of deposits to other banks in other places which had less than the amount allowed. But the distribution of the treasury surplus among the several States produced this effect of arbitrary dislocation on a larger scale. On January 1, 1837, the surplus available for distribution amounted to $37,468,859. That surplus was nominally in the banks, but really in the hands of borrowers, who used it for legitimate business or speculation. Withdrawing it from the banks meant, therefore, withdrawing it from the business men or speculators who had borrowed it. The funds so withdrawn were made for some time unavailable."

The failure of the banks did not occur, however, until May, 1837, after Jackson had retired from the presidential chair. The general suspension necessitated a meeting of Congress, for the federal officials could lawfully receive and pay out the notes of specie-paying banks only; and as the deposit banks had suspended with the others, the fiscal machinery of the Government was stopped, and action by Congress was therefore needed.

PROPOSAL OF THE INDEPENDENT TREASURY BY VAN BUREN.

President Van Buren summoned an extra session for September 4, 1837. In his message the President recalled the history of the various methods of keeping the public money, and remarked that, although advocates of the use of national and state banks were still to be found, "it is apparent that the events of the last few months have greatly augmented the desire, long existing among the people of the United States, to separate the fiscal operations of the Government from those of individuals or corporations." Van Buren himself argued against the reestablishment of a national bank, on the ground that the people had declared against it in two elections. He maintained, too, that the United States Bank did not or could not prevent overissue and depreciation, an assertion which could hardly be sustained by the facts, at least in the days of the honest management of the bank's affairs. He further declared that it was no part of the Government's business to regulate domestic exchange,[a] and therefore advocated the entire separation of the Government from the banks, proposing that it collect, keep, and disburse its own funds. The possibility of doing so was greater than ever before and continually growing more so as the country developed, because the difficulties of transfer were constantly being lessened. This was a recommendation of the independent or constitutional treasury, as it was called by its friends, or the subtreasury, as its opponents named it. The system was, in fact, virtually in operation already; for, under the circumstances, it had become necessary for the Government to discontinue the use of state banks as depositaries and to revert to the older method of leaving the money with the receivers and collectors, on whom drafts were directly made. The Gov-

---

[a] Contrast the statement of Secretary Shaw in 1907. See Finance Report, 1906, p. 40.

ernment deposits, of course, could not be withdrawn immediately from the banks, and therefore the administration was much hampered. Late in 1837 Congress passed an act authorizing the Secretary to withdraw the deposits, but he was obliged under the circumstances to be somewhat indulgent.[a] Secretary Woodbury informed Congress in his report, that although on the suspension of specie payments six banks had been retained as depositaries, part of the public money was kept as a special deposit in Washington, part at the mint, and the rest with the officers collecting it. The Secretary urged on Congress either an enlargement and adaptation of this method, which he was employing on his own responsibility, or a new organization of commissioners and receivers-general, "to gather the collections to more central points, and to keep the public money, or such as could not be kept safely and expended conveniently, in the hands of the collecting officers."

The President and the Secretary were not alone in suggesting plans of relief and future action. Congress was deluged with memorials and petitions suggesting plans of one kind and another. Some had points of merit, but most were chacterized by that sublime indifference to history, experience, and economic principles that is a marked feature of the empiric schemes of which, in all such crises, political charlatanism and ignorance are prolific.[b]

The schemes actually considered in Congress were three: The revival of a national bank; the revival, or continuance,

---

[a] U. S. Stats. L , V : 206.

[b] For an interesting specimen see Sen. Doc. No. 6, 25th Cong., 1st sess.

of the deposit system established by the act of June 23, 1836; and the keeping of the public money by public officers. The last, or independent treasury plan, which, as already said, received the support of President Van Buren, has been proposed as long ago as 1834, by Senator Gordon, of Virginia. It was dropped at that time from lack of support, but was now brought forward as the measure of the administration by Senator Silas Wright,[a] of New York, who had been a stanch and consistent supporter of the Jacksonian financial policy. The bill now proposed was entitled a bill "imposing additional duties as depositaries, in certain cases, on public officers," and its provisions, as amended during discussion, were essentially those that afterwards became the law of the land in the final establishment of the constitutional treasury, or independent treasury, or subtreasury, as it was variously called.

The measure was keenly debated, the specie clause, requiring public dues to be paid in specie, being the main object of attack. The adoption of this clause, it was argued, would leave the bank notes in the hands of the people and give the specie to the Government. It was argued that convertible state bank notes should be received for government dues; that the adoption of the independent system would render the public money insecure; that it would open the way to favoritism in such ways as, for instance, accommodating political friends in the payment of customs; that it would contract the currency; and, finally, that it would increase executive patronage and so give the President too much power. The Whigs, more-

---

[a] Gillet, R. H.: Life and Times of Silas Wright, I: lxiv, and elsewhere.

over, represented the measure as an attack on the banks and the whole credit system of the country, and designated it as an experiment, novel and contrary to the habits of the people. Webster characterized the bill as a backward step, from dependence on credit to bolts and bars. "The use of money," he further said, "is in the exchange. It is designed to circulate, not to be hoarded. All the Government should have to do with it is to receive it to-day, that it may pay it away to-morrow. It should not receive it before it needs it, and it should part with it as soon as it owes it. To keep it—that is, to detain it, to hold it back from general use, to hoard it, is a conception belonging to barbarous times and barbarous governments."[a] That is sound doctrine even for to-day.

On the other side it was urged that under the proposed system the public money would be more secure, that a specie circulation would be promoted, and the currency made more uniform; that the action of the banks had made the separation of the Government from them necessary, and that a government was not worthy of its name if it could not manage its own finances. Further, it was maintained, the failure of the banks might at any time sweep the public deposits away and jeopardize the credit of the country; and, finally, that the independent treasury system would be more plain and simple in its arrangements, and truer to the spirit of the Constitution. The bill succeeded in passing the Senate, but met with defeat in the House, being laid on the table by a vote of 120 to 107. The contest over it showed the Whigs ranged in defense of the use of state banks, which they

[a] Speech on the subtreasury, delivered in the Senate March 12, 1838.

formerly opposed, and the friends of the administration supporting the measure which but lately they had condemned. During the three months that elapsed before the first regular session of the Twenty-fifth Congress began, the measure apparently did not gain aught in the estimation of the public. The subject had, indeed, been a matter of wide and earnest public discussion; and on it, aside from mere political argument, much that was logically sound had been said and written. The most elaborate defense of the plan was set forth by William M. Gouge in a pamphlet *a* which deserves consideration as the best exposition of the aims and hopes of the promoters of the system.

Gouge estimated the number of depositaries that would be necessary for the transaction of the business of the Treasury at 36, their locations to be those of the banks formerly used for the purpose. He thought that the expense would be less than that of the banks, probably aggregating not more than $101,600. "So plain would be the accounts," he goes on to say, "that we might choose for chief bookkeepers of these subtreasuries the disciples of the ingenious cordwainer who daily threw into the leg of one boot a slip containing a statement of his receipts for the day, and into the leg of the other a slip containing a statement of his expenditures."

The probabilities of loss, Gouge declared, would be less with independent depositaries than with banks; for there would be less loss from fire, since the deposits would be in specie; less from peculation, because the accounts

a An Inquiry into the Expediency of Dispensing with Bank Agency and Bank Paper in the Fiscal Concerns of the United States, Philadelphia, 1837 : 56.

would be simpler; and less from robbery, because thieves could carry off but little of the metallic money, on account of its weight. To the objection that the system would lock up money the author replied that there should be no surplus to lock up. The inconvenience of transfer could be obviated, he declared, by the use of drafts; and gold and silver payments could be easily maintained. Gouge held, contrary to the general opinion, that the system would decrease executive patronage. These views of Gouge's were exceedingly interesting because they show how widely even the most intelligent of the advocates of the independent treasury miscalculated the scope and influence of the system and underrated the growth of the fiscal life of the Government.

In 1838 the practice of leaving the public money with the collecting officers was pretty general,[a] yet some state banks continued to be employed. Where suitable banks could be found, the Secretary used them as depositaries, under the terms of the act of January 23, 1836. If a bank could not comply with the requirements of that law, the public money was sometimes left with it as a special deposit. But by far the larger part of the public money was kept, as has been remarked, in the hands of the collectors and receivers. About four-fifths of the expenditures for the year, or nearly $20,000,000, were made by drafts on collecting officers.[b] That it was thus kept proved fortunate when the banks collapsed again in 1839. Their recovery from the panic of 1837 had been too rapid. Of nearly 1,000 banks in the country, including branches,

---

[a] Finance Report, December 5, 1838.

[b] Cf. Remarks of President Van Buren, in his message, Dec. 2, 1839.

343 suspended specie payments entirely in 1839, 56 went out of business, and 62 resorted to partial suspension. As before, the larger number of these was in the West and South.

Congress assembled again on the 4th of December. President Van Buren again recommended his favorite measure, and again it was brought before the Senate by its champion, Mr. Wright, but only to have its success in the Senate once more offset by defeat in the House of Representatives. The debate was participated in by Clay, Calhoun, Webster, and others, in speeches of the power and brilliancy that characterized their great authors, but the arguments were mainly political.

The subject was again brought up in the session of 1839–40, after it had been urged, as usual, by President Van Buren in his message. And then at last the bitter struggle came temporarily to an end. The independent treasury was established. It barely escaped its former fate in the House; for it passed that body, June 30, 1840, after long and bitter debate, only by the small majority of 17 in a total vote of 231. According to the act, one-fourth of all government dues had to be paid in specie after June 30, 1840, and an additional one-fourth had to be so paid each successive year until the whole should become thus payable.

Thus was at length established the system for which Van Buren had risked his office. For the idea was adopted by him as his own, and although he pushed it perseveringly on to success, in the very achievement of that success "it helped sink the originator." But the

country owes a debt of gratitude to him for his persist-
ent adherence to a "hard-money" system. The sever-
ance of the Government from the banks, as banks were
then constituted, relying largely as they did on government support for the convertibility of their notes, was
the means of removing a large element of uncertainty
from the credit of the Government, and of insuring to
the currency the soundness for which the people had
struggled so long. It was, therefore, an act of wise
statesmanship, commendable to its promoter, and worthy
of the gratitude of all who believe in maintaining the
credit of the country; and a large share of this credit
must be accorded to Mr. Van Buren.

REPEAL OF THE SUBTREASURY LAW.

The shortness of Harrison's administration prevented
any action on the subtreasury and the currency. But
Tyler, on his accession, declared his intention of adher-
ing to the policy which Harrison and the party were
known to favor. Under a proclamation which had
been issued by Harrison, Congress assembled in special
session on the last day of May, 1841. In calling attention in his message to the state of the revenue and the
currency, Tyler proposed no definite plan of reform.
The people had, he thought, sustained Jackson in his
course against the national bank; the state-bank deposit
policy and the subtreasury had both been condemned;
therefore he left the whole question to Congress, saying:
"I shall be ready to concur with you in the adoption
of such a system as you may propose, reserving to myself
the ultimate power of rejecting any measure which may

in my view of it conflict with the Constitution, or otherwise jeopard the prosperity of the country."

Bills were immediately introduced into Congress for
the repeal of the subtreasury act and for the incorpora-
tion of a bank. As usual a large number of petitions and
resolutions for and against the movement were sent to
Congress, but, as usual also, they could be regarded as only
expressions of party fealty and not as intelligent opinions
based on careful consideration of the merits of the question. During the year since its establishment the subtreasury system had worked more smoothly than might
have been fairly expected. Secretary Ewing took occasion, in a report in July, 1840, to argue against the
system. He maintained that it exposed the government
funds to risk of loss; that it was cumbrous, expensive,
and inconvenient; that it tended to center disbursements in some eastern cities, especially New York; and
that it injured business by contracting the currency.
He reviewed the history of the government policy in the
matter of keeping its own money, recalling the fact that
there had been two periods of twenty years each in which
a national bank was used, and intervals, comprising a
period of nine years, in which state banks were employed,
and that during the rest of the time the funds were ad-
ministered by individual officers and agents.

The Secretary said that the losses under the state bank
system from 1811 to 1816 had been about $1,000,000;[a]
from 1833 to 1837 there had been no money loss, but much
inconvenience. There had been no loss through either of
the national banks, and no delay or expense in trans-

---

[a] Finance Reports, 1833 and 1837.

mitting public money, so far as the banks were concerned. The Secretary recommended the establishment of a bank, for which he afterwards submitted a plan. In fact, the results of the trial of the subtreasury failed to justify any of the prophecies of the Whigs. It may be fairly said, however, that this was as much the result of circumstances as of the merits of the system; for the conditions were, on the whole, favorable to success. However, the subtreasury act was repealed August 13, 1841, thus necessitating a return to the use of state banks. The conditions made with the banks were in substance what Taney had agreed on seven or eight years before. The banks had become so much safer that there was general satisfaction, and the Secretary wrote, in response to a Senate inquiry, that, in his opinion, the public money was safe and that he had no reason to apprehend any loss.[a]

The truth of the matter is that the disasters of the panic had produced a healthier mode of doing business, both banking and mercantile, and public deposits were therefore not made a basis of speculative mania such as had culminated in the panic of seven years before. The safety of the deposits was therefore no longer an issue, but this was due to the improvement in banking morals and knowledge.

A bill was immediately reported by Henry Clay for the establishment of a bank. Clay preferred a bank after the old pattern, but yielded to the wishes of the President and his friends and recommended an institution substantially such as they desired. The course pursued by President Tyler with reference to the establishment of the

---

[a] Sen. Doc. No. 88, 28th Cong., 2d sess.

bank was curious. He vetoed Clay's bill, although it had been passed by both Houses in the confident expectation of his approval. He asked his Secretary of the Treasury to draft a bill, and his request was complied with, even to naming the proposed institution to suit his whim. He approved the plan when read at a Cabinet meeting. Congress passed it unchanged except in two points, and sent it to him. He talked over it, wept over it, prayed over it—and vetoed it, on constitutional grounds that militated equally against the proposal of Secretary Ewing, which he had approved.

Yet it was fortunate, perhaps, that both the bills mentioned were defeated, for either of them would have been likely to work great mischief. Some of the provisions of Ewing's proposed plan were as follows: The bank, which must be in the District of Columbia, was to have a capital of $30,000,000. It could establish branches in the different States, but only with the consent of the States and under their control. The government subscription of $6,000,000 was to be in "stock" created for the purpose, and the States were to be allowed the privilege of subscribing in a similar way. The bank was to perform the usual duties of a fiscal agent of the Government, and all government debts were to be discharged by checks payable in the notes of the bank, which were also receivable for government dues. Dividends were to be limited to 6 per cent, and all surplus above $2,000,000 was to go to the Government. The bank could not incur a debt of over $20,000,000 more than its deposits, or make loans to more than one and three-fourths times its capital. Its specie reserve must be at least one-third of its circulation. Its dealings were to be in coin, bullion, notes, and inland bills of exchange. No loan could be made for more than six months, and no debt could be renewed. The limit of a government loan from the bank was to be $3,000,000, for not more than six months. As usual, the charter was to be for twenty years. In adopting the plan, Congress raised the dividend rate to 7 per cent, stopped all discounts and loans when the note circulation amounted to three times the specie on hand, and rejected the provision requiring the consent of the States to the establishment of branches.

In criticism of this plan it may be said, first, that if the Government is to own shares at all, it should pay in its capital like any other stockholder. This same mistake was made in the case of the United States Bank. In its financial aspect it resembles the conduct of railroad "promoters" who issue stock certificates, a certain amount of which they divide among themselves without paying in a dollar of the capital. It was an effort to share the gain without sharing the risk of loss. The burden was thrown on the other stockholders. Still, this was less vicious financially than some of the other provisions. The absolute prohibition of the renewal of debts, the debt limitations, and the support given to the credit of the bank notes by the government credit were bad features. The limitation placed upon loans to the Government was a ridiculous attempt to check the possible abuse of executive power and patronage. The limitation on discounts, if put into rigid operation on the verge of a crisis, would have precipitated a panic, exactly contrary as it was in effect to the method of freely discounting at such times that has received the sanction of experience and the judgment of wise bankers.

THE FINAL ESTABLISHMENT OF THE INDEPENDENT
TREASURY.

During the next few years the subject was less discussed,
as it was supplanted in public attention by the questions
of the tariff and the annexation of Texas. In the third
session of the Twenty-seventh Congress, however, the
matter came up again. The Committee of Ways and
Means made a report on the President's proposed "Plan
of an exchequer," condemning the subtreasury, passing
by the state-bank system as already rejected by the
people and as unsafe on account of the failure of the
banks, and praising the old national-bank system. The
committee's opinion of the subtreasury is shown by the
following remarks: "Its model may be found in the
imperial institutions of Darius, the King of Persia, and
its principles have descended, with little modification
and slight improvement, it is believed, through all
governments where banks do not exist, and are now
found in perfect operation in the island of Cuba."

According to the committee, the exchequer plan in its
details was essentially the subtreasury with certain
banking functions added, and herein lay the main objection to the scheme. When the bill came before Congress
a remarkable amendment was submitted by one member. [a]
He proposed the issue of $100,000,000, bearing interest
for ten years at 2½ per cent, *based on the public lands as
security* and to be distributed among the States in proportion to their respective "federal numbers." According
to this plan, "fiscal agencies" were to be established,

[a] Horace Everett, of Vermont.

whose beneficent operations, combined with the blessings of the land currency, would bring on a millenium of prosperity of which later advocates of "coining all the land of the country" never dreamed. The proposed scheme is one of the most curious of the monetary vagaries that have been brought to public attention in our short history as a nation.

During all this time the government officials kept the public money as best they could. That is, the unlegalized system of government agents as depositaries continued, and the operations of the Treasury rested on the law of 1789 and the resolutions of 1816. Many of the public officials deposited in selected banks.

In his message at the opening session of the Twenty-ninth Congress, President Polk revived the matter and urged the reestablishment of the subtreasury. Secretary Walker came to the President's aid in his annual report and brought forward anew the arguments so often presented against the use of banks. Though he advocated their complete and final rejection, he pointed out the uselessness of establishing a constitutional treasury "if it is to receive or disburse the paper of banks." The proposed measure again underwent earnest public discussion and again met with strenuous opposition. The arguments which were brought forward were pretty much the same as had been used before, but the long discussion enabled them to be presented in a more complete form. It was again urged in favor of the independent treasury that the union of the Government with the banks was unconstitutional. The constitutional argument on both sides is of only historical interest now, but it is perhaps worth while to note its points. The constitutional argument for the subtreasury was based on the words of the Constitution that "no money shall be drawn from the Treasury but in consequence of appropriations made by law." This, it was maintained, meant "a substantive treasury, substantial treasurer, and a real treasurer." Again, the First Congress, in establishing the Treasury Department, declares that "it shall be the duty of the Treasurer to receive and keep the moneys of the United States." Of course the argument from this provision depends on the logical content of "receive" and "keep." If "keep" is, as the adherents of the proposed system urged, to be understood literally, why not also "receive?" But for the Treasurer personally to handle all the receipts of the Government is impossible. Moreover, what is the literal meaning of "keep" in this connection?

The whole constitutional argument against the use of banks by the Government was but a phase of the old doctrine of states rights and supremacy which prevented Congress from assuming such control over the banking system of the country as would have made it safe, would have prevented "wild-cat" banking, would have saved the financial good name of the country, and would have made the subtreasury system unnecessary by making the banks as safe for government use as they are to-day.

The arguments urged in favor of the banks were the safer keeping and the free and safer transmission of the public moneys; the easier and more inexpensive collection of the government revenues; the greater facility of obtaining loans, and the receipt of interest by the Government on its deposits. The first of these arguments, as to the safer keeping and transmission of the government money, is patently weak. As Mr. Niles had remarked years before, a Government is not worthy of its name if it can not protect its own property. And if it can not protect its own property, how could any bank do so when the Government is the ultimate source of protection to the bank? The only strength of the argument lies in the fact that if a bank should lose government deposits it would have to replace them if it could, if it had any means left wherewith to do so. The matter of interest is unimportant, and should have no weight by the side of other considerations. A far more weighty objection to the system under discussion was brought forward when it was said that the continued payment of government debts in coin was impracticable. The use of treasury notes, it was said, would become necessary, and they would remain at par only so long as public deposits were on hand. The argument had some truth in it, but it was not true to the extent its advocates maintained. Aside from political exigencies, under a sound system of finance, payments in actual specie are only inconvenient and costly, not impracticable, in some varying proportion to their amount and frequency.

In a review of the subject the editor of the Bankers' Magazine[a] asserted: "That scheme [the subtreasury] we consider utterly impracticable and indefensible." Such a law "can not be in force for six consecutive months, nor will it be, in our opinion, strictly complied with for forty-eight hours."

---

[a] I: 15 (1845–46).

The subject went the old weary round of discussion in Congress, supported and attacked with arguments that applied and arguments that did not, with arguments to the point and arguments aside from the point, and emerged at last into light from behind the clouds of personalities, party animosities, and "counsel without knowledge," that more or less darkened the subject during the whole ten years from the time when it had been first proposed.

As before, the hottest fight was made over the provision requiring receivers and disbursers of the public money, including all postmasters, to receive and pay out specie only. On the face of it, this was, of course, the most probably impracticable provision of the bill. Objection was also made to the employment of so large a portion of specie in the payment of duties, on the ground that it would embarrass business; and the expensiveness of the system was held up as a further reason for condemnation.

However, the tide had turned, and the ship of state was being guided by the political compeers and descendants of Jackson and his policy, and public opinion was less pronounced against the measure than it had been. Thus it happened that the subtreasury was reestablished. The bill was reported by the Committee of Ways and Means, and passed the House, April 2, 1846, by a vote of 123 to 67. It received the sanction of the Senate, on the 1st of August, by a strict party vote of 28 to 24, and went into effect immediately, thus consummating the policy of the "divorce of bank and State" which was begun by Jackson and carried on by Van Buren, and in his time lasted "just long enough to prostrate the party which brought it into being; which expired with the elevation of the opposing party, was revived with the restoration of 'the democracy,' and has since continued, through changes of administration, undisturbed; having received the general acquiescence of the popular will, if not the positive approval of the public judgment."[a]

And so the divorce of bank and State, which had for a time been "*a mensa et thoro*," now became "*a vinculo*." The act found its justification in the nature and condition of the banking system of the time, which made the reliance of the Government on the banks for financial safety dangerous and, therefore, undesirable. Under the old national banks the issue of notes was, indeed, fairly well under government control. But that system of issue was unsuited to the rapidly growing needs of the country, and threatened a social differentiation incompatible with the preservation of the democratic equality necessary to the vitality of republican government.[b] The State banking system had been well denominated "wild-cat." Utterly irresponsible, and beyond control in the strength of the doctrine of state supremacy, in its evil and untenable form which was swept away by the necessities of the Government in the civil war, these banks were a veritable powder magazine by the explosion of which the credit and good name of the nation, if it trusted them, might at any time be shattered.

It is in this danger that we must look for the justification of the removal of the government finances to a sounder

a Young, A. W.: American Statesman, 739.

b Cf. Schurz, Carl: Henry Clay (American Statesmen Series), II: 48–50.

and safer basis. Whatever may be the influence of its operation now, the establishment of the subtreasury was, under the circumstances, justifiable and necessary. Whether its continuance is so, is another question, the answer to which it remains to discover from the history of its operation.

Chapter III.—Development of the Independent Treasury.

THE PROVISIONS OF THE LAW.

The first section of the new law [a] defined the Treasury thus:

"The rooms prepared and provided in the new Treasury building, at the seat of government, for the use of the Treasurer of the United States, his assistants and clerks, and occupied by them, and also the fireproof vaults and safes erected in said rooms for the keeping of said moneys in the possession and under the immediate control of said Treasurer, and such other apartments as are provided for in this act as places of deposit of the public money, are hereby constituted and declared to be the Treasury of the United States." The other places of deposit provided for were Philadelphia, New Orleans, New York, Boston, Charleston, and St. Louis. The appointment of assistant treasurers was provided for in the last four places, while in the other two the treasurers of the mints were to perform the duties of assistant treasurers.

The sixth section contains the provisions which essentially modified the nature of the Treasury. It provides "That the Treasurer of the United States, the treasurer of the mint of the United States, the treasurers, and those acting as such, of the various branch mints, all collectors of the customs, all surveyors of the customs acting also as collectors, all assistant treasurers, all receivers of public

---

[a] The act is given in full in Appendix 2.

moneys at the several land offices, all postmasters, and all public officers of whatsoever character be, and they are hereby, required to keep safely, without loaning, using, depositing in banks, or exchanging for other funds than as allowed by this act, all the public money collected by them, or otherwise at any time placed in their possession and custody, until the same is ordered, by the proper department or officer of the Government, to be transferred or paid out; and when such orders for transfer or payment are received, faithfully and promptly to make the same as directed, and to do and perform all other duties as fiscal agents of the Government, which may be imposed by this or any other acts of Congress, or by any regulation of the Treasury Department made in conformity to law; and also to do and perform all acts and duties required by law, or by direction of any of the executive departments of the Government, as agents for paying pensions, or for making any other disbursements which either of the heads of those departments may be required by law to make, and which are of a character to be made by the depositaries hereby constituted consistently with the official duties imposed on them."

Sections 7 and 8 provide for the giving of bonds; section 9 provides for deposits by collectors; section 10, for transfers by the Secretary of the Treasury; sections 11 and 12, for examinations of the condition of the subtreasuries and depositaries; section 13 provides means, such as fireproof vaults, etc., for the safe-keeping of the public funds; section 14, for the transfer of balances from one depositary to another by the Secretary of the Treasury; section 15 directs the method of deposit by marshals, district attorneys, etc.; section 16 defines and provides penalties for embezzlement, and for violations of the act; and section 17, for temporary quarters. Sections 18 and 19 contain the provisions around which debate had raged most fiercely. In them occurs the famous specie clause, which requires the payment of public dues and disbursements in gold or silver coin or Treasury notes only. The specie clause was not to go into effect until the 1st of January, 1847. Section 20 supplements the two previous sections by requiring that all exchanges of funds must be on a gold and silver basis. The mode of payment of drafts is prescribed by the twenty-first section and that of salaries by the twenty-second. In the twenty-third and final section provision is made for immediate incidental expenses.

From this brief summary it is clear that the act completely accomplished the separation of bank and state. It made the Government its own banker, even to the furnishing of the paraphernalia of office rooms; and, taken in connection with the law sanctioning the emission of Treasury notes, the subtreasury act virtually made the Treasury a bank of issue.

The provision of vaults was simply a result of that play on words which, after all, was part of the basis of the constitutional argument. There was no good reason why, even though the government financial operations were separated from the banks, the public money might not have been kept in bank vaults as special deposits.

The places selected for the establishment of subtreasuries were those in which the government operations were most considerable, and which were centers for the collection of revenue from the country round about and for the payment of public creditors. The establishment of a subtreasury or depositary appears to have been regarded as advantageous to a locality from a business point of view, because it was thought to make trade brisker through the concentration of larger amounts of money. The selection of the localities was made, however, on the supposed needs of the public service; and, as a matter of fact, the ground covered by the new sub-treasuries and depositaries was substantially that formerly occupied by the banks through which the Government had done its business. At a later time the feeling that the presence of a subtreasury is advantageous to business led to an attempt to secure the establishment of one at Louisville, but the request was refused by Congress.[a]

The requirement that all public officers should safely keep the public money committed to their charge without depositing it in banks was as absurd as it was unjust to the officers and unsafe for the money. For no proper places for safe-keeping were provided. The banks had vaults far safer than any place of deposit that could be provided by most of the officers of the Government. The new provision, then, made the public money less, rather than more, safe, so far as fire and theft were concerned. Moreover, it was unjust to throw so great a responsibility on the holders of the public money without furnishing them suitable accommodations for keeping it. To be sure section 13 did provide for fireproof

[a] See p. 80.

vaults, and section 17 for temporary quarters, but not in sufficient number; and, besides, they could not be secured for some time to come. The specie clause was a return to the provision passed by the First Congress, that the Treasury should receive only coin in payment of public dues. Of this clause Edward Everett said that "if the attempt could be forced through, it would be like an attempt on the part of the Government to make use of the ancient modes of travel and conveyance, while every citizen in his private affairs enjoyed the benefits of steam navigation and railways." [a] In a certain sense Everett was right; but the remark seems to indicate that he misconceived the whole drift of the subtreasury act, and especially of the specie clause. As Secretary Walker had pointed out, the act without the specie clause would have been useless or worse. If the Government were to be no longer connected with banks, especially in the way of having no control over their issues, it was right that it should not use their notes. The only other way whereby it could provide itself with the "steam navigation and railways" of paper money, or the "aerial wagon way," to use Adam Smith's better figure, was to issue notes of its own. Every lover of sound finance must always fear that operation, which, under the circumstances existing at that time would have caused untold trouble if it had been largely resorted to. The only alternative was the use of specie, and to that, in the main, the Government wisely committed itself. The clause was not, indeed, could not be, observed to the very letter. Even as late as 1855 we are told it was little, if

---

a Bankers' Magazine, August, 1885.

at all, observed by postmasters.[a] Notwithstanding the imperfect manner in which the law was executed, the clause was productive of great good. " All receipts from lands, customs, and other public dues were paid in gold and silver and treasury notes; and these were employed by the Treasurer in making payments. In this way a stream of gold and silver was set in motion, limited, indeed, and running chiefly from the public depositaries to the banks and then returning. But it swelled to larger dimensions." [b] In short, the specie clause, although it was impeded and limited in its operation, was wholly productive of good, and the departure from it under financial stress in later times was a misfortune.

So far as the banks were concerned the new system meant the loss of the government deposits, with the consequence of lessened discounts and the withdrawal of the support of government credit from their notes. The banks might suffer from the first incident, but had no right to complain of it; and as for the second, it was no fault of the Government if bank notes could not be kept afloat at par without government support. It is the duty of a bank to see that its notes are convertible at par without the aid of the public credit.

The work which the new system had to accomplish seemed simple enough, consisting as it did merely of the receipt and payment of the public money. It seemed that the organization of such a system should not be any more difficult than that of such a group of branches as was developed under the Second United States Bank.

[a] Young, A. W.: American Statesman, 847.
[b] Bolles, A. S.: Financial History of the United States, 1789–1860, 356.

But having declared its purpose to pay specie, the Government was bound to do so at every agency, however remote from a great business center. To refuse to do so, or even to hesitate or delay, was to discredit itself.

The new system began its career under many difficulties. No appropriation was made for the salaries of assistant treasurers, or for additional salaries for treasurers of the mint who were to assume new duties under the law, or for the payment of any special examining agents. Neither were any appropriations made for the expense of transfers, nor "to enable disbursing agents to pay the public creditors at all times and places with punctuality and despatch." Moreover, the provision for incidental expenses was inadequate; no adequate security was provided by the law for public money in the hands of disbursing agents, and the powers of the department as to the method of making payments abroad were not sufficiently defined. There were, in addition, certain external difficulties to be overcome. Chief among these were the opposition of the banks and the distrust and friction incident to an untried system.

On the 25th of August, 1846, Secretary Walker issued a circular to collectors, subtreasurers, and other officers, directing them to make all government drafts payable to order, not bearer. The drafts were to be transferable only by special indorsement, and payable only at designated places. If a draft were payable at a place not more than 50 miles from Washington, it must be presented for payment within twenty days from the date of the draft; if at a point distant between 50 and 100 miles, it must be presented within forty days; between 100 and 200 miles, within sixty days; between 200 and 400 miles, within eighty days; and over 400 miles, within ninety days. All drafts not so presented had to be sent to the Treasurer to be paid as he should direct. No exchange of funds between disbursing officers or other government agents was allowed, except for gold or silver. Because of the specie clause, the Secretary directed that no payments be made in treasury drafts, even though a creditor should prefer that mode of payment.[a]

THE INDEPENDENT TREASURY DURING THE MEXICAN WAR.

During the next two years the country had the Mexican war on its hands, and in 1847 the Government was compelled to issue over $20,000,000 of treasury notes, and to contract a $28,000,000 loan.[b] But the notes were issued at par, and the bonds commanded a premium. Throughout the war specie payments were kept up, and the treasury notes at no time fell more than one-half of 1 per cent below par in New York. In his report the Secretary gives the subtreasury much of the credit for the success of the financial operations of the war. "The Constitutional Treasury," he says, "has been tried during a period of war, when it was necessary to negotiate very large loans, when our expenditures were being increased and when transfers unprecedented in amount were required to distant points for disbursement. During the last eleven months the Government has received, transferred, and disbursed more specie than during the whole

---

[a] Finance Report, 1846, Appendix H.
[b] Including the conversion of treasury notes.

aggregate period of fifty-seven years preceding since the adoption of the Constitution." Over $24,000,000 of specie were imported during the year, a net gain of more than $22,000,000 of imports. This specie, the Secretary maintained, would have been made the basis of a paper inflation that would have produced a ruinous revulsion in business if it had been deposited in the banks. Gouge, writing at the time, took the same view. The Secretary wrote: "From this revulsion we have been saved by the Constitutional Treasury, by which the specie imported, instead of being converted into bank issues, has been made to circulate directly, to a great extent, as a currency among the people. * * * The Government is now disconnected from banks, and yet its stock and notes are at par, although we have been constrained to contract heavy loans, and to keep larger armies in the field than at any former period. But during the last war, when the Government was connected with banks, its 6 per cent stock and treasury notes were depreciated 25 per cent, payable in bank paper 20 per cent below par, thus amounting to a loss of 45 cents upon every dollar in the operations of the Government."

Although Secretary Walker's view of the beneficial influence of the independent treasury may be regarded as too favorable, we may readily admit that the credit of the Government was upheld largely by the specie clause of the law, which virtually bound it to redeem its notes and bonds in coin, and that the operation of the act was to keep up a specie circulation which gave a sound basis to the whole currency.

How far these results would have been accomplished—and how far, therefore, they were due to the subtreasury—if, while the Government was under the stress of the war, trade had not assumed a tremendous bound, is at least problematical. The large grain exports of 1847, amounting to over $37,000,000, brought in, as already noted, a large amount of specie; the abolition of the corn laws in England was attaining its full effect, and the revolutionary disturbances in Europe in 1848 also tended to help American commerce. The balance of trade was settled largely by imports of specie which remained in the country, thus showing that it was satisfying a lasting need. The permanence of demand was doubtless largely caused by the demand of the Government. If the conditions of business had not been favorable to securing specie, however, very likely the stress produced by the demand of the Government for it, would have strained the financial virtue of Congress to the point of breaking or annulling the act. Consequently the subtreasury can not be credited with the whole of the good influence of the increase in metallic circulation. The increase was largely due to favorable commercial and financial conditions. Still the independent action of the Government had a beneficial influence on the currency by restraining bank issues. If the government money had been deposited in the banks, as the banks were then conducted, they would have made it the basis of further issues of notes, forcing up prices and leading to an export of specie. But it is not surprising that the contrast between government finances and credit, in the wars of 1812 and of 1846, should have reconciled the people to the new system.

One small advantage of the system that had not been foreseen was reported by Secretary Walker. This was in the fact that, whereas under the régime of the banks it had been necessary to keep $4,000,000 in the treasury to supply the mints with bullion for coinage, it was found under the subtreasury system that $3,000,000 would do.

The experience of the first two years developed some defects of detail in the system. In his report for 1848, Secretary Walker writes of losses from delay in shipping foreign coin received in New York for customs dues to Philadelphia for recoinage. Therefore he advocated the establishment of a branch mint at New York. He still insisted, however, on the advantages of the independence of the Government in money matters, asserting that "a system which has operated so beneficially, both in war and in peace, must, in the main, be wise and salutary."

A side light is thrown on the working of the subtreasury system in a speech of Webster's, delivered in Faneuil Hall, Boston, October 24, 1848.[a] He asserted that on the 25th of the preceding August, the New York banks had $5,800,000 in specie, and the New York subtreasury had $1,400,000. On September 29, the banks had but $4,600,000 and the subtreasury had $2,400,000, thus having absorbed $1,000,000 in a single month, with the evil results of a scarcity of money and a curtailment of discounts. It must be remembered, however, that Webster was making a political speech. It is not at all probable that the specie lost by the banks was all gained by the subtreasury. Money was moving westward at that season of the year.

[a] Writings and speeches of Daniel Webster (National Edition) IV: 154.

DEFECTS SHOWN IN EARLY YEARS OF OPERATION.

In the following year (1849) other inconveniences became manifest. According to the provisions of the law, when a draft was issued to a disbursing officer he was obliged to receive the whole amount of the payment, no matter how large, in one sum, even though he was to use it in making many separate small payments. Hence these officers were compelled to assume custody of the money and bear the burden of transferring it to the places where it was due. In this way the money was exposed to risk of loss or theft. Moreover, the actual carriage of coin was expensive and unsafe; there was great inconvenience from the accumulation of coin where it was not needed, and the number of clerks employed to do the work of the various offices was too small. On account of these disadvantages, as he affirmed, the new Secretary of the Treasury, Mr. Meredith, questioned the expediency of continuing the system. He proposed that disbursing officers be allowed to deposit their drafts with an assistant treasurer and draw on the deposit as they needed the money. But, although the matter had been repeatedly urged on its attention, nothing was done by Congress even with reference to disbursing agents until 1857.

As to the transfer of the public funds, obviously one way was to transfer specie by agents appointed for the purpose. But this could be done only at great expense and risk and loss of time. A second method of transfer was to give drafts to bankers and brokers and permit them to use the money long enough to compensate them for the expense of transporting the specie. This method had been used early in subtreasury history and became common after 1850.

When Secretary Guthrie assumed office in 1853, he found that "$475,000 was in the hands of agents under agreements to transfer the same for the department to different places of deposit, together with the sum of $2,226,982.27 unaccounted for and designed to pay interest."[a] The Secretary abolished this method of making transfers and effected them "by the sale of treasury drafts at the points where the money was needed for disbursements, as authorized by law, or by an actual transfer by an officer of the department."[b] Secretary Guthrie required the assistant treasurers and officers of depositaries to receive the deposits of disbursing agents, so as to render the use of banks by these agents unnecessary. But not all collecting officers adopted the practice, and the Treasury continued to draw on them directly. It was well that the Secretary held this opinion of the proper method of making transfers, for the use of bankers and brokers as agents was a vicious makeshift. It opened the way widely to favoritism toward particular banks and was a source of great risk. Some of the drafts were not accounted for for long periods. Moreover, it was a virtual abandonment of the principle of the complete separation from banks, which was the underlying principle of the Independent Treasury. That this mode of transferring funds was much abused is shown by the increase in the amount of transfers when the method was used. When the transfers were made in cash, they amounted, in New Orleans, to about $38,000 a

---

[a] Finance Report, 1853: 13   [b] Ibid.

month; under the system of employing bankers and brokers the transfers swelled to $227,000. In Washington they rose from $135,000 a month to $225,000.[a] The evil was corrected, however, in 1854, and the transfers were thereafter made in money.

In May, 1854, Mr. William M. Gouge was appointed special agent to examine the condition of the various sub-treasuries and their operations. As has been already mentioned, the system, at the time of its establishment, was under great disadvantages from lack of proper buildings. In only a few of the places designated as the seats of depositaries were such to be found. Gouge reported[b] that the Government had not "in the whole valley of the Ohio a building or a vault in which to deposit a dollar or a paper." Boston was the only place provided with suitable buildings for the subtreasury. Most of the buildings actually used for the purpose were unsuitable,[c] being only such as each agent could secure under his special circumstances; so that, as hitherto, the provisions for the safe-keeping of the public money against fire and burglars were totally inadequate. But the zeal and honesty of the officials made up for these defects, showing, as the Secretary pointed out, that the objection to this system, founded on probable loss from the personal dishonesty of the assistant treasurers, was unfounded.

Gouge recommended that the transfers of specie be reduced to a minimum and supplemented by the use of drafts on some specified subtreasury. These drafts, he

---

[a] Gouge's Report. In Finance Report, 1854, Doc. No. 30.

[b] Ibid.

[c] For an interesting description of a United States depositary in a tavern, see Finance Report, 1854:257.

recommended, should be issued at any subtreasury on deposit of the amount in specie at the issuing office. This mode of transfer was essentially adopted afterwards. The object of making these proposed drafts payable at a particular depositary was to prevent their passing from hand to hand as currency. For with the restriction as to the place of redemption, if they circulated at all it would be in the neighborhood of the subtreasury at which they were payable.

Gouge incorporated in his report a résumé of the advantages of the independent treasury as he saw them. He insisted that it gave greater stability to the banks, not only by its restrictive influence on note issues, but also by keeping specie in circulation. For the banks are sustained, he argued, not only by the specie which they have in their vaults, but also by all in the country to which they may have immediate access by the sale of securities. Gouge further maintained that the amount of specie in the country had been more than doubled by the action of the constitutional treasury system. Summarizing his opinions, he declared that if the constitutional treasury system were faithfully carried out it would increase the amount of gold and silver in circulation, weaken the force of bank expansions and contractions, prevent the losses that had formerly arisen from the use by public officers of public funds intrusted to their care, give the Government at all times complete control of its own funds, prevent the derangement of business caused by Government's effecting large loans through bank credits, and tend to prevent a general suspension of specie payments, or facilitate their restoration if suspension should occur. "The less Government has to do with banks, and the less banks have to do with Government, the better for both." That doctrine was eminently sound as banks were then constituted.

It may fairly be admitted that experience with the independent treasury, up to the time when Gouge wrote, justified him in the first four opinions mentioned in the summary above, gave plausibility to the fifth, and showed that there was a considerable amount of truth in the last. For, notwithstanding its many imperfections, the system seems to have been at this time in good working order, and was apparently accomplishing all that its advocates had claimed for it. But since its establishment the financial operations of the Government and the conditions of business had been favorable to its success. At no time had there been in the Treasury any very large surplus, and there had been no crisis to cause financial distress. To be sure the Mexican war had caused a pressure in the market, but there was no real disturbance. On the whole, business had been good and commerce had increased. Consequently there was little to cause friction in the working of the new fiscal machinery.

These conditions made it possible for the Secretary of the Treasury to write, in 1855, that the independent treasury was "still eminently successful" in all its operations. The transfers for disbursement for the fiscal year were $39,407,674, made at a cost of $19,762, and the premiums on the sale of Treasury drafts amounted to $30,431. The receipts and expenditures of the Government for the year were all paid in gold and silver, and according to the Secretary were without any perceptible effect on currency or business.

During the year 1854–55 the vaults at Washington had been made safe, but those at other places remained in pretty much the same condition. Gouge again made an examination of them, but developed nothing new. The only loss from robbery, he says, was in the previous year at Pittsburg, and amounted to $10,000.

The system of transfer drafts recommended by Gouge the year before had been adopted and had worked well. He reported that further experience had strengthened his opinion of the advantages of the system.

EARLY INFLUENCE ON THE MONEY MARKET AND RENEWAL
OF CONNECTION WITH BANKS.

Although in its administration the system was working well, it had already begun to exert an influence on business through the money market, which had attracted some attention. About this time the California gold mines began to have an influence on business by making gold a commodity for export. The excess of gold exports over imports rose from a little less than $3,000,000 in 1850 to $24,000,000 in 1851, to $37,000,000 in 1852, and became $34,000,000, $52,000,000, $41,000,000, and $56,000,000, respectively, in the four following years. The large gold production must have had a tendency to make prices more irregular than they would otherwise have been. At the same time, the irregular action of the subtreasury was a disturbing factor. In 1853 the receipts of the Government exceeded its expenditures, so that there was a considerable accumulation of money in the Treasury. To prevent any stringency that might be caused thereby the Secretary issued a circular, on the 30th of July, offering to buy

$5,000,000 worth of 6 per cent bonds. He secured them by paying a premium of 21 per cent.

During the year 1854, according to the report of Secretary Guthrie, the Treasury kept up the demand for coin by receiving and paying more than $75,000,000 of it. Thus, the circulation of specie was maintained despite the tendency exerted by the small notes of the banks to drive it out; for so long as the Government insisted on using specie, it could not be wholly driven from use. The Treasurer stated in his report that no difficulty had been found in the working of the law, and that the money in the various subtreasuries was "as safe and secure as that in the Treasury."

Nevertheless, the existence of a surplus was evidently a source of anxiety to the wellwishers of the independent treasury. For in his next report, December, 1856, the Secretary of the Treasury took occasion to explain its action on the volume of money and attempted to show that the influence was beneficent. He declared that "the independent treasury, when over-trading takes place, gradually fills its vaults, withdraws the deposits, and, pressing the banks, the merchants, and the dealers, exercises that temperate and timely control which serves to secure the fortunes of individuals and preserve the general prosperity." Secretary Guthrie went on to say that the subtreasury may "exercise a fatal control over the currency, the banks, and the trade of the country, and will do so whenever the revenue shall greatly exceed the expenditure." This was clear to the Secretary from his own experience that year. There was a surplus and prices were rising. Therefore the Treasury had repeated its attempt to afford relief to the money market by that method of forced debt payment with which we have since become so familiar. "There has been expended, since the 4th of March, 1853, more than $45,525,000 in the redemption of the public debt. This debt has been presented, from time to time, as the money accumulated in the National Treasury and caused stringency in the money market. If there had been no public debt, and no means of disbursing this large sum and again giving it to the channels of commerce, the accumulated sum would have acted fatally on the banks and on trade. The only remedy would have been a reduction of the revenue, there being no demand and no reason for increased expenditure." [a]

The amount of transfers during the year had amounted to $38,088,113.92, at a cost of $12,945.87; and the premium on the sale of Treasury drafts had been $54,924.16, leaving $41,978.29 over the expenses of transfer. The Secretary expressed the opinion that hereafter the transfers of public money would be made without charge and without risk.

By an act of March 3, 1857, the law was amended so as to require disbursing officers to deposit in some subtreasury. Up to this time many of them had continued to use the banks for safe-keeping of the public money in their charge, usually leaving it with them as a special deposit. After the amendment, the Secretary directed the treasurers of the mints, of the depositaries, and of the subtreasuries to receive deposits of disbursing officers, but not to honor drafts on them unless made in favor

---

[a] Finance Report, 1856: 32.

of some person known to the treasurer. If for sums of $20 or less, the drafts might be drawn in favor of the disbursing officer himself or to bearer. Disbursing officers might also draw for money to pay the salaries of employees, but they were required to furnish lists of such employees. Public depositaries were not required to pay drafts made out to A. B., or *order;* but they might pay to A. B., or *bearer.* There were many obvious difficulties in the way of the strict enforcement of the amendment, and it is probable that it was not widely observed to the letter. The Treasury report of 1858 pointed out, what might have been easily forseen, that there were some conditions under which compliance with the law was impracticable. Sailors in a foreign port, or on a long cruise, could not be paid according to the law, and pursers must carry money with them. Indian agents could not pay so, neither could disbursing officers remote from a depositary, and disbursing agents of the army would have some difficulty. Much additional labor and expense were entailed by the act requiring the assistant treasurers and depositaries to hold the money of disbursing officers and pay it out in detail. According to Secretary Cobb, the additional labor amounted to " 100 per cent." This labor increased as the government revenues grew, and assumed enormous proportions on the breaking out of the civil war. According to the report of 1861, the amounts so deposited rose from $8,000,000 to $190,000,000.

The year 1857 witnessed a panic in the money market. As the pinch grew more severe, the Secretary of the Treasury sent to the various depositaries silver change of all denominations, and small gold from the mint, with instructions to pay out the coin to applicants in exchange for large coin. This furnishing of "change" was a real convenience, and it could not but have had a good educational effect by keeping specie in daily use among the people.

Writing of the effect of the amendment requiring disbursing officers to deposit in the government depositaries, Secretary Cobb said: "The present condition of money affairs is a significant indication of the consequences that must have been anticipated if this regulation had not been adopted, and the public money advanced to disbursing officers had continued to be deposited in banks and with bankers, and had been used by them as a basis for increasing their business and extending their circulation. Not only would the contraction now going on, and the consequent embarrassment and distress of the commercial community have been much greater than it is, but the public moneys themselves would have been placed in imminent danger."[a] In fact, the situation was such that there would probably have been a repetition of the events of 1837, and the "divorce of bank and state" was justified by the danger which it had evidently enabled the Government to avoid. In 1837 the failure of the banks caused the Government great embarrassment. In 1857 the banks had again failed; but the Government, having its money in its own hands, was able to pay its debts, and met every liability without trouble. Said the Secretary of the Treasury: "It has resorted to no expedient to meet the claims of its creditors, but with promptness pays each one upon presentation." It is not to be won-

[a] Finance Report, 1857.

dered at that such a showing should wed people to the system. Its practical success in preserving the credit of the Government, or at least in making its financial operations easier, was an object lesson that appealed to the public.

Secretary Cobb's claim that the specie disbursements of the Government afforded relief to the money market was doubtless true. But this fact by itself does not prove that the operations of the subtreasury system were wholly beneficial. It must also be shown that its previous absorption of this specie did not bring on or intensify the monetary pressure. Certainly it could not now be said that the system had prevented overissue by the banks, in face of the prostration of credit that had overtaken them. It is possible that the Treasury absorption of money made place for the bank issues. Thus one of the claims, of which most was made in favor of the "constitutional treasury," that it would check excessive issues of bank notes, was shown by the occurrences of 1857 to have less ground than had been supposed. Even Mr. Howell Cobb, the Secretary of the Treasury, ardent supporter as he was of the policy, was compelled to admit that the anticipations of its friends that it would so operate were true only "to a limited extent." The obvious explanation is that contraction of the circulation by Treasury absorption is good only when the circulation is redundant.

The collection and disbursement of the revenue went on during the panic, according to the Secretary, without "loss or embarrassment," and the subtreasury system was "eminently successful." There was no loss from faithless officers, the expense of its operation was small, and it had, in the opinion of the government officers, no bad effect on business. President Buchanan took the same view as did his Secretary of the beneficial operation of the subtreasury. In his annual message, December 7, 1857, he said: "Thanks to the independent treasury, the Government has not suspended [specie] payments, as it was compelled to do by the failure of the banks in 1837. It will continue to discharge its liabilities to the people in gold and silver. Its disbursements in coin pass into circulation and materially assist in restoring a sound currency."

During the financial year, 1858, bond purchases were continued to the amount of nearly $4,000,000, and contributed somewhat to the mitigation of the disasters of the revulsion. However, in view of the fact that the excess of exports of specie over imports for the year amounted to over $33,000,000 it is clear that the influence produced on the whole volume of currency by the amount set free from the Treasury must have been very insignificant.

After the country recovered from the effects of the panic its progress was very rapid. From 1858 to 1861 it was prosperous, and the banks held a strong specie reserve. The expenditure of the Government for three years exceeded its receipts by about $90,000,000, and the deficit was met by loans. Under an act of December 23, 1857, over $52,000,000 of treasury notes were issued. They were redeemable in one year, bore interest ranging from 3 to 6 per cent, and were sold at par. In June, 1858, bonds to the amount of $20,000,000, redeemable in fifteen years, were sold at a premium. In June, 1860, came

$7,000,000 more, which also sold at a premium, though a smaller one; and in December of the same year an issue of $10,000,000 of treasury notes was authorized. They sold at par. The needs of the Government under the stress of war necessitated the placing of several more loans, both in bonds and treasury notes, all of which, with one exception, were placed at, or above, par. This is true even of the demand notes of 1861, although it was only with some difficulty that the employees of the Government were persuaded to receive them. As yet the Government was true to its resolution to maintain itself on the specie basis that formed the keystone of the independent treasury system. However, under the act of July 17, 1861, Secretary Chase applied to the banks for a loan of $50,000,000 in seven-thirty bonds, payable in three years. The loans of the Mexican war had been placed independently of the banks. The Treasury had been its own broker. This solicitation of aid from the banks was, therefore, another step away from the principle on which the independent treasury system had been built. It was a little step. The banks were not yet to handle the government receipts or to have the custody of its money. But it was a look backward to the policy abandoned in 1846. The act, however, was a necessity. The Government needed gold, and the only large accumulated stock of that metal was in the banks. Their specie reserve amounted to about $87,000,000, and they were strengthening their position. In August the Secretary had a conference in New York with representative bankers of New York, Philadelphia, and Boston, with reference to the requested loan. The Government was provided with money, which, being expended in military operations, found its way back to the banks and enabled them to make a further advance of a similar amount soon afterwards. Between August 19 and November 19, 1861, Secretary Chase borrowed more than $140,000,000 from the banks. The specie held by them in August, the time of the first loan, was $47,000,000; in December, after most of the last loan had been paid, it had decreased only by about $5,000,000. The recuperative power of the banks was thus clearly shown.

But, while borrowing the gold of the banks, Mr. Chase was also driving their notes from circulation by the issue of treasury notes, and the bank notes coming in for redemption created a new drain on the gold reserves of the banks. The banks could furnish the Secretary with gold, or they could sustain the credit of their notes. But they could hardly be expected to do both. Accordingly they urged the Secretary to cease the issue of the treasury notes and to use bank notes. The Government refused to do so, however, and in December, 1861, the banks suspended specie payment. Had the Secretary withdrawn the treasury notes and accepted the bank issues, it would have been a departure from the independent treasury law. But possibly the banks would not then have been compelled to suspend, and the Government could have kept the spirit of the specie clause of the law inviolate. In avoiding Scylla Mr. Chase fell into Charybdis. That the banks would have avoided suspension if the Government had accepted their notes is, of course, by no means certain. It is possible, perhaps probable, that the briskness of business caused by the war would soon have induced the banks to overissue, and specie payments might have been suspended just the same. Certainly the mere acceptance of the notes by the Government, while it would have greatly strengthened the credit of the banks, could not have prevented their notes from depreciating unless at the same time the Government could have limited their issue.

It is not, indeed, true that the main responsibility for the suspension of specie payments by the banks can fairly be laid on the independent treasury, for the banks could have refused to lend to the Government, and so could have kept their gold for the redemption of their notes; but if they had done so, treasury notes would early have been issued, in even greater numbers than they actually were, and they would inevitably have increased beyond the power of the Government to keep them at par. The independent-treasury law permitted the issue of treasury notes, and so far contributed toward the tendency to suspension. But the real force making for suspension was the policy of Congress and the Treasury Department in trying to meet the expenses of the war by loans, with as slight an increase of taxation as possible. The treasury notes contemplated by the independent-treasury law were convertible, and to be issued for a short time. The notes of the war period evidently violated the spirit of the law, though keeping within its letter. There is reason for thinking, however, that if the Government had used bank notes instead of treasury notes suspension could have been postponed and perhaps avoided.

Independent Treasury of the United States

The suspension of specie payments by the banks was necessarily followed, and that within a week, by a similar action on the part of the Government. On January 6, 1862, "it dishonored its own promises—it ceased paying coin," and gold immediately went to a premium of 2 per cent. Of the two evils, acceptance of bank notes in payment of government dues and the suspension of specie payments, the first, of course, was infinitely the less. The mistake of Secretary Chase was in thinking he could avoid both.

Thus the most important provision of the independent-treasury act of 1846 was made of no effect. The Government had been solicitous about keeping the public money safe from banks and bankers that would not, or could not, redeem their notes; but it turned itself to the manufacture, by the hundred million, of "greenbacks," which were forced on creditors in payment of the hard-earned dollars they had loaned. From this time on, then, certainly until the resumption of specie payments, the subtreasury law was largely a dead letter.

Still, the abandonment of the system of " divorce of bank and state" was not complete. The subtreasury remained in form. The legal-tender notes were not receivable for customs dues, because the Government had to have some specie, and there was now no way of getting it as a current receipt except by making these duties payable in gold.

We read nothing more in the treasury reports about the subtreasuries beyond the mere official reports of their transactions until 1863. During that financial year, we are told, the receipts and disbursements of the assistant treasurers at San Francisco and St. Louis, and of the designated depositaries, especially at Baltimore, Cincinnati, and Louisville, were "large beyond precedent." Of course, this simply meant that government financial matters had, in the conduct of the war, suddenly leaped to gigantic proportions. The duties of the officers, the Secretary assures us, were well performed. Meantime the plan of paying government dues by means of transfer checks on the assistant treasurers at New York, Philadelphia, Boston, and San Francisco had been adopted, and Treasurer Spinner informs us, in 1863, that the plan had proved of signal "benefit to the public creditors and an essential aid to the business of the department." The number of these checks had increased form 1,484 in the financial year of 1861 to 30,526 in 1863. In the latter year $159,864,954 were thus transferred. By the use of these the necessity for the actual transfer of specie was obviated.

In 1880 an effort was made to extend the system by the establishment of a subtreasury at Louisville, Ky. The petition was refused, the Finance Committee of the Senate pointing out that the only advantage that the establishment would bring to Louisville would be to save its people the expense of carrying coin to the nearest subtreasury for redemption and exchange, and that it would be cheaper for the Government to pay express charges on all these shipments than it would be to maintain a subtreasury.

The following table[a] shows the extent of the use of banks by the Government for the deposit of public money,

[a] Finance Report, 1906: 196.

Independent Treasury of the United States

from the establishment of the Treasury Department until the creation of the present national banking system.

Date.	Number depositary banks.	Balances.
Dec. 31, 1789	3	$28,239.61
Mar. 31, 1790	3	60,613.14
June 30, 1790	3	155,320.23
Sept. 30, 1790	3	349,670.23
Dec. 31, 1790	3	570,023.80
June 30, 1791	3	571,699.00
Sept. 30, 1791	4	679,579.99
Dec. 31, 1791	6	973,905.75
Mar. 31, 1792	6	751,377.34
June 30, 1792	9	623,133.61
Sept. 30, 1792	9	420,914.51
Dec. 31, 1792	8	783,212.37
Mar. 31, 1793	....	1,035,973.09
June 30, 1793	....	561,435.33
Dec. 31, 1793	....	753,661.69
Dec. 31:		
1794	....	1,151,924.17
1795	....	516,442.61
1796	....	888,995.42
1797	....	1,021,899.04
1798	....	617,451.43
1799	....	2,161,867.77
1800	....	2,623,311.99
1801	....	3,295,391.00
1802	....	5,020,697.64
1803	14	4,825,811.60
1804	16	4,037,005.26
1805	15	3,999,388.99
1806	....	4,538,123.80
1807	....	9,643,850.07
1808	....	9,941,809.96
1809	....	3,848,056.78
1810	....	2,672,276.57
1811	....	3,502,305.80
1812	....	3,862,217.41
1813	....	5,196,542.00
1814	....	1,727,848.63
1815	....	13,106,592.88
1816	94	22,033,519.19
1817	....	14,989,465.48
1818	29	1,478,526.74
1819	....	2,079,992.38

Date.	Number depositary banks.	Balances.
Dec. 31—Continued.		
1820...	....	$1,198,461.21
1821...	....	1,681,592.24
1822...	58	4,193,690.68
1823...	55	9,431,353.20
1824...	58	1,887,799.80
1825...	60	5,296,306.74
1826...	59	6,342,289.48
1827...	59	6,649,604.31
1828...	56	5,965,974.27
1829...	40	4,362,770.76
1830...	40	4,761,409.34
1831...	42	3,053,513.24
1832...	41	911,863.16
1833...	62	10,658,283.61
1834...	50	7,861,093.60
1835...	44	25,729,315.72
1836...	91	45,056,833.54
1837...	54	5,779,343.01
1838...	43	5,364,887.61
1839...	27	3,992,319.44
1840...	11	290,532.18
1841...	19	170,361.73
1842...	26	1,699,709.09
June 30:		
1843...	30	10,525,267.10
1844...	34	8,222,651.19
1845...	43	7,385,450.82
1846...	49	8,915,869.83
1847...	....	....
1848...	....	....
1849...	....	....
1850...	....	....
1851...	....	....
1852...	....	....
1853...	....	....
1854...	....	....
1855...	....	....
1856...	....	....
1857...	....	....
1858...	....	....
1859...	....	....
1860...	....	....
1861...	....	....
1862...	....	....
1863...	....	....

"The Secretary of the Treasury determines the number of such depositories, the amount of public money required in each for the transaction of the public business, fixes the amount of balances they may hold, and requires the banks thus designated to give satisfactory security, by the deposit of United States bonds and otherwise, for the safekeeping and prompt payment of the public money deposited with them and for the faithful performance of their duties as financial agents of the Government. The regular depositories receive and disburse the public moneys, and are required to pay interest at the rate of 1 per cent per annum on the average monthly amount of public deposits held in excess of the sum needed for the transaction of the public business, while the special depositories hold only the moneys transferred to them from the Treasury. They pay interest at the same rate on the average monthly amount of public deposits held."[a]

[a] Finance Report, 1909, 142

Chapter IV.—The Organization and Work of the Independent Treasury.

PROVISIONS FOR KEEPING THE PUBLIC MONEY.

The independent treasury, as at present organized, consists of the Treasury offices at Washington and nine subtreasuries under the charge of assistant treasurers. In carrying on its monetary operations in 1908–9 the Government has also utilized a varying number of designated depositaries, including the treasury of the Philippine Islands, the American Colonial Bank of Porto Rico, the Banco de la Habana, and the National Bank of Cuba.

The supervision of the independent treasury comes under the charge of the chief of the division of public moneys in the Treasury Department. Among other duties, according to the rules of the Treasury, that division must perform the following:

"The supervision of the several independent treasury offices, the designation of national-bank and other depositaries, and the obtaining from them of proper securities.

"The directing of all public officers, except postmasters, as to the deposit of public moneys collected by them.

"The issue and enforcement of regulations governing independent treasury officers, and the several depositaries and public disbursing officers, in the safe-keeping and disbursement of public moneys intrusted to them.

"The direction for special transfers of public moneys and generally all matters pertaining to the foregoing."[a]

---

[a] The Organization of the Office of the Secretary of the Treasury, published by Treasury Department, July, 1884. Department circulars describing methods of issue and redemption of currency, treatment of disbursing officers' checks, etc., are given in the appendix.

Independent Treasury of the United States

The places at which subtreasuries are at present located are Baltimore, Boston, Chicago, Cincinnati, New Orleans, New York, Philadelphia, San Francisco, and St. Louis. The relative importance of each is shown by the amount of business done for the fiscal year 1909.[a]

	Receipts.	Disbursements.
Baltimore...	$102,815,135	$102,565,652
Boston...	156,504,725	157,312,586
Chicago...	398,002,896	385,817,865
Cincinnati...	66,392,568	63,452,111
New Orleans...	54,464,360	56,636,350
New York...	1,802,315,952	1,859,063,475
Philadelphia...	313,687,394	313,290,852
San Francisco...	90,846,461	84,480,240
St. Louis...	140,776,861	136,006,667

The following table shows the comparative growth of the staff and expense of the subtreasuries from 1849 to 1909:

	1849.		1909.	
	Officers and clerks.	Salaries.	Employees.	Salaries.
Baltimore...			24	$34,000
Boston...	2	$3,400	31	45,710
Charleston...	2	3,400		
Chicago...			50	72,650
Cincinnati...			17	24,410
New Orleans...	2	1,400	20	28,890
New York...	6	9,100	130	206,510
Philadelphia...	2	1,400	36	49,440
St. Louis...	2	3,400	30	40,540
San Francisco...			18	30,420
Total...	14	18,700	356	532,570

Contingent expenses and salaries of special agents amounted to $20,000 more in 1849, making the total ex-

[a] Finance Report, 1909: 74

penditure on the independent treasury at that time $38,000.[a] At present, in addition to the expenses for salaries and wages, $3,000 are appropriated for salaries of special agents and expenses of examiners of subtreasuries and depositaries; $14,000 for paper for checks, drafts, etc.; and $260,000 for contingent expenses in the collection, safe-keeping, transfer and disbursement, and for transportation of notes, bonds, and other securities. These amounts added to that for salaries and wages give us a grand total of $809,570 for the expenses of the independent treasury for the fiscal year 1909–10.[b]

A law of March 2, 1853, fixed the compensation of the officers of appointed depositaries at one-half of 1 per cent on the first $100,000 received; one-fourth of 1 per cent on the second equal amount; and one-eighth of 1 per cent on all sums over $200,000. The depositary paid his own rent out of the sum thus received. These provisions were not, however, to apply to offices in which the maximum compensation allowed by law was already received. Nor could any officer receive a commission that would make his total income greater than such maximum; and the whole amount received by any one depositary could not exceed $1,500.

The exigencies of the civil war rendered an enlargement of the number of depositaries necessary until the national banks were established in considerable numbers. Depositaries have existed at one time or another in the following places, in addition to the subtreasuries mentioned in the

[a] Exec. Doc. No. 4, 31st Cong., 1st sess.
[b] Estimates of appropriations, House Doc. 177, 61st Cong., 2d sess., 48ff., 395.

table above: Buffalo, N. Y.; Charlotte, N. C.; Dahlonega, Ga.; Denver, Colo.; Dubuque, Iowa; Jeffersonville, Ind.; Little Rock, Ark.; Louisville, Ky.; Mobile, Ala.; Nashville, Tenn.; Norfolk, Va.; Pittsburg, Pa.; Richmond, Va.; Santa Fe, N. Mex.; Tallahassee, Fla.; and Wilmington, Del. Some of these were made assay offices by the coinage law of 1873 and others were dropped entirely.

The assistant treasurer and all officers authorized by law to act as such are required to give bonds for the faithful discharge of their duties, the amount to be fixed by the Secretary of the Treasury, and the sureties to be approved by the Solicitor of the Treasury.[a]

Not only has the amount of work of the kind originally performed by the subtreasury largely increased, but the character of the work has greatly changed. As originally conceived the subtreasury was, in its organization, so simple that its accounts might possibly have been kept in the simple manner ascribed to Gouge's "ingenious cordwainer." [b] Its duties were simply the receipt and payment of public money, in coin and treasury notes. Their enlargement is due to the financial operations connected with and consequent on the civil war; to the monetary and banking policy of the country; and to the great increase of government receipts and expenditures.

The work of the subtreasuries consists, in general, in receiving and paying all public money, receiving deposits of collecting and disbursing officers, and in issuing and redeeming, under proper regulations, all money of the United States. Besides the nine assistant treasurers

---

[a] U. S. Rev. Stats., 3600   [b] See above, p 38.

appointed as such, the superintendents of the mints at Carson City and Boise City are required by law to perform the duties of assistant treasurers. In addition to the subtreasuries the national banks also are keepers of the public money. By the act establishing them provision was made for depositing the receipts from internal revenue in these banks, and they have been used by the Government for that purpose ever since. An effort was made in 1868 to rescind the provision of the law making them public depositaries. On January 28 of that year a bill [a] passed the House of Representatives prohibiting the deposit of public money in banks in any cities or places in which there was a treasurer or an assistant treasurer, and prohibiting collectors and disbursers of public money from depositing public money in banks if they were within 50 miles of a subtreasury. The bill failed, however, to become a law.

The banks were to be allowed to hold public money on providing security by the deposit of United States bonds and otherwise, under regulations prescribed by the Secretary of the Treasury. The custom for a long time was to allow the banks to hold public money up to 90 per cent of the par value of the bonds deposited as security. But after the bonds rose so as to command high premiums, it became unprofitable for the banks to deposit them in advance as security for public money, because the money reached them only as it was collected in taxes, and this was often too slow a process to be to their advantage. Moreover, the practice in the earlier years of the system

[a] H. R. bill 450. See House Journal, 40th Cong., 2nd sess., 265.

was for the Treasurer to draw against his bank balances whenever funds were needed. "In consequence the balances were not uniform, but fluctuated from 60 per cent to par of the face value of the security. About October, 1886, the practice became quite general to allow a fixed balance equal to 90 per cent of the face value of the United States 4 per cent bonds, and a somewhat smaller amount on 4½ and 3 per cent bonds. This rule was changed in May, 1887, and a balance equal to par allowed on 4 per cents. Later, in October, in view of the stringency of the money market and the amount of surplus in the Treasury, and as an inducement to banks to become depositaries, the rule was again changed and a balance was allowed equal to 110 per cent of the face value of 4 per cent bonds and par of the 4½ per cents whenever a sufficient margin remained to cover the largest deposit likely to be received in any one day." [a]

Secretary Fairchild also increased the number of depositary banks at this time, and raised the limit of the amount of money that could be held by any one bank from one-half to one million dollars.[b]

When Secretary Windom assumed the Treasury portfolio, he changed the policy of his predecessor as to the extent of the use of the national banks as depositaries, and the amount of money held by them was reduced. Under the law and the regulations of the Treasury, collectors and surveyors of customs, collectors of internal revenue, and other receivers of public moneys who live

[a] Ex. Doc. No. 243, 50th Cong., 1st sess. (Secretary Fairchild in a letter to the House of Representatives.)

[b] Commercial and Financial Chronicle, October 15, 1887.

in a town in which there is a subtreasury or a national
bank depositary are required to deposit their receipts
daily. Officers who are unable to do this on account
of their distance from a depositary are required to forward
their receipts when they reach the sum of $1,000, and
at the end of each month whether they reach this amount
or not. Attorneys, marshals, and court clerks of the
United States who have occasion to receive public money
are also required to deposit according to the regulations above mentioned. Disbursing officers are required
to deposit disbursing funds to their official credit, and
must deposit such moneys with a treasurer or assistant
treasurer or a national bank depository authorized by
the Secretary for that purpose. It will be noticed that
under the law disbursing officers may not place their
funds in national bank depositaries without special
permission of the Secretary of the Treasury. If neither
a subtreasury nor a national bank depositary is available,
the Secretary may, under the law, authorize disbursing
officers to keep their funds as he thinks best. Failure
to comply with the provisions of the law as to making
deposits renders the offender indictable for embezzlement. Depositaries are required to keep accounts of
post-office deposits separate from other accounts of public
money.

Disbursing clerks, agents of the executive department,
independent officers, and commissions are directed to
make their deposits on or before the 5th and 20th of
each month in the United States Treasury, and any cash
balances drawn to meet pay rolls which have not yet
been paid out are held until the next regular pay day, and

after that they are therefore obliged to make payment by check.

Circulars issued from time to time by the Treasury Department give instructions concerning the proper discharge of the various duties of assistant treasurers.

The sources of the receipts of a subtreasury are new currency from Washington; deposits for transfer by the Treasury Department to other points; customs; transfers of public money from depositary banks; sales of gold by the assay office; internal revenue; patent fees; the annual tax on national banks; deposits of postmasters for the account of the Post-Office Department; deposits for the shipment of silver coin; and deposits by individuals, banks, and firms for redemption and exchange. These last may be mutilated or worn money, or it may be money of one kind, in good condition, deposited in exchange for another kind, as greenbacks for gold, or vice versa. The subtreasury is a money-receiving, money-paying, and money-exchanging establishment.

The subtreasury at New York is divided into departments, as follows: The receiving and the paying departments, the minor-coins department, the bonds department, and the checks department. As a matter of fact the classification is in practice carried further, so that there may be distinguished the general receiving and the gold-receiving departments, the general paying and the coin-paying departments, the coupon division, the registered interest division, the accounting and auditing division, and the bookkeeper's division.

The general receiving department is that into which all money other than gold is paid. All notes paid in are counted and sorted here, and counterfeits detected and thrown out. National-bank notes as well as government notes are received, for the Government accepts them now in payment of all dues except customs.

The "checks division" has charge of the receipt, payment, and issue of all checks. It is really a part of both the receiving and the paying departments.

The number of checks handled is very large. Probably at least two-thirds of the whole number of pensions are paid in checks on New York, making a million and a half or more checks annually from this source alone. Besides these, the New York subtreasury pays checks of several hundred disbursing officers, paymasters, quartermasters, and others, who use in all nearly half a million checks a year.

In the coins division a subdivision of labor is necessary on account of the great number of coins that are received of different denominations. Hence in the minor-coins division there are clerks whose whole time is taken up in receiving, counting, and sorting coins of only one or two different denominations, as 1-cent and 5-cent pieces.

The coupon and the registered interest divisions are, of course, really divisions of the bonds department, and their business is confined to dealing with the public debt.

The accounting department is the one in which all checks are finally gathered, classified, entered, and verified; and all accounts of disbursing officers are rendered monthly. It may be noticed in this connection that the accounts of the General Treasury are kept separate from those of disbursing officers. In the work of this department we find an explanation of a fact which we shall have occasion to note later, that sometimes the reported receipts and disbursements of the subtreasury do not correspond with the amounts of money actually received or disbursed, for there are many transfer transactions which appear only on the books. For example, the Treasurer transfers from the cash in the office, held on account of the General Treasury, $1,000,000, to be placed to the credit of a pension agent, against which the latter issues checks. On the books, that is treated as a payment from the General Treasury and a receipt by the pension agent's account, although no money is actually paid out until the pension agent's checks begin to come in.

The names of the other departments carry with them a sufficient explanation of the work done in them.

There are many interesting points of detail that are worth noticing. The visitor to the Treasury, or to a subtreasury, is always interested in seeing the provisions for the safe-keeping of the money on hand. It is kept in vaults, or strong rooms, usually in the basement of the building. There are five of these vaults in the New York subtreasury. Four of them are bright apartments, well lighted by electricity, on the main floor of the building, one on each side, and one under each of the Pine street side corners of the rotunda floor. These "vaults" are simply large safes, or strong rooms, full of steel drawers, and fitted with steel walls, ceilings, floors, and doors. The fifth strong room may be accurately termed a vault; it is the largest of the five and is situated in the basement. "Just where all this money is stored, on the site of the subtreasury, once stood old Federal Hall, where the first Congress of the United States met when the future of this country was in the balance; and in front of the sub-treasury building was George Washington inaugurated as first President of the United States."[a]

Fitted into the walls of the vaults in which silver is kept are iron boxes, or closets, of uniform size, each large enough to hold 100 bags of silver containing $5,000 apiece. As much as $40,000,000 or $50,000,000 of silver is sometimes collected in a single vault. The notes are stored in packages, each denomination by itself, and 1,000 notes to a package. This arrangement is convenient both for storing and for counting.

There is a large portion of the money in the subtreasury that is constantly on deposit—that is, is seldom paid out. This is true of the larger part of the silver, which is represented in circulation by certificates. This money is kept in vaults sealed with the seals of the assistant treasurer and of some representative of the Treasurer of the United States. When it becomes necessary to open one of these vaults, the seals must be broken and the vault unlocked in the presence of both parties interested, or in that of their duly appointed representatives.

The ordinary vaults, those which are in use every day, are in the charge of a vault keeper, can not be entered except in his presence, and even then only during business hours, because most of the vaults are fitted with time locks.

The accounts of the subtreasury are, of course, balanced every day, and a statement of the day's business is forwarded to Washington.

[a] New York Times, November 9, 1890.

Not the least interesting work performed at the sub-treasury is, to the casual visitor, the details of the redemption of currency. Mutilated currency usually reaches the subtreasury in the form of deposits, or is sent in for redemption by the banks, while very often men come alone and make inquiry about doubtful bills. The deposits contain new as well as old notes, and sometimes counterfeits. The clerks assort the bills as they are counted, putting together those that are still fit for circulation. The larger part of the mutilated money consists of bills of small denominations, ones, twos, and fives forming the heaviest contribution. The good bills are sent over to the paying department for disbursement, while the mutilated ones are tied up in packages of 100 bills each, and are canceled by having a hole of about the same diameter as that of a lead pencil punched through them. The punched bills are then sent on to Washington, where they are counted; they are then split in halves lengthwise, and are recounted twice. If the count is found to be correct, the canceled bills are then ground to pulp, and so destroyed.

The clerks in the receiving department, besides culling out the mutilated bills that come into the Treasury, are on the constant lookout for counterfeits. So quick are they in detecting spurious paper that, although they may be counting bills at the rate of 100 a minute, the momentary glance at a bill as it passes under their eyes is sufficient to let them know whether it is good or bad. On an average between 200 and 300 counterfeit bills a month are brought into the subtreasury. When a counterfeit is found, it is stamped with a steel die that cuts the word "counterfeit" in large letters out of the bill. Counterfeits are not, however, confined to notes. There are counterfeit coins also. Filled coins are the most dangerous of this class, especially filled gold coins, as they are the most profitable. The coin in this case has been cut open and a portion of the gold taken out; it is then filled in with some base metal which gives it approximately correct weight. These coins circulate with the public, but the subtreasury clerks promptly detect them and throw them out.

The precautions taken for preventing robbery are, of course, great. The contrast between the defenses of the New York subtreasury and those which Gouge so graphically described in 1854 [a] is, in its degree and kind, of the same general character as that between the state of the progress of the country then and now. Iron shutters, steel barred doors, and a dozen or more armed watchmen and detectives furnish security to a mass of treasure greater probably than the founders of the independent treasury ever dreamed would be in its possession.

BANKING FUNCTIONS OF THE INDEPENDENT TREASURY SYSTEM.

The independence aimed at by the establishment of the independent treasury was independence of the banks of the country, first, as to the safe-keeping of the public money; and, second, as to the steadiness of value of the currency. To accomplish the first purpose the Govern-

---

[a] See Finance Report, 1854.

ment provided its own depositaries. To secure the second it refused to receive bank notes, and, when the civil war broke out, it issued its own notes. The Treasury became, in a way, a bank of issue, and thereby opened the way for as far-reaching and mischievous interference with the money market as has ever been produced by the alternate contractions and expansions of the currency caused by its independence in the matter of deposits.

The evils of the attempt to have an independent government currency became evident when Secretary Chase made his attempts to borrow the specie of the New York banks in 1861 and 1862. The Government, under the independent treasury law, was obliged to be independent of the banks in the sense that it must not use their notes. If, therefore, the Treasury was to get money to carry on its now extensive operations it must use specie or issue Treasury notes. Secretary Chase felt that he must actually secure and put in the government vaults in the form of specie the amounts of the loans made him by the New York banks. But if he locked it up the banks could not keep it as a reserve against their notes. It could not be in both places at once. Therefore Secretary Chase's policy involved a double contraction of the currency— the withdrawal of the specie from the banks and the contraction of the bank-note circulation in consequence. As we shall see when discussing the relation of the sub-treasury to the management of loans, the banks could not stand such a strain. The Secretary therefore maintained the independence of the Treasury in the matter of currency by resorting to Treasury notes. This was a kind of independence which was not specifically contemplated, although it was distinctly enough implied, by the act of 1846.

After the country entered upon the policy of the use of fiat paper it made several attempts to maintain its independence of the banks in the currency it used. To be sure, with the establishment of the present national banking system, the Government acquiesced in the use of notes issued under it, but was not content to let these serve its purpose altogether. The use of irredeemable paper continued until 1879, and the notes, though now redeemable, are still in use. In addition, the Government entered upon a curious career in its silver policy in 1878 and 1890. The evils of the independence of the Treasury as to the kind of currency it shall use were especially evident in the period when the Treasury showed an excess of expenditures over receipts and at the same time stress in the money market and depression in business caused a run upon it for the exchange of its independent money for the specie with which the world is willing to settle its debts. The most serious portion of the experience was, of course, in the five years following 1890; although students of the subject need not be told that evils of no little magnitude had been caused in this way in the preceding twenty years. The lessons of the experience of the years from 1890 to 1895 were strong enough to force us a few years later to adopt some reasonable measures of protection in the management of the Treasury as a bank. To a full understanding of the independence of the Treasury, therefore, it is necessary to give some attention to what may properly be called its banking functions.

Independent Treasury of the United States

The history of the independent treasury shows that for long periods it has performed some of the functions of a bank of deposit and issue. It has redeemed United States notes since they came into use, and has for many years undertaken the service of transferring funds from one part of the country to another. Of late years, however, its banking activities have been greatly enlarged.

To the extent that it is required by law to receive money on deposit, and to pay it, or to issue notes and redeem them on demand, it is engaged in a business which can not be conducted without having ability to comply promptly with its obligations. As Secretary Carlisle wrote in 1893:[a] "Under existing legislation the Treasury Department exercises to a larger extent than all the other financial institutions of the country combined the functions of a bank of issue * * *. While the laws have imposed upon the Treasury Department all the duties and responsibilities of a bank of issue, and to a certain extent the functions of a bank of deposit, they have not conferred upon the Secretary any part of the discretionary powers usually possessed by the executive heads of institutions engaged in conducting this character of financial business." The subtreasuries act as banks of deposit, issue, and redemption, and as agents for the transfer of currency from one part of the country to another. In addition to performing these services, the New York subtreasury is also a storage warehouse or depot for gold and silver bullion used in international exchange to settle trade balances. If we were to enumerate the specific banking functions of the Treasury, they

---

[a] Finance Report, 1893: lxxiii.

would be as follows: (1) It issues and redeems paper money—United States and Treasury notes; (2) it exchanges various kinds of money for one another; (3) it prepares and supervises the issue of, and redeems, national bank notes; (4) it transfers money to move the crops; (5) it supervises the division of the money of the country into proper denominations so as to furnish the proper supplies of large and small notes, respectively; (6) it acts as a regulator of the rate of discount by contracting and expanding the currency through its operations upon the deposits in banks and in its own vaults; (7) it keeps the gold reserve of the country.

A brief account of the mode and conditions of the issue and redemption of currency by the subtreasury system will be interesting. All United States notes, and all national bank notes, that are unfit for redemption, are replaced with new notes at the Treasury, or at a subtreasury, free of charge; and United States notes are redeemed in gold, in sums not less than $50, at the subtreasuries in New York and San Francisco; gold certificates are issued for not less than $20 on deposit of gold coin at a subtreasury; silver certificates are issued for silver deposits, or for other, worn-out, certificates; and treasury notes of the law of 1890 are exchanged for silver bullion.

Silver dollars are exchanged at the Treasury or a subtreasury for silver certificates; and fractional silver is issued in any amount desired in exchange for government or bank notes. On the other hand, fractional silver coin and minor coin may be deposited in sums of $20, or multiples of twenty and "lawful money" received in exchange. Standard silver dollars are exchangeable for silver certificates only.

Since the issue of the United States notes known as greenbacks it has been the business of the Treasury to receive or redeem and reissue these notes. They are issued, to be sure, not on the basis of discount, as they would be if the Treasury were a true bank, but in the payment of other obligations. Moreover, their amount is fixed. The extent to which these practices of redemption and reissue are carried is scarcely realized by the majority of our people. To go back only a few years, we find that in 1897 the issue of United States paper currency and certificates was $374,848,000 and the redemptions $330,710,020. The Secretary of the Treasury, in his report for the same year, adds that the presentation of national-bank notes for redemption was so large as to overtax the staff of employees who counted and sorted them, so that it was necessary to secure some of the general funds of the Treasury to meet the expenses. For the years following 1897 the issues and redemptions of all kinds of paper currency were as follows:

Year.	Issued.	Redeemed.
1898	$1,310,677,000	$338,357,020
1899	301,276,000	309,808,330
1900	495,545,000	327,257,424
1901	407,102,000	358,891,490
1902	466,908,000	408,083,600
1903	551,038,000	488,558,220
1904	650,026,000	565,340,300
1905	637,540,000	623,026,600
1906	629,826,000	577,445,100
1907	698,273,000	582,902,000
1908	804,326,000	665,220,000
1909	764,510,000	722,395,000

In the fiscal year 1908–9 the United States notes issued and redeemed were $132,940,000. These redemptions were, of course, largely exchanges of notes of one denomination for those of other denominations. The largest number of exchanges is due to a demand for small denominations for circulation, on the one hand, and for large denominations to be used by the subtreasury in the settlement of clearing-house balances, on the other. Gold certificates were issued in the same year to the amount of $294,710,000 and the redemption of these certificates amounted to $261,892,000. Silver certificates were issued to the amount of $336,860,000 and redeemed to the amount of $326,796,000. Under existing conditions the annual redemption of United States notes and treasury notes in gold is, of course, relatively unimportant. In 1908–9 United States notes were redeemed in gold to the amount of $19,984,536 and treasury notes of 1890 to the amount of $31,405. We are not likely to have a repetition of the "endless-chain" process of 1893. For several years about that time the redemptions, of course, were very large. They rose from a little under $6,000,000 in 1891 to $102;100,345 in 1893 and to more than $158,655,956 in 1896. After that the amount thus redeemed gradually fell to $8,267,245 in 1903. Since that time it has increased slowly, until in 1909 it was a little over $20,015,941. These statements are sufficient to show the extent of the business of the Treasury in the matter of issue and redemption.

The exchange of one kind of money for another is, of course, included in what is called redemption in the treasury reports. Redemption in the proper sense refers to the acceptance of notes in exchange for gold, and the figures last given in the above paragraph are the ones that have reference to this process in its true sense. The Treasury has been obliged at times to make a distinct effort to push certain kinds of money into circulation. This has been notably true several times of the standard silver dollars. Standard silver dollars presented at the Treasury office for exchange during the fiscal year 1908–9 amounted to $23,488,604, which was a considerable decrease over that of the preceding year. Subsidiary coin is also redeemed by the Treasury to a considerable extent, and the amount in the fiscal year ending June 30, 1909, was over $56,000,000. One service which the Treasury is rendering now is to retire the treasury notes of 1890 as fast as silver dollars are coined.

Under the head of "Issue and redemption of currency" is included the transfer of money from one part of the country to another. The transfer here spoken of must be distinguished from the transfer of the Government's own money. This transfer relates to the money of individuals or of banks deposited at some subtreasury. Formerly the banks themselves paid the full expense of shipping money to the interior to meet the demand for "moving the crops." But after the Bland silver law went into effect it was soon found that the silver dollars were accumulating in the Treasury instead of passing permanently into circulation. To overcome this difficulty the Secretary of the Treasury took advantage of the usual fall movement of the currency to send silver to the interior and at the same time to increase the Treasury reserve of gold. In September, 1880, he issued a circular authorizing the delivery of silver certificates at subtreasuries in the interior in exchange for gold deposited at the subtreasury in New York, and the Government paid the express charges. The order was rescinded in January, 1885, and the present system adopted instead.[a]

In the crisis of 1890 a further step was taken. To relieve the money market at that time, the Secretary of the Treasury authorized the assistant treasurer at San Francisco to receive deposits of funds from bankers who desired to transfer them by telegraph to the assistant treasurer at New York. The purpose was to enable those having money in San Francisco, which was not needed there, to transfer it for immediate use in New York. The same privilege was promised to other places at which there were subtreasuries, if it proved of any service in affording relief. The order was soon complained of, however, by the San Francisco bankers, on the ground that it diminished their available reserve. The amount of transfers under the circular was over three million dollars.

The regulations which cover the issue and redemption of paper currency and the specie of the United States give an adequate idea of the work of the subtreasuries in the matter of issue and redemption. According to these regulations, (1) new currency is sent in return for currency unfit for circulation, and for national-bank notes and minor coin received for redemption. (2) Silver certificates are issued also by assistant treasurers in exchange for standard silver dollars. (3) Gold certifi-

[a] See p. 105 and Appendix 3.

cates are issued for gold coin. (4) Gold coin is paid out by the treasurer or subtreasurers for gold certificates, United States notes, and treasury notes of 1890. (5) Standard silver dollars are sent by express at the expense of the consignee in exchange for silver certificates or treasury notes of 1890. Charging the expense to the consignee is a departure from the old policy noted above whereby the Government paid the express charges in order to induce the banks in the interior to take silver dollars and put them into circulation. (6) Subsidiary silver coin is exchanged for United States notes or bank notes, and it is sent from the nearest subtreasury at the expense of the Government. If the consignee prefers to have the coin come by registered mail, it will be so sent at his risk, but with postage registration free. (7) Nickels and pennies are exchanged for United States notes or bank notes, and sent by express on the same terms as subsidiary silver coin. Both subsidiary silver coin and notes may be obtained, however, by drafts sent to the Treasurer or assistant treasurer in New York, payable to the order of this officer. The transportation charges on new silver or minor coin sent direct from the mints must be paid by the consignee. (8) Gold is paid out, of course, in the redemption of United States notes, treasury notes of 1890, and gold certificates. Silver certificates are redeemable in silver dollars at the Treasury or any subtreasury. National-bank notes are redeemed at the United States Treasury only, and not at the subtreasuries.

Provisions are made for the redemption of overworn currency, and careful instructions are given by the department as to the mode of packing and sending currency for redemption and exchange. One of the latest circulars on the subject will be found in the appendix.

The national-bank notes redeemed during the fiscal year 1909 amounted to $461,522,202, and were 67.8 per cent of the average outstanding circulation for the year. The amount redeemed varies considerably from year to year.

The words "money for moving the crops" have come to be a familiar heading in the Treasury reports of the United States. The service to be performed in this connection is not only to furnish the proper amount of small denominations of currency, but also to see to its proper geographical or economic distribution. As has been said, the method of transfer is for the banks in the interior cities to call on their New York creditors to deposit gold at the subtreasury and in exchange for this the Secretary of the Treasury orders payment of the amount to the creditor bank in the kinds of money called for at the home bank. In the fiscal year ending June 30, 1909, the subtreasury at New York received $10,250,000 in gold coin and certificates during the months of April, May, June, August, and September. The Treasurer and assistant treasurers of the United States paid for this deposit with $450,000 of United States notes to banks in Washington, $9,500,000 to banks in San Francisco, and $300,000 to banks in New Orleans. "The Treasury is called upon every year to provide small denominations of paper to facilitate the movement of the crops. A large part of this business is done by the deposit of funds with the assistant treasurer in New York, for which payment is made by the assistant treasurers in New Orleans, St. Louis, or Chicago, respectively." [a]

The supply of notes of small denominations is of course a matter of great importance. Notwithstanding the great development of our bank-check system, what is needed in the country districts during the spring and autumn is a sufficient amount of currency. This must be of such denominations as suits wage payments. Consequently the United States Treasurer takes especial care to furnish denominations of the proper amount. In the opinion of the Treasurer, as expressed in his report for 1909, there had been so considerable an increase in the volume of small denominations of currency during the past few years, and its distribution had become so much more general throughout the country, that the volume of requests for money to assist in moving the crops during the fall of that year was much less than formerly. According to the same report, all denominations of ten dollars and less was 53.85 per cent of the total paper currency on October 1, 1909. This shows a small relative decrease, though, as the Treasurer says, there has been an absolute increase.

We need not here expatiate upon the action of the Treasury as a regulator of the rate of discount. The whole story of its operations for nearly fifteen years, and especially for the past eight years, is a history of its attempts to keep the money market steady and the rate of discount equable by alternate deposits and withdrawals of the public money in the national banks, as well as by the sale of bonds and other devices that we will discuss later.

---

[a] U. S. Treasurer's Report, 1900: 21.

The Treasury keeps the gold reserve of the country. This function was assigned to it, by implication, by that clause of the specie-resumption law which established the gold reserve. But it is the act of March 14, 1900, which specifically and in great detail fixes and describes the banking functions of the Treasury, especially its duty to keep the gold reserve of the country. By that act the Treasury was divided into two departments, one of them the ordinary fiscal department of the Government, and the other the department of issue and redemption, virtually a bank. Under the provisions of the law the Treasurer is required to redeem in standard gold coin all United States notes and Treasury notes of 1890. For this purpose the Secretary of the Treasury is required to set apart a reserve fund of $150,000,000 in gold coin and bullion. This fund succeeds the old $100,000,000 reserve which had been kept by the Secretary of the Treasury under the implied authority of the resumption act. This fund of $150,000,-000 was made for redemption purposes only, as above specified. Whenever the Treasurer redeems United States notes he is required to use the notes which come into his hands for purposes of restoring and maintaining the gold reserve. Three methods are prescribed for doing this. In the first place he may exchange the notes redeemed for gold coin in the general fund of the Treasury. By the second method he may accept deposits of gold coin at any subtreasury or at the main office of the Treasury in exchange for redeemed United States notes. Or, finally, he may obtain gold for such notes.[a] If he finds that he is not able by any one of these means to keep the gold

---

[a] See sec. 3700, Rev. Stats.

reserve up to $100,000,000, he is required to sell bonds in order to restore it to the maximum, $150,000,000. The gold coin received from the sale of bonds first goes into the general fund of the Treasury, and is then exchanged for notes which have been redeemed and are held in the department of issue and redemption. The Secretary is given discretion to use notes which have thus come from the department of issue and redemption to redeem United States bonds, or for any "other lawful purpose the public interests may require," excepting to meet deficiencies in current revenue. Redeemed notes must therefore be held in the reserve fund until exchanged for gold. The reserve fund must be entirely of gold or gold and redeemed notes and may not exceed the maximum already mentioned.

The Division of Issue and Redemption of the Treasury Department, as has been remarked, has been assigned the banking functions of the Treasury so far as relates to issue and redemption of paper money. All records and accounts relating to the issue and redemption of United States notes, gold certificates, silver certificates, and currency certificates are now in charge of this division. It keeps the gold coin held against outstanding gold certificates, United States notes against which currency certificates have been issued, and silver dollars representing silver certificates, and is obliged to redeem notes and certificates by the respective funds held against them. These are known as the trust funds of the Treasury.

Under the law the Secretary may issue gold certificates against deposits of gold coin in sums of not less than twenty dollars. This right of issue, however, becomes inoperative when the gold in the reserve fund is below $100,000,000

Another provision of the law indirectly made it the duty of the Treasury Department to provide currency of small denominations by prescribing the denominations under which silver certificates may hereafter be issued. There are other provisions, but these are the essential and important ones for our purpose.

An examination of this law shows that it makes the issue and redemption department of the Treasury a bank of deposit and issue. Under the law the Treasury receives deposits of gold and issues warrants or certificates against them. It issues its own notes and holds the specie reserve against them. It exchanges money of one kind for other kinds. It performs exchange operations by a transfer of currency. Under the national banking law it virtually issues notes against a deposit of bonds without reserve. All these services it performs at considerable expense to the Government. In other countries the banks perform most or all of them at their own expense. In the function of issuing bank notes against bonds it is virtually discounting the paper of the issuing banks without direct charge. All that is necessary to make the Treasury a bank of discount is to permit it to accept securities other than United States bonds against note issues. If the law permitted it to accept commercial paper from the banks and to give them additional circulation in exchange, in times of crisis for example, it would be performing practically all the functions of a great central government bank and have all the functions and power necessary to "regulate the currency."

The history of the independent treasury since the creation of the national banks is a record of gradual departure
from independence, both in practice and in law. The
increasing revenues and disbursements of the Government and the irregularity of its fiscal operations have
produced interference with business to a larger extent
with the passage of the years. Efforts by the Treasury
to correct or prevent the consequent ill effects have
become much more frequent and brought the Government into closer relations with the banks. On some occasions, too, the necessities of the Treasury have compelled
it to rely on the help of the banks, and so brought them
together in their operations.

The law establishing the present national banking system, passed February 25, 1863,[a] took two more steps away
from the act of 1846. The first was that which allowed
national banks, designated by the Secretary of the Treasury, to be depositaries of public moneys, except receipts
from customs, under regulations to be prescribed by the
Secretary of the Treasury. The reason for prohibiting
the deposit of customs receipts in the banks was that
these were paid in coin, which the Government needed,
and the banks had suspended specie payments. They
were required to give security by the "deposit of United

---

[a] U. S. Stat. L., 37th Cong., 3d sess., p. 58, sec. 54; 38th Cong., 1st sess.,
p. 106, sec. 45.

States bonds and otherwise for the safe-keeping and prompt payment of the public money deposited with them." Postmasters in counties which had no designated depositaries, treasurers of mints, or assistant treasurers, or the Treasurer of the United States, might deposit in the national banks at their own risk. This was practically a reversal of the act of seven years before, which required collecting and disbursing officers to use the government depositaries. The second step backward, under the national banking law, consisted in giving a semi legal-tender character to the notes issued by banks formed under the new law. These notes were to be received at par in all parts of the United States in all payments to and by the Government, except customs and interest on the public debt, respectively.[a] Had this same use of the banks' notes been legalized two years before, Secretary Chase's hands would not have been tied; even the shadow of excuse for suspension would have been taken from the banks, the "greenbacks and depreciation" could have been easily avoided, and the monetary history of the succeeding forty years would doubtless have been a brighter record. This provision of law was almost a complete withdrawal from the position of 1846. The banks might also, by this law, be employed as the financial agents of the Government.

In this same year, 1863, to avoid the inconvenience of handling specie for the payment of duties and of interest on the public debt, the deposit of gold coin and bullion with the Treasurer or subtreasurers, in sums of not less than $20, was authorized; and certificates were issued for

---

[a] Section 20 of the bank act of 1863.

these, in denominations of not less than $20, and corresponding with the denominations of United States notes. The metal had to be kept for the redemption of the certificates, which were used in the payment of interest and customs. Thus the use of the vaults of the Government was given free of charge to bankers, brokers, and bullion dealers for the storage of their specie.

The suspension of specie payments had thrown gold on the market as a commodity, and speculation in it soon became rife. The violent fluctuations in the value of gold "reacted upon prices and turned the most legitimate of business enterprises into a kind of gambling." The principal causes of this unfortunate state of affairs were bad legislation and the accumulation of gold in the Treasury. The amount of coin received for customs dues had exceeded the payments of interest on the public debt until, in 1864, about $50,000,000 were stored in the government vaults. To relieve the situation Congress authorized the Secretary of the Treasury to sell the surplus gold for other currency. He did so to the extent of $11,000,000, but the effect was only for a day. The fluctuations of the value of the metal continued and were aggravated by the alternate accumulation and sale of gold by the Government.

In 1866 the organization of national banks was well under way, and the system had proved a great convenience. The Treasury report for 1866 says: "The employment of national banks as depositories of public moneys and fiscal agents of the Government has been a great aid to the department in the placing of loans, and especially to this office, in the collection of the revenues of the Government. They have within the three years ending with the

month of September, 1866, received moneys on deposit to
the credit of the United States as follows:

[Cents have been omitted.]

On subscription to United States stocks............... $1, 116, 151, 286
On account of internal revenue..................... 599, 936, 712
From miscellaneous sources........................ 37, 443, 637

    Total collections............................. 1, 753, 531, 636

"They have paid in various ways, and at points as
directed by this office, and without expense to the Government, during the same time, $1,722,554,656."

So close was now the connection between the banks and
the financial operations of the Government that the
"divorce of bank and state" could no longer be said to
exist. Said the Commercial and Financial Chronicle of
April 4, 1868: "The Treasury, so far from being severed
from the banks, may now at certain critical periods
possess great influence over them, and has had for some
weeks past almost despotic control over them, because it
could at any time take away their legal-tender reserves
by sales of gold, by sales of bonds, or by drawing down the
balances in the national-bank depositories." Yet the gap
still remaining between them, due to the fact that customs
receipts, which were in gold, could not be deposited in the
banks, gave Treasury operations a dangerous influence,
made more so because the country was on a fiat money
basis.

During the next few years the subtreasury remained
substantially the same in its influence and mode of operations, the extent of the latter adapting itself, of course, to
the needs of government business.

In 1873 the Government undertook virtually to perform the office of safe depositary for the banks by allow-

ing them to deposit legal-tender notes in exchange for certificates of deposit prepared at the expense of the Government. The deposits were withdrawable on demand. This meant that the banks could use the subtreasury to keep them in notes of convenient denominations at public expense.

The banking work of the Treasury received an additional impulse in this year by the reissue of legal-tender notes that had been once paid, but which Secretary Boutwell brilliantly regarded as a "reserve" that he could put out again to increase the currency and so relieve a stringency. This was, however, but a trifling interference with business relations compared with others that had been made since the day when the country had cut loose from the safe moorings of specie payments to which she had been definitely tied in 1846. In 1873 came the panic and the scarcity of money was severely felt. Had the country been on a specie basis the distress would probably have been much less, perhaps scarcely felt, for there lay in the vaults of the Treasury and subtreasuries $50,000,000 of gold which could not be used to relieve the situation because the specie was not wanted to pay private debts, for its use would have entailed a sacrifice equal to the amount of the premium on gold. Secretary Boutwell's "reserve" was brought into requisition again. In October Secretary Richardson thought to afford some relief by instructing the subtreasury officers to pay out silver coin to public creditors who wished it in sums not exceeding $5 in any one payment. But the Treasury held too few small coins to make an impression of any importance on the situation by such a step.

The next part of importance played by the subtreasury system was at the time of the resumption of specie payments, in 1879. Secretary Sherman decided to pay interest in coin at the New York subtreasury only. Other subtreasury officers were to pay interest to all who would accept legal-tender notes. The subtreasury at New York also became at this time a member of the clearing house, "to a certain extent and for certain purposes." The Government agreed to collect its checks through the clearing house and the latter to receive the balances due it at the counter of the subtreasury and to accept legal-tender notes in payment of all government drafts. Thus the connection of the Government with the banks became closer than ever. As the notes to be redeemed were government notes, the gold necessary for purposes of resumption was accumulated in the Treasury vaults and not in the banks. But resumption could probably not have been successful without the aid of the banks. The banks of New York City alone held $40,000,000 of government paper, and the presentation of these doubtless would have shipwrecked the Treasury plans. But the banks held them back and so strengthened the government credit. Moreover, so far the largest part of the drafts on the subtreasury passed through the clearing house, and as that organization had agreed not to call for specie the actual demand for coin payments, when resumption began, was very small.

The independence of the Government in financial operations could not well have been maintained under the financial conditions into which the nation drifted during the war. In fact, the national banks were avowedly created for the purpose of aiding the Government, and their very establishment was an abandonment of the principle of the subtreasury act of 1846. Whether it would have been possible to get on during the war without the aid of the banks in placing loans, even if the government finances had been differently conducted, is a question the correct answer to which could hardly be given in the affirmative.

But it was not only in loaning to the Government and in aiding resumption that the banks rendered valuable services. The refunding operations that have from time to time taken place would have been at least exceedingly difficult without their aid. The amount of labor and expense which they saved the Government in these was very great. But for the use of the banks as depositaries the money paid for the bonds sold "would necessarily have been placed in the subtreasury to await the maturity of the bonds called under the three months' notice required by law."[a] At the end of April, 1879, the banks had sold $389,944,295 worth of bonds, which sum would otherwise have gone into the subtreasury vaults, to be paid out only as the bonds matured or were called in. Thus more than one-half the paper circulation of the country would have been withdrawn from use and the results would have been disastrous.

A DECADE OF VACILLATING POLICY AFTER RESUMPTION.

Before the resumption of specie payments in 1879 the extent of the use of national banks by the Government was mainly dependent on the amount of the government fiscal operations; since then it has varied mainly accord-

---

[a] Proc. Amer. Bankers' Assoc., 1880.

ing to the views of the Secretary of the Treasury or the President.

In his report for 1885, Treasurer Conrad Jordan said that "a more extended use of the banks as depositaries would result in a large saving to the Government, and very much lessen the chances of loss from peculation and frauds in the conduct of the operations of the Treasury."

In 1885 the intimate connection of the Government with the banks was shown very emphatically by the reliance of the Treasury on the banks to extricate it from the difficulty into which it was brought by the reduction of its gold reserve.

Silver certificates had accumulated at money centers on account of the dullness of business, and were largely used in payments to the Government. So fast did they come in that anxiety was caused as to the ability of the Government to maintain gold payments. In March the New York clearing house, in order to relieve the Treasury, offered to receive silver certificates in part settlement of government balances due it. But even this was not sufficient. By the last of May the government holdings of gold had sunk to $115,810,533, including the greenback reserve of $100,000,000. In July the banks of New York agreed to purchase from the Government from ten to twenty million dollars' worth of subsidiary silver, and to pay for it at par in gold. The difficulty passed away after $5,000,000 of gold had been advanced.[a]

---

[a] The transaction was really a loan of gold by the banks to the Government, with the subsidiary silver as security, rather than a sale; and the banks soon afterwards got back their gold. There is some doubt whether the transaction was really necessary, for gold began very soon to flow into the Treasury. For an excellent account of the difficulty and the means whereby it was tided over, see Taussig's "The Silver Situation in the United States," Publ. Amer. Econ. Assoc., vii: 1: 30–37.

In 1886 Mr. Jordan again declared that the arrange-
,ments for collecting and disbursing the revenue were
defective, and recommended a larger use of the national
banks. A bill was introduced [a] in the House of Representatives to reduce the amount of bonds required from
national bank depositaries and so restore to the channels
of business the excessive accumulations of money in the
Treasury. The bill was never acted on, and nothing came
of Mr. Jordan's suggestion.

In pursuance of the policy of a larger use of national
bank depositaries, which animated the treasury management during the Presidency of Mr. Cleveland, the government deposits in banks were allowed to increase. On
January 1, 1887, they were about $20,000,000. In De-
cember the amount was $52,199,917, and in April, 1888,
it had become $61,921,294. The purpose, of course, was
to restore to circulation the money taken therefrom in
taxation by the Government and locked up in the vaults
of the subtreasuries, on the ground that its withdrawal
contracted the currency and so caused distress. The
policy was reversed, however, by Mr. Windom when he
became Secretary of the Treasury. In his report for the
fiscal year 1889 he condemns the use of the banks except
for the deposit of such sums as are necessary for the business transactions of the Government. Under his management the bank deposits were reduced by October, 1889,
to $47,495,479, and he declared his intention of making
a further reduction of $30,000,000. "The national bank
depositaries have been, and are," he says, "useful aux-
iliaries to the subtreasury system, but the deposit of pub-

---

[a] Dec. 20, 1886; H. R. bill No. 10324, 49th Cong., 2d sess.

lic funds therewith to an amount largely in excess of the needs of the public service is wholly unjustifiable. Such a policy is contrary to the spirit of the act of August 6, 1846, which contemplates a subtreasury independent of the banks." Whether or not Mr. Windom's opinion of the benefits of the subtreasury is correct, he was certainly justified in his wish and endeavor to observe the law.

Throughout these twenty-five or thirty years there occurred only two instances of loss to the Government from the use of national bank depositaries. Treasurer Hyatt wrote in his report for 1887: "The only losses suffered by the Government on this account, since the present system was adopted, occurred over twenty years ago. Under the present method of Treasury supervision it is hardly possible for any losses to occur."

"The early losses to the Government were caused by the failure of two banks, one in 1863 and one in 1864.[a] These losses have been more than counterbalanced by the benefit derived from the increased conveniences for collecting and disbursing the revenues of the Government without incurring any expense for transportation of funds to places where money was needed for the payment of its creditors."

We have seen that according to the provisions of the banking law the national banks were made the legal depositaries of all public money excepting customs receipts. Of course the bulk of the deposits was, therefore, internal-revenue receipts. Postmasters were at liberty to deposit in banks on their own responsibility where there were no government depositaries at hand.

---

[a] See the Finance Reports for these years.

The significance of the word "deposit" in connection with placing public money in the banks should perhaps be noted. The intent of the law was that the banks could receive this money as it was collected by the proper officers. The law did not give authority to any public officer to transfer to the banks money already actually deposited in the Treasury, subtreasury, or a government depositary other than a bank, except to the credit of disbursing officers for the payment of their drafts. There was a change in the meaning assigned to the word "deposits" about 1903. Whereas depositing in the banks originally meant permitting the accumulating revenues to go into the banks from the hands of the collecting officers, the Secretary in this year actually took money from the Treasury and deposited it in the banks. This gave a new significance to the word "deposit." It is probable that the previous interpretation of the law was due not so much to the actual prohibition of the transfer of money from the Treasury to the banks as to the difficulty of distinguishing internal revenue from the proceeds of customs in money once covered into the Treasury. As only the former could be put into the banks, it would have been unsafe to make any transfer when it was impossible to distinguish what part of the money came from this source.

There was no change in the interpretation of the law concerning the use of national banks as depositaries of public money until about 1898, although, as we have seen, Secretary Fairchild had allowed the public deposits to increase, in conformity with the interpretation of the law followed by his predecessors. Notwithstanding his explanations, his larger utilization of the banks raised a good deal of criticism and protest. Under the administration of Secretary Gage, however, the volume of deposits increased pretty rapidly, and we have the first clear evidence of the adoption by the Treasury Department of the policy of accumulating a volume of deposits determined by the state of the money market. The machinery which had been used as a means of relieving stringencies was now to be made a continuous regulator of the money market and the rate of discount.

In 1898 Secretary Gage prepaid interest and redeemed bonds and so relieved the money market, while at the same time he allowed the deposits in the banks to rise to $95,000,000. The next year he increased them to $111,000,000, nearly twice as much as the public had criticised Secretary Fairchild for making only a few years before. Secretary Fairchild had limited the amount in any one bank to $1,000,000, but in the year mentioned Secretary Gage allowed something over $15,500,000 to accumulate on deposit in the National City Bank at one time, and more than $4,500,000 in the Hanover National Bank of the same city. Secretary Gage did not, indeed, escape criticism for these increasing deposits, and he was accused of showing favoritism to the banks just mentioned.[a] In reply to a congressional inquiry on this point, however, he succeeded in satisfying Congress that he had been impartial.

The law was amended by the act of June 6, 1900,[b] authorizing the Secretary of the Treasury to designate

---

[a] See article "The Partial Responsibility of Secretaries Gage and Shaw for the Crisis of 1907," by A. P. Andrew, Bankers' Mag., 76: 493 ff.

[b] U. S. Stats. L., 56th Cong., 1st sess., 797 : 658.

depositary banks in the Philippine Islands, Porto Rico, and in Cuba, while occupied by the United States. Whereas bank depositaries on the continent proper were required by the old law to secure their deposits by "United States bonds and otherwise," the meaning of which we shall presently discuss, these insular depositaries were required to secure their deposits with United States bonds only to an amount not less than the deposits.

One other point in the development of the use of banks as depositaries is worthy of notice. According to an act of March 3, 1901,[a] the Secretary is required to "distribute the deposits herein provided for, so far as practicable, equitably between different States and sections." This is a reflection of the demand from banks in different sections of the country that no special advantage shall be given to any party or any bank by government deposits. There is no sound reason for the provision. It is impossible for anyone to say what is an equitable distribution. Moreover, what will be an equitable distribution in the sense of affording profits to the depositary banks might be a very vicious distribution from the point of view of the general welfare. If we are to use depositary banks at all, the Secretary of the Treasury should be required to utilize them in such a way as to promote the general interest, without regard to sectional prejudice and demand. "When Secretary Cortelyou came into the Treasury he found himself flooded with applications from national banks for deposits of the public funds. * * * It is a difficult problem to distribute deposits properly, and the head of the Treasury Department is under constant pressure. If there are

---

[a] U. S. Stat. L., 34: 1290.

two national banks in a town and one gets a deposit of public money, the other, in all probability, enlists the influence of a Member of Congress or Senator to help it get a deposit."[a]

The futility of the provision was shown in 1907 by the fact that "the allotment of deposits to the banks selected was made principally to relieve local needs for currency, but it was observed that many of the banks had their allotments placed with their correspondents in New York City, influenced no doubt by the high rates of interest prevailing there."[b]

The Secretary certainly should not be subjected to any such pressure. Either he should be left entirely free, without any legal restriction, or some definite plan of distribution should be provided for him. There is no reason why the public money should be scattered all over the country simply to accommodate banks which want to increase their profits; yet it is difficult to devise a plan that would be likely to meet general approval. It has been suggested that the government money should be kept in reserve cities.

In 1902 the act was further changed so that the treasurer of the Philippine Islands and banks in the islands chartered by the United States, or any State thereof, which had a capital of not less than $2,000,000, might be designated as depositaries by the Secretary of War and the Secretary of the Treasury. According to this act, the treasurer of the Philippine Islands was not required to

[a] Boston Evening Transcript, May 6, 1907.
[b] Finance Report (Treasurer) 1908: 161.

deposit bonds as security, nor to give other security unless required by the Secretary of War.[a]

THE ABANDONMENT OF THE POLICY OF INDEPENDENCE.

Much as Secretary Gage had done to establish a larger use of the banks and to aid the money market, it was under his successor, Secretary L. M. Shaw, that the policy of continuous regulation of the money market became fully developed. Here it is necessary only to narrate the successive steps by which the policy of the law of 1846 was virtually abandoned. The operations which led to them will be recounted later.

Secretary Shaw made a new departure in policy in two respects: He accepted other than United States bonds as security for public deposits, and told the banks that they need not keep a reserve against them. This last provision, of course, is open to serious criticism, for it made available as a basis of new loans, or for an expansion of credit, about $100,000,000 in the banks of New York alone. The Clearing House refused to avail itself of the privilege. However, the practice thus established by Mr. Shaw was legalized[b] by Congress in 1908.

On August 27, 1903, however, Mr. Shaw departed from the policy of allowing public money simply to accumulate in the banks, and announced his purpose to transfer money from the Treasury to the banks in order to prevent or relieve a stringency in the market. He then said that he had about $38,000,000 to assist the banks if a panic came.

In 1907 what had actually become a practice was legal-

---

[a] U. S. Stat. L., 57th Cong., 1st sess., 1369: 711.
[b] U. S. Stat. L., 35: 552.

ized by the act of March 4,[a] amending the depositary section of the law by providing that banks might receive on deposit the receipts from customs. It may fairly be said that with the passage of this act, permitting the banks to receive deposits of customs receipts, the last vestige of compulsory independence of the United States Treasury as the depositary of government revenue disappeared. Under the old law the customs receipts, more than half of the government revenue, could not so be used. Since the public had become accustomed to expect the Secretary of the Treasury to "ease the market," it seemed foolish to continue to insist that half the revenues of the Government should be unavailable to him for this purpose, while of course the original reason for making an exception of the customs revenues had in a sense disappeared. That reason was to make sure that the receipts from the customs, which had to be in gold, got into the hands of the Government rather than those of the banks. As circumstances were in 1907, therefore, there was a good reason for making this change in the law. Moreover, it was obviously one of the steps toward the ultimate abolition of the independent treasury and the possible establishment of a central bank as the agent of the Government.

The amendment to the law in 1907 found the Treasury, however, poorly equipped with the machinery necessary to carry out its provisions. This remark applies, for example, to the receipt and custody of the securities required from the banks. Moreover the enlargement of the government deposits in the banks emphasized the cumber-

---

[a] U. S. Stat. L., 34: 1290; 59th Cong., 2d sess., 2914.

someness of the lawful method of getting the money out of the banks and back into the Treasury.[a] The legal method of making payments is by subtreasury drafts. The Government can not check on its deposits in the banks but must cover the money back into the sub-treasury, a process which involves many complicated formalities in the surrender of the securities deposited by the banks. So many were the difficulties of carrying out the depositary law, especially with the provision included in the amendment of 1901 that the Secretary "should distribute the deposits herein provided for, so far as practicable, equitably between the different States and sections,"[b] that the Secretary of the Treasury, Mr. Cortelyou, appointed a commission to work out a systematic plan relative to the deposits of public money. The commission included the United States Treasurer, the Director of the Mint, the Comptroller of the Currency, one representative of the Division of Loans and Currency, and one from the Division of Public Moneys.[c] It seems that the commission had several meetings and discussed the subject pretty thoroughly, but never made a formal report. An avalanche of protests was received from banks all over the country, which had, or wanted, public deposits, against any plan which might deprive them of this source of gain.

In May, 1908, another amendment was made to the law, whereby all regular national bank depositaries are

[a] Cf. Boston Evening Transcript, May 7, 1907, article on Government Bank Deposits. Of course, in those places in which the subtreasury is a member of the clearing house the difficulty is less.

[b] Act of March 3, 1901.

[c] See "Cortelyou Plans Reform," Boston Evening Transcript, May 6, 1907.

required to pay interest upon public deposits at the rate of 1 per cent per annum on the average monthly amount of the deposit. The rate of interest must be uniform throughout the country. This last provision is bad, for it makes no allowance for differences of rates in different localities. The rate fixed is so low that very likely little mischief will be done; but if the rate were higher, it might easily happen that in some places a local stress would make the local rate of discount lower than the interest to be paid on the public deposits, and in other places higher. Thus we see that the legislative provisions of recent years emphasize the truth of what has been said in another connection, that the only conditions under which the public money should be deposited are those of safety, convenience, and reasonable profit consistent therewith.

It appears therefore that recent legislation has virtually destroyed the distinction between the subtreasury and the national banks as places for the depositing of public money. So far as appears on the face of the law, it would be proper for the Secretary of the Treasury to deposit all receipts of the Government in the national banks. If he had the authority to check against such deposits instead of having to cover them back into the Treasury, the use of the independent treasury for depositary purposes would pass away. It is not impossible that some Secretary of the Treasury may take the view that it is not forbidden to do this. If so, the policy of the independence of our Treasury, so far as concerns the safekeeping of the public money, will have passed away.

The number of banks used as depositaries of public money has largely increased in the past few years. Some of them are regular depositaries and some special or temporary. For example, on September 30, 1909, there were 207 regular and 974 special depositaries.[a] The use of the latter first became large in the panic of 1907. The following table shows the number of depositary banks, and the receipts and balances of bank deposits, from the beginning of the national-banking system.[b]

Date.	Depositary banks.	Bonds to secure deposits.	Receipts.	Balances end of fiscal year.
1864	204	$30,009,750	$153,395,108.71	$39,980,756.39
1865	330	32,707,500	987,564,639.14	24,066,186.19
1866	382	38,177,500	497,566,676.42	34,124,171.54
1867	385	39,177,950	351,737,083.83	25,904,930.78
1868	370	38,517,950	225,244,144.75	22,779,797.62
1869	276	25,423,350	105,160,573.67	8,597,927.34
1870	148	16,072,500	120,084,041.79	8,206,180.34
1871	159	15,536,500	99,299,840.85	6,919,745.59
1872	163	15,329,000	106,104,855.16	12,501,595.08
1873	158	15,210,000	169,602,743.98	7,233,551.11
1874	154	15,390,200	91,108,846.70	7,435,966.69
1875	145	14,547,200	98,228,249.53	11,562,679.52
1876	143	14,578,000	97,402,227.57	7,520,194.76
1877	145	15,377,000	106,470,261.22	7,299,999.28
1878	124	13,858,000	99,781,053.48	46,928,268.56
1879	127	14,421,400	109,397,525.67	208,033,840.24
1880	131	14,777,000	119,493,171.94	7,771,233.90
1881	130	15,295,500	131,820,002.20	8,704,830.83
1882	134	15,925,000	143,261,541.41	9,381,712.90
1883	140	17,116,000	145,974,256.86	9,803,381.79
1884	135	17,060,000	129,100,449.35	10,488,827.63
1885	132	17,607,000	119,056,058.94	10,770,579.96
1886	160	19,659,900	123,592,221.68	13,822,070.80
1887	200	26,485,500	128,482,769.20	18,975,315.41
1888	290	56,128,000	132,591,946.77	54,698,728.36
1889	270	45,222,000	139,316,214.49	43,090,750.53
1890	205	29,713,000	147,761,566.81	26,779,703.32
1891	185	26,349,500	152,389,837.70	21,399,689.16
1892	159	15,852,000	159,380,415.47	10,450,130.01
1893	160	15,247,000	166,257,566.29	9,962,526.00
1894	155	14,736,000	147,326,916.13	10,423,767.61
1895	160	15,278,000	169,440,435.46	10,978,505.80

a Finance Report, 1909: 234ff.
b Finance Report, 232ff. Cf. table of deposits for years preceding, on p. 81.

Date.	Deposi-tary banks.	Bonds to secure deposits.	Receipts.	Balance end of fiscal year.
1896..............	160	$16,928,000	$181,705,917.74	$11,415,474.42
1897..............	168	16,930,500	149,306,649.29	12,162,158.05
1898..............	172	30,851,500	207,178,119.61	33,843,700.81
1899..............	357	78,564,540	283,276,222.20	70,295,326.94
1900..............	442	107,253,580	303,903,655.56	92,621,371.72
1901..............	448	105,765,450	313,373,160.38	93,442,683.00
1902..............	577	124,718,650	281,234,091.57	117,141,564.13
1903..............	713	152,852,020	244,947,528.71	140,001,016.70
1904..............	842	112,902,550	251,970,862.51	104,459,638.45
1905..............	837	80,404,950	251,255,327.39	64,803,466.30
1906..............	928	95,575,725	267,418,788.43	80,731,058.05
1907..............	1,255	193,244,052	313,824,771.09	166,803,951.96
1908..............	1,436	180,459,419	293,869,490.31	147,692,036.79
1909..............	1,414	81,244,071	300,924,352.92	60,427,525.69

The table given is compiled from tables 50, 52, and 54 in the report of the United States Treasurer for 1909 and corresponding tables in other reports. The balances are those on deposit at the close of the fiscal year. It should be noted, however, that these balances differ from the balances given in Table 54 of the Treasurer's report for 1909.[a]

A study of the columns giving the number of depositary banks since 1864 shows, as has been already stated, a

---

[a] The explanation of the difference, kindly given by the United States Treasurer is as follows:

Table 54, on page 240 of the report, is an aggregated statement of ledger balances, including the unavailable funds and the deposits in the treasury of the Philippine Islands. The balances standing to the credit of the Treasurer of the United States with the depositaries, when brought together, verify the amount stated in the table referred to, as follows:

In national-bank depositaries (p. 19).................. $60,427,525.69
In treasury of Philippine Islands (p. 19).............. 957,628.34
Unavailable balances in banks (p. 188)............... 214,761.38

Total..................................... 61,599,915.41
Less warrants outstanding (p. 19)................... 1,432,027.18

Balance as stated in Table 54 (p. 240)........... 60,167,888.23

very great variation, indicating the changeableness of policy. In 1867 the number of depositary banks rose to 385; after this it fell rapidly to the low point of 127 in 1879. It should be noted, however, that the balance in the latter case, although the number of banks was smaller, was nearly nine times as much in the former-mentioned year. From 1879 the number again increased to 290 on June 30, 1888. The number again fell to 155 in 1894, and then rose each year until in 1904 it became 842. The following year the number fell to 837 and has steadily increased since, the numbers for the four following years being, respectively, 928, 1,255, 1,436, and 1,414.

As to the total receipts in recent years, the sum in 1890 was $147,761,566; the amount increased every year with two exceptions, 1894 and 1897, until it reached the high total of $313,373,160 in 1901. It was less during each of the following five years, but rose again in 1907 to $313,824,771, fell to $293,869,490 in 1908, and became $300,924,352 in the fiscal year of 1909.

The balances on hand in the depositary banks at the close of the fiscal years also show great differences. The balances are significant because they throw some light on the policy of the department as to the amount of money left in the control of the banks. The balance in 1893 was $9,962,000. It did not vary much for four years, but took a sudden leap in 1898 to over $33,000,000. In 1899 the balance at the close of the fiscal year was more than double that of the preceding year and increased steadily until in 1903 it was $140,000,000. In each of the two following years there was a large decrease, but in 1907 the balance rose again to the large sum of

$167,000,000. In 1908 it was $147,692,000 and on June 30, 1909 it was $60,427,525.

The warrants paid by the banks in 1890 were $20,548,-812. They remained within a million or two of this figure until 1902, and have since increased until in 1909 they aggregated over $79,000,000.

As to the amount transferred to the banks from the Treasury, it never rose to as high a figure as $100,000,000 before 1899, but in that year it suddenly jumped to $226,173,117 from $82,971,223. Two years later it had fallen to $125,000,000. In 1903 it became $201,000,000, in 1906 $233,000,000, in 1907 $349,000,000, in 1908 $297,000,000, and in 1909 $192,000,000.

SECURITY FOR DEPOSITS OF PUBLIC MONEY.

According to the law passed April 2, 1864, providing for the use of national banks as depositaries of government revenue, it was provided that such deposits should be secured by United States bonds and otherwise. The necessity has never arisen for courts to pass upon the meaning of the words "and otherwise." From a study of the debates of Congress it appears that the words were intended to mean a personal bond. The words were inserted as an amendment to the original bill by Mr. Hooper, of Massachusetts. On inquiry on the floor of the House as to the meaning intended by the amendment, Mr. Hooper replied: "By the present arrangement or rules of the Department, the Secretary requires a personal bond in addition to a deposit of United States stock, and it was to cover that point that I offered the amendment." [a]

It does not seem to have occurred to any Secretary of the Treasury that the security to be accepted for a deposit of public money in the banks could be other than United States bonds until the time of Secretary Leslie M. Shaw. He ruled that other kinds of securities might be accepted, so that United States bonds might be released and become the basis of new note issues. This was virtually making the phrase "United States bonds *and* otherwise" read "United States bonds *or* otherwise."

The action of the Secretary aroused much discussion and criticism, but was defended on the ground that the phrase "United States bonds and otherwise" is verbally capable of that interpretation. Against this opinion, however, certain considerations must be set. These are:

1. The intention of the framers of the law clearly was to restrict the bonds used to those of the United States. This is evident from the remark of the mover of the amendment by which the words "and otherwise" were inserted in the law.

2. The other interpretation reduces the phrase to absurdity. If "United States bonds and otherwise" means a mixture of United States and other bonds, the Secretary could accept as security for any amount of deposits two United States bonds of the lowest denomination and let the rest of the security be in the form of other bonds. If it were the intention of Congress to permit this, the requirement of United States bonds at all is foolish.

---

[a] Congressional Globe, 38th Cong., II : 1401.

3. Every Secretary of the Treasury before Mr. Shaw since the passage of the act under discussion has construed the phrase in the sense intended by Congress. All have uniformly refused to accept other bonds as security for public deposits.

4. The intent of Congress may be inferred also from the fact that it has always refused to amend the national banking law so as to permit the use of other than United States bonds as security for note issues.[a]

How far we have broken away from our older practice may be seen from a letter of the Secretary of the Treasury, under date of February 27, 1908, transmitting a response to the resolution of the House of Representatives as to the number, capital, circulation, deposits, etc., of the national banks.[b] The variety and character of the bonds held by the different banks is remarkable. Besides United States securities we find railway, municipal, county, and state bonds.

The attitude of the present administration of the Treasury on the relation of the Government to the banks may be gathered from these words of the Secretary: "The tendency to affiliate the subtreasuries with the clearing houses of their localities is, I think, clearly in the right direction. There seems to be no good reason why the receiving and paying work of the Government should not be on the lines of the receiving and paying work of other business organizations, and so far as the discretion lies with the Secretary of the Treasury I shall consider with great

---

[a] Cf. the proposals of Hon. M. A. Harter, of Ohio, in bill 5442, introduced in Congress February 5, 1892.

[b] House Ex. Docs., 714, 60th Cong., 1st sess.

interest suggestions for the adjustment of the ordinary paying and receiving business of the Government to the convenience of the people.

"I even hope for, and I beg to suggest to the consideration of the Congress, a reconsideration of the methods of the payment of customs duties so that these transactions may cease to be so very inconvenient and may conform themselves to the ordinary practices of business. The spectacle should not be possible of a detail from the navy carrying $30,000 in cash through the streets of New York from the subtreasury to the custom-house to pay duties on navy importations and of a return trip from the custom-house by the representatives of the collector back to the subtreasury with this same money, all because the collector of customs could not legally accept a check of the Navy Department upon the subtreasury.*a*

Under the pressure of a growing deficit, the present Secretary was obliged in 1908–9 to recall a large part of the government deposits from the banks. He says: "In previous years it was deemed advisable to restore accumulating revenues in the Treasury to the channels of trade by making direct deposits thereof in national banks; consequently, with the growth in disbursements in later years not equaled by the income, such deposits have been gradually recalled to the Treasury as needed. The balance in depositary banks to the credit of the general fund at the beginning of the last fiscal year was $149,004,924. Calls for the return of deposits to the Treasury were made as follows: July 2, 1908, $33,403,120; November 18, 1908,

*a*Finance Report, 1909: 13–14.

$4,864,750; January 11, 1909, $24,716,760; February 4, 1909, $28,478,000; and June 30, 1909, $24,954,900. The total amount of these calls had not been paid by the close of the fiscal year, but the balance in banks to the credit of the general fund had been reduced to $60,427,525.69." [a]

From all this it appears that from being a passive agent in not contracting the currency by simply allowing the internal revenue to accumulate in specified national banks, the Treasury has become an active, positive, agent by making actual transfers of money once covered into the Treasury. It has enlarged its power to deposit, and has not only accepted a larger variety of securities, but allowed a larger volume of deposits. We have seen it first in a condition where the deposits simply accrued; second, a condition in which not only were deposits allowed to accrue, but money once in the treasury was actually transferred; third, adding to the source of these deposits by including customs as well as internal revenue; fourth, increasing the number of depositary banks; fifth, changing the character of securities, first by the Secretary of the Treasury, and then by law; sixth, increasing the payment of government obligations by bank warrants. "Thus we see that in the sixty years of its existence, the independent treasury has become an institution of a very different character from what its creators intended. In 1846 it was a depositary of the public moneys, intended to keep them safe from the manipulation of banks. In 1861 it established a permissible but slight connection with the banks. In 1903 we find

---

[a] Finance Report, 1909: 34.

the law interpreted so as to take the money actually already in the Treasury for deposit in the banks, and from then until now we see the independent treasury made an active and dominating factor in determining the volume of money in circulation, in other words, the elasticity of the currency."[a]

OPERATIONS OF THE INDEPENDENT TREASURY UNDER THE POLICY OF REACTION.

The functions described as gradually added to the independent treasury in the past ten years in the efforts to neutralize its ill effects have become a regularly recurring part of the Treasury operations. The cases of interference due to the occurrence of crises will be described in connection with that topic. A sketch of the ordinary Treasury operations for the past few years will bring out strongly the other services described.

For five or six years after 1890, as a result of the independence of the Treasury in creating its own circulating medium for some years previously, the monetary affairs of the country were so deranged that its independent method of keeping the public money was of secondary importance and interest. The alternate intake and output of money from circulation continued, indeed, as before. But their influence was lessened because of deficits in revenue and the increasing use of depository banks. The operations connected with the currency can be described more appropriately in discussing the panic of 1893.

---

[a] Publ. Amer. Econ. Assoc., 3d series, 9: 1: 204.

With the advent of Secretary Gage into the Treasury Department we find the beginning of a period of positive reaction from the policy of independence and a definite attempt toward closer affiliation with the banks. In the matter of keeping the public money, Secretary Gage inaugurated no new policy, but extended existing practices. In the matter of Treasury issues he stood for further advance in the direction of sound currency, which had been taken with the repeal of the silver purchase law. His object was largely attained by the action of Congress in passing the currency law of 1900.

To Mr. Gage's successor, Secretary Leslie M. Shaw, is to be ascribed the wide departure from established policy and practice, which, although afterwards sanctioned by act of Congress, invited sharp criticism from business men and students of financial affairs. With the stoppage of constant inflation from silver coinage, with the recurrence of an "endless chain" redemption of greenbacks prevented by the law of 1900, and with the return of a surplus in the revenue of the Government, public attention was turned once more to the evils of the other phase of the independence of the Treasury, that concerned with the safe-keeping of the public money. The condition of the bank reserves and the state of the money market became matters of concern to the Secretary and started him in the policy of closer union of bank and Treasury, which, more than anything else, distinguishes his career from that of any of his predecessors since the passage of the act of August 5, 1846.

During the summer of 1902, the bank reserves, contrary to custom, showed almost continuous decrease. The

Secretary of the Treasury consequently anticipated trouble in the fall and prepared to meet it. He ordered as many bank notes as could be engraved to be prepared in advance, so that they would be ready for immediate distribution on the call of the banks, and thereby avoid the delay in issuing them to which the banks had been previously subjected in times of sudden stringency and increased demand for circulation. In order to induce the banks to take out additional circulation the Secretary about this time also offered to accept other bonds than those of the United States as security for deposits.

A third preparatory move was the announcement that the Secretary would anticipate the payment of interest due in November on the public debt. He announced, in the fourth place, an increase in the deposits of public money in the banks, and finally gave out the information that he would not put into liquidation banks which failed to maintain reserves against public deposits. This was granting permission to the banks so to interpret the law requiring a reserve against their deposits as to exclude public money from counting as deposits in the sense of the law. This practice, which at this time was based entirely upon what the Secretary supposed the law gave him permission to do, was legalized six years later. The Secretary of the Treasury seemed to believe that upon him was placed the burden of regulating the money market in the interests of what he regarded as the public welfare.

In the following year, 1903, the Secretary, being of the opinion that the deposits of current internal revenue and miscellaneous receipts in the banks were insufficient to prevent the possibility of a serious stringency, took another radical step. Of course, the daily or weekly receipt of the proceeds of the internal revenue by the banks enabled them to increase their discounts, and of this opportunity they took advantage. The receipt of this public money, therefore, did not necessarily put them in any stronger position to withstand a shock. Accordingly the Secretary ordered the receipts from internal revenue and miscellaneous sources to be accumulated in a separate fund "so as to be prepared in case of an emergency to grant prompt relief by large deposits." [a] He was preparing to transfer to the banks money already covered into the Treasury. By the means thus far described, and also by bond purchases, in the neighborhood of $27,000,000, were "restored to the channels of trade" in the fall of 1903.

One new feature presented in the year 1904–5 was a decrease in the national revenue. The year closed with a deficit of $23,000,000. Confronted with this deficit the Secretary found it necessary to strengthen his position by reducing the deposits with the banks. He withdrew $50,000,000 in the summer, and from this and other causes the surplus reserve of the New York banks fell to less than $7,000,000. The benefits received by previous actions were being offset by the present one.

In 1906 was announced Secretary Shaw's much criticised plan of depositing in banks against gold imports. He is charged with showing partiality in this move to one of the larger banks of New York City.[b] The plan was to

a Finance Report, 1906, 38.

b A. Piatt Andrew: The Partial Responsibility of Secretaries Gage and Shaw for the Crisis of 1907; Bankers' Magazine, 76:493.

make deposits in any bank that would import gold equal to the amount of gold engaged, the deposits to be returned when the gold arrived. In this way, he tells us, approximately $50,000,000 of gold were brought from abroad. It is said that permission to do this was given to the National City Bank of New York two weeks before public announcement of the policy was made. In his report for 1906, Secretary Shaw defends the policy on the ground that it had caused the importation of gold without expense to the Government and with great benefit, although without profit, to the banks. This is a matter about which there is room for a difference of opinion.

This was regarded by many people as an extraordinary action. A somewhat similar proposal was made to the Secretary of the Treasury in 1873. It is interesting to compare his action with that of Secretary Shaw as contrasting the different views of the two men as to the scope of their discretion in their interpretation of the law. In September, 1873, the New York Produce Exchange asked the Secretary of the Treasury "that currency be immediately issued to banks or bankers, upon satisfactory evidence that gold has been placed upon special deposit in the bank of England, by their correspondents in London, to the credit of the United States, to be used solely in purchasing commercial bills of exchange." The Secretary replied:

"If your object is to induce the Treasury Department to loan United States notes to banks in New York upon the pledge and deposit in London of gold, it is asking the Secretary of the Treasury to loan the money of the United

States upon collateral security for which there is no authority in law. If the Secretary of the Treasury can loan
notes upon a pledge of coin he can loan them upon a
pledge of other property in his discretion, as he has re-
cently been requested to do, which would be an extraordinary power as well as a most dangerous business to engage in, and which my judgment would deter me from
undertaking, as the Secretary of the Treasury, even if by
any stretch of construction I might not find it absolutely
prohibited by law."[a]

Another remarkable operation for which Secretary Shaw
was responsible in 1906, was the reduction of deposits of
public money secured by other than United States bonds,
and an increase of deposits secured by United States
bonds, in order to make the latter bonds scarce and push
up the price to furnish a better market for the sale of the
new Panama bonds. Under the circumstances, the Panama bonds sold at 1.0436 as against a market price of
1.0325 for 2 per cent nineteen-year consols. To quote the
Secretary's own words: "In other words, a market for
government bonds was created which stimulated their
price."[b] We may doubt whether the cause assigned for the
rise in the price of bonds at the time is the true one. But
even if not, one is amazed at the opportunity for manipulation of the market afforded by this mode of procedure. It
was virtually an attempt to corner the market for existing
United States bonds in order to get a higher price for the
new debt.

The fall of 1906 brought the expected stringency, and
the Secretary took new steps in the application of his

---

[a] Finance Report, 1873, XIII.   [b] Finance Report, 1906: 40.

policy to care for the business interests of the country. He again made deposits against gold imports to the amount of fifty millions; he accepted other than United States bonds as security for deposits of public money, to the amount of $18,000,000, on the same condition as before, that the extra circulation based on the released bonds be taken out by the banks and be retired not later than the following spring or summer. He was looking forward to a contraction of the currency at a time when he thought it ought to be contracted, just as he was providing for its expansion at the season when he thought that necessary.

But the limits of the Secretary's beneficent policy were not yet reached. Not content with keeping, or trying to keep, the money market of our own country in stable equilibrium, he felt it incumbent upon himself to do what he could to help the rest of the world on the same matter. He declared that no government operations in this country should be permitted to interfere with prosperity either at home or abroad,[a] and then went on as follows: "The Treasury now holds (November 20) in its own vaults a working balance of $78,000,000, as much as can possibly be spared of which will be deposited if business conditions require it, though it become necessary to pay current expenses of the Government with checks on depositary banks.[b] The money of the country belongs to the people, and Treasury operations must be

---

[a] Finance Report, 1906 : 40.

[b] The authority for so doing, it is alleged, is found in the general powers of the Secretary and the Treasurer. In the writer's opinion this assumed authority is inferred, rather than specific, like the authority assumed by Secretary Shaw to transfer money from a subtreasury to a bank.

made subordinate to the business interests of the country."[a] This is remarkable language for an officer sworn to uphold the law. Such an interpretation of the law would give to the officer in question discretion of more far-reaching consequence to the welfare of the business interests of the country than most of us would care to intrust to one man. But the Secretary of the Treasury had the courage of his convictions, and insisted in his report that it would be better squarely to put such responsibility upon the Secretary.[b] His views can best be given in his own words. He realized, as he remarked, that "the Treasury has always been a bloody angle of criticism of the administration," and felt it necessary to explain and defend the steps he had taken and his own general policy. "The Government quarantines against yellow fever; it spends millions to protect the people against unwholesome food; it inspects banks in the interests of depositors; it has thought of every means to safeguard the people against disaster of various kinds. * * * Believing it to be the duty of the Government also to protect the people against financial panics, which, in this country, have caused more mental and more physical suffering than all the plagues known to man * * * the Secretary of the Treasury undertook the task of making some slight provision for the inevitable." After paying his compliments to the people who write articles without studying actual conditions, and giving a graphic description of the blockade of traffic in the fall, through lack of adequate transportation facilities, he tells us that

---

[a] Finance Report, 1906 : 40.   [b] Finance Report, 1906 : 49.

he deemed it wise to relieve the blockade by importing gold. It was for this reason that he made deposits against importation, as already described. But it is not necessary to expatiate upon the radical character of the policy of the Secretary at this time. Suffice it to say that evidently he acted for what he thought the best business interests of the country in broadening the interpretation of the scope of the Secretary's duties in connection with the money market. It is worthy of notice that some of the precedents which he established were so strongly approved by the business interests he favored that later they were adopted into law.

The year 1906 showed a surplus of $25,669,322 on June 30, as contrasted with a deficit of $23,004,228 for the preceding fiscal year. Accordingly "national-bank depositaries were utilized during the fiscal year as a medium through which the excessive accumulation of money in the Treasury was restored to the channels of trade."

On March 4, 1907, Mr. Cortelyou became Secretary of the Treasury. He came into his office at a difficult time, and it is not surprising that he followed in the steps of his predecessors. Indeed, it is doubtful whether, under the conditions that prevailed, he could have done otherwise. The policy of the Treasury Department had been fixed, and conditions of business were such that a departure from that policy would have made matters worse; hence, whether or not the incoming Secretary believed in the established policy, his hands were tied. Accordingly, he followed his immediate predecessors in

increasing the bank-deposit accounts because of a stringency that arose from depreciation in the money market.
He accepted railroad bonds as security; he anticipated
interest payments; and he redeemed bonds. All these
measures, however, failed to relieve the situation sufficiently, in his opinion. On August 23 he announced his
plan of depositing the public money each week for five
successive weeks, and declared that he would not give
out any information as to the amount or distribution of
these deposits. Under this deposit policy the aggregate
of public money in the banks by October reached the
great sum of $176,000,000. Within three days the Secre-
tary deposited more than $31,000,000 in the New York
banks alone, and the total deposits throughout the country rose first to $209,000,000 and later to $242,000,000.
The features and the effects of these measures are considered in the discussion of the panic of 1907.

CHAPTER VI.—THE INFLUENCE OF THE ORDINARY OPERATIONS OF THE INDEPENDENT TREASURY SYSTEM ON BUSINESS.

THE DIFFERENT PERIODS OF SUBTREASURY ACTION.

The most important phase of the operation of the independent treasury is its influence on the business of the country in ordinary times. During the early years of the operation of the system the annual receipts and expenditures of the Government were small compared with what they have been in recent years and, moreover, were approximately equal. As the outgo virtually equaled the income and was fairly equable in its flow, there appeared but little of the evil of the disturbance of the money market due to the irregular locking up and disbursement of the medium of circulation. There was no great surplus such as for a good many years since has been a permanent feature in the financial operations of the country. This is an important consideration. When the system was established the receipts of the Government were about $1,000,000 a week. So unimportant was the influence of the fiscal operations of the Government for some years after 1846 that, as Professor Sumner remarks,[a] "the bankers and merchants could afford to laugh at the insignificance of the government on their arena." To-day, however, conditions are very different. The Treasury is the greatest single handler of money in the country, and

---

[a] History of American Currency: 167.

its annual revenue frequently runs much beyond its expenditure.

This is an important consideration. For the influence exerted, on the amount of the circulating medium, for example, by a government which keeps its own money may be very different under a policy of surplus financiering from what would prevail when income and outgo are nearly equal. Certainly there would be an element in the situation due to the possible prolonged withdrawal of money from circulation in the one case which would not exist in the other.

For another considerable period of the existence of the subtreasury system the country was under a régime of fiat paper money, issued under circumstances which practically involved a departure from the doctrine of complete divorce of bank and state, of the advantages of which so much was said at the time when the subtreasury system was established. During this period gold was not part of the money of exchange of the country, nor, indeed, of the bank reserves. Yet the law of the land required it to be collected in payment of customs dues and, therefore, caused its accumulation at times in the vaults of the subtreasury. The result was the establishment of a current of disturbances in the gold market independent of any influence which the system may have been exerting at the same time on the currency of the country. During this period there were, therefore, two possible areas of disturbance of business through subtreasury action, one exerted through its operations on gold and the other through its operations on the paper currency.

Therefore, although during both the period of the civil war and the period of paper inflation that followed it, the Government was obliged to depart from its policy of the complete separation of its operations from those of the banks of the country, by using them as depositaries and also as fiscal agents, nevertheless it would be difficult to trace the influences due exclusively or principally to the independence of the Treasury in its relation to the banks, because of the disturbing causes due to the war and the currency system.

Moreover, whatever the influence of such a system, it must have been largely increased, if not changed in character, by the mere growth in magnitude of the fiscal operations of the Government, as well as by the rapid industrial and commercial development of the country, and especially by the tremendous growth of credit which the past generation has witnessed. Commerce has multiplied many times and there is a far greater solidarity of business interests, due to improved means of communication, business reorganization, consolidation of capital and development of corporate organization. Consequently, in a way, business is much more sensitive to disturbing influences, although at the same time its power to withstand serious shocks has also increased.

For a period of twelve or fifteen years following the resumption of specie payments, we find the independent treasury system operating in a way that enables us to study its effects with the smallest number of entangling influences. During this period the independence of the Treasury continued as it had been modified by the national-bank act at the beginning of the civil war. Its evils were not so constantly felt nor so clearly understood as to produce a positive policy of constructive amendment of the subtreasury law, such as has been followed in the past ten years. It operated, therefore, during the decade or more following 1880, with less active interference on the part of the Secretaries of the Treasury than at any time since. During this period, therefore, its operation is more easily studied.

During the past ten or fifteen years, on the other hand, in consequence of the realization, on the part of Secretaries of the Treasury and business men, of the evil influences of the subtreasury system on business, there has grown up a policy of active interference on the part of the Treasury Department. To prevent these evils succeeding Secretaries have deliberately set themselves at work to counteract and even to anticipate the effect of subtreasury action. This action, therefore, is not so clearly traced in the statistical registers of business as it would have been in the absence of such interference.

In other words, the sixty years of existence of the independent treasury system is pretty clearly divisible into five periods, in only two of which, the first and fourth, has it operated under normal conditions; and in the first of these two its operations were not sufficiently extensive to teach us many lessons. Briefly stated, these periods are: (1) A period of quiescence, during the first fifteen years of its life; (2) the period of the civil war, when a departure from independence was made; (3) the period of fiat paper money, extending to 1879; (4) a second period of quiescence, with increasing government revenue and rapidly enlarging business, extending down to the early nineties; (5) the period of active interference by the Secretaries of the Treasury to prevent the injurious influence of sub-treasury activities under a policy of surplus financiering.

Moreover, as we have already seen, the functions of the independent treasury have themselves changed, both in extent and character. In addition to its intended duties of receiving and disbursing Government money, the independent treasury has for years performed some of the functions of a bank of deposit and issue. "The duties of the subtreasuries," said Treasurer Jordan in 1886, "have changed since the passage of the laws authorizing the issue of the various kinds of certificates of exchange, and redemption of the silver coinage and paper currency of the country. Each subtreasury is now a bank of issue and redemption. Whether such functions should be performed by these offices is a grave question."[a] These activities, extending as they do far beyond the scope of the subtreasury system as first established, make its influence on business different from what it would be if these duties were not performed.

It may seem, at first thought, that the influence of the independent treasury on business might be directly traced; that prices and the rate of interest might be shown to vary with the absorptions and disbursements of money by the Treasury, and that thus there might be shown to exist between business and the fiscal machinery a connection so close as to amount to a demonstration of the influence of the latter. Unfortunately, however, this can not be done. For large amounts of money may be withdrawn

---

[a] Treasurer Jordan, on proposed subtreasury at Louisville. Senate Com. Rept., No. 1834, 49th Cong., 2d sess., II.

from circulation without any apparent effect on the rate of interest, or on business; and the effects of changes in the circulation are modified by the widely extended use of credit. Credit instruments of one sort and another perform a very large, perhaps the larger, part of our exchanges. Price changes, therefore, depend more directly on variations in the amount of credit than of the money in circulation. Moreover, the elements that enter into the determination of prices are so numerous, so variable, and sometime so obscure, that we can not eliminate those which are not material to the problem of finding the causes of variation at a given time. Direct proof of the effect of subtreasury action on prices is, therefore, impossible. The same is true of variations in the rate of interest. So far as they are caused by the independent treasury, they are due to the changes effected by it in the amount of loanable funds. But usually no direct connection can be positively shown, because variations in the amount of loanable capital are not the only cause of variation in the rate of interest.

THE REACTION OF THE SUBTREASURY SYSTEM ON THE BANKS.

The influence of the independent treasury on business is exerted mainly through its action, direct or indirect, on the volume and character of the purchasing medium of the country. The independent treasury at one time absorbs, at another disburses, considerable sums. There is nothing in its organization that makes its receipts and payments necessarily concomitant with a free and stringent condition of the money market respectively. Its action is, in the main, independent of either condition. That it must have a tendency to influence prices, depending on the extent of its absorption, retention, and disbursement of money is, therefore, clear.

A series of tables and diagrams are presented below, representing the receipts and disbursements of the New York subtreasury, the amounts to and from the clearing-house banks in New York City, customs receipts of the Government, etc., for different periods. Table 1 gives the receipts and disbursements of the New York subtreasury from September, 1890, through June, 1891.

TABLE 1.—*Receipts and disbursements of the New York subtreasury, September, 1890, to June, 1891, inclusive.*

[Expressed in millions of dollars.]

Week ending—	Receipts.	Disbursements.	Net gain.	Net loss.	Balance of gain.	Balance of loss.
1890.						
Sept. 5........	14.1	14.3	....	0.2	....	....
12........	16.8	19.6	....	2.8	....	....
19........	19.5	42.7	....	23.1	....	....
26........	17.1	25.6	....	8.5	....	....
Month ..	67.5	102.2	....	34.6	....	34.6
Oct. 3........	17.7	16.6	1.1	....	....	....
10........	18.3	15.8	2.5	....	....	....
17........	14.8	14.0	.7	....	....	....
24........	13.9	12.5	1.4	....	....	....
31........	15.9	14.8	1.2	....	....	....
Month ..	80.6	73.7	6.9	....	6.9	....
Nov. 7........	12.3	11.1	1.2	....	....	....
14........	13.7	14.6	....	.9	....	....
21........	14.6	14.5	.1	....	....	....
28........	11.0	10.6	.4	....	....	....
Month ..	51.6	50.8	1.7	.9	.8	....
Dec. 5........	16.6	13.0	3.6	....	....	....
12........	13.5	22.5	....	9.0	....	....
19........	14.2	15.8	....	1.6	....	....
26........	12.7	13.8	....	1.1	....	....
Month ..	57.0	65.1	3.6	11.7	....	8.1

TABLE 1.—*Receipts and disbursements of the New York subtreasury, September, 1890, to June, 1891, inclusive*—Continued.

Week ending—	Receipts.	Disbursements.	Net gain.	Net loss.	Balance of gain.	Balance of loss.
1891.						
Jan. 2........	20.3	16.1	4.2	....	....	....
9........	14.2	15.5	....	1.3	....	....
16........	15.0	17.2	....	2.1	....	....
23........	17.5	17.7	....	.2	....	....
30........	17.1	12.4	4.8	....	....	....
Month ..	84.1	78.9	8.9	3.6	5.3	....
Feb. 6........	13.6	13.0	.6	....	....	....
13........	16.9	13.4	3.5	....	....	....
20........	13.3	9.1	4.1	....	....	....
27........	12.1	9.5	2.6	....	....	....
Month ..	55.9	45.0	10.8	....	10.8	....
Mar. 6........	13.3	12.4	.9	....	....	....
13........	12.8	14.9	....	2.1	....	....
20........	16.0	18.7	....	2.7	....	....
27........	14.3	14.8	....	.5	....	....
Month ..	56.4	60.8	.9	5.3	....	4.425
Apr. 3........	14.6	15.0	....	.4	....	....
10........	20.3	22.2	....	1.9	....	....
17........	17.7	19.7	....	2.0	....	....
24........	19.1	20.4	....	1.3	....	....
Month ..	71.7	77.3	....	5.6	....	5.6
May 1........	17.7	17.5	.2	....	....	....
8........	19.3	20.0	....	.7	....	....
15........	23.2	23.8	....	.6	....	....
22........	36.1	36.8	....	.7	....	....
29........	22.3	23.4	....	1.1	....	....
Month ..	118.6	121.5	.2	3.1	....	2.9
June 5........	26.6	27.7	....	1.1	....	....
12........	18.7	21.7	....	3.1	....	....
19........	19.6	25.5	....	5.9	....	....
26........	17.7	20.6	....	2.8	....	....
Month ..	82.6	95.5	....	12.9	....	12.9

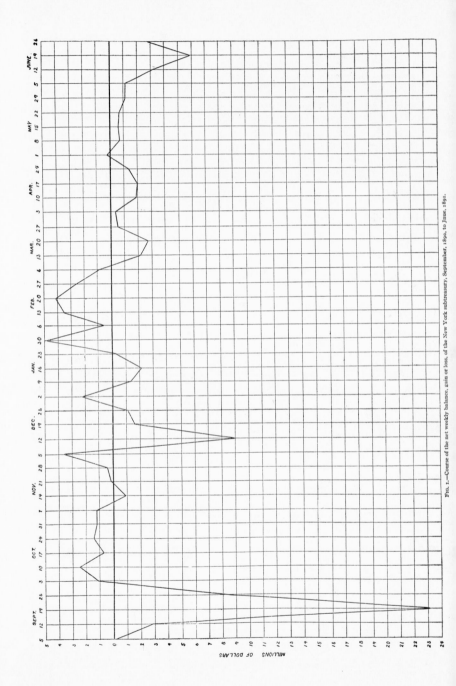

FIG. 1.—Course of the net weekly balance, gain or loss, of the New York subtreasury, September, 1890, to June, 1891.

In the ten months here represented there was a continual variation of the amount of money in the channels of business, due to the ordinary operations of the subtreasury at New York. It poured out over $34,000,000, net, in September; withdrew nearly $8,000,000 in the following two months; let out over $8,000,000 in December, and in the last four months of the period made a net addition to the money afloat of nearly $26,000,000. The changes are shown graphically in figure 1. All points below the line represent net loss and all above it net gain for the subtreasury. Each square running horizontally represents two weeks, and vertically, $1,000,000.

Table 2 gives data, which are presented graphically in figure 2, showing the net weekly balance of gain or loss of the New York subtreasury from September, 1899, to August, 1900.[a]

The striking fact again shown by the table and diagram is the sharp variations in the balances of receipts and disbursements. The important thing, of course, from the point of view of disturbance of the market is the suddenness and extent of the changes in the balance.

We see that the high points in the excess of receipts were about the first or second week of September, December, March, May, June, and August, while the excess of disbursements over receipts, shown by the low points of the curve, are toward the end of December, January, March, May, June, and August. The changes are very sudden.

If we look at the returns by months, it appears that during eight of the twelve the subtreasury receipts

---

[a] These figures and those in the next table were kindly furnished me by the assistant treasurer at New York.

exceeded disbursements; while the opposite was true in January, April, July, and August. The excess of receipts over disbursements for the year was $64,136,000. This meant a contraction of the currency to that extent except so far as offset by government deposits in banks or by bond purchases. Whether this contraction had any influence in producing the low scale of prices[a] for domestic goods, which led to the tremendous exports of 1900, would be an interesting study. Such a contraction might induce a reduction of loans to an extent between $200,000,000 and $300,000,000.

TABLE 2.—*Receipts and disbursements of the New York subtreasury, September 1, 1899, to August 31, 1900.*

[Expressed in thousands of dollars.]

Week ending—	Receipts.	Disbursements.	Net gain.	Net loss.	Balance of gain.	Balance of loss.
1899.						
Sept. 1	30,252	27,181	3,071			
8	35,924	30,107	5,817			
15	33,975	26,744	7,231			
22	34,977	31,417	3,560			
29	34,049	28,879	5,170			
Month			24,849		24,849	
Oct. 6	30,664	26,556	4,108			
13	27,703	26,212	1,491			
20	27,676	22,669	5,007			
27	21,985	21,233	752			
Month			11,358		11,358	
Nov. 3	21,931	18,466	3,465			
10	19,770	16,032	3,738			
17	22,351	22,463		1,112		
24	25,624	24,939	685			
Month			7,888	1,112	6,776	

a Compared with European prices.

Independent Treasury of the United States

TABLE 2.—*Receipts and disbursements of the New York subtreasury, September 1, 1899, to August 31, 1900*—Continued.

Week ending—	Receipts.	Disbursements.	Net gain.	Net loss.	Balance of gain.	Balance of loss.
1899.						
Dec. 1........	20,538	22,082	....	1,544	....	....
8........	25,804	17,714	8,090	....	....	....
15........	23,601	19,365	4,236	....	....	....
22........	24,465	27,749	....	3,284	....	....
29........	15,672	17,127	....	1,455	....	....
Month ..	....	....	12,326	6,283	6,043	....
1900.						
Jan. 5........	17,642	19,621	....	1,979	....	....
12........	23,472	25,882	....	2,410	....	....
19........	28,879	28,458	421	....	....	....
26........	22,789	25,636	....	2,847	....	....
Month ..	....	....	421	7,236	....	6,815
Feb. 2........	25,003	23,449	1,554	....	....	....
9........	24,866	21,810	3,056	....	....	....
16........	20,133	19,099	1,034	....	....	....
23........	20,022	16,966	3,056	....	....	....
Month ..	....	....	8,700	....	8,700	....
Mar. 2........	25,283	19,828	5,455	....	....	....
9........	23,062	16,399	6,663	....	....	....
16........	20,886	19,259	1,627	....	....	....
23........	19,876	19,993	....	117	....	....
30........	18,742	23,201	....	4,459	....	....
Month ..	....	....	13,745	4,576	9,169	....
Apr. 6........	21,921	24,431	....	3,510	....	....
13........	24,929	29,519	....	4,590	....	....
20........	26,262	27,690	....	1,428	....	....
27........	22,631	24,212	....	1,581	....	....
Month ..	....	....	....	11,109	....	11,109
May 4........	32,117	27,554	4,563	....	....	....
11........	34,592	26,994	7,598	....	....	....
18........	26,228	26,290	....	62	....	....
25........	21,913	24,667	....	2,754	....	....
Month ..	....	....	12,161	2,816	9,345	....

TABLE 2.—*Receipts and disbursements of the New York subtreasury, September 1, 1899, to August 31, 1900*—Continued.

Week ending—	Receipts.	Disbursements.	Net gain.	Net loss.	Balance of gain.	Balance of loss.
1900.						
June 1........	18,884	19,843	....	959	....	....
8........	24,495	23,664	831	....	....	....
15........	36,019	27,209	8,810	....	....	....
22........	28,790	28,003	787	....	....	....
29........	21,343	21,005	338	....	....	....
Month...	....	....	10,766	959	9,807	....
July 6..........	17,878	21,230	....	3,352	....	....
13........	26,586	27,355	....	769	....	....
20........	27,529	25,902	1,627	....	....	....
27........	22,539	23,804	....	1,265	....	....
Month...	....	....	1,627	5,386	....	3,759
Aug. 3........	27,117	28,016	....	899	....	....
10........	42,760	32,862	9,898	....	....	....
17........	40,245	38,244	2,001	....	....	....
24........	21,638	27,733	....	6,095	....	....
31........	20,041	26,073	....	6,032	....	....
Month...	....	....	11,899	12,127	....	228

Figure 2 presents the same facts graphically and brings out very strikingly not only the extent but the sharpness of the changes.

The third table shows the changes in the reserves of the associated banks of New York City for the period covered by the preceding table and furnishes the means of comparing the relation of subtreasury receipts and disbursements to reserve losses and gains. The tables are compiled from the reports of the Commercial and Financial Chronicle.

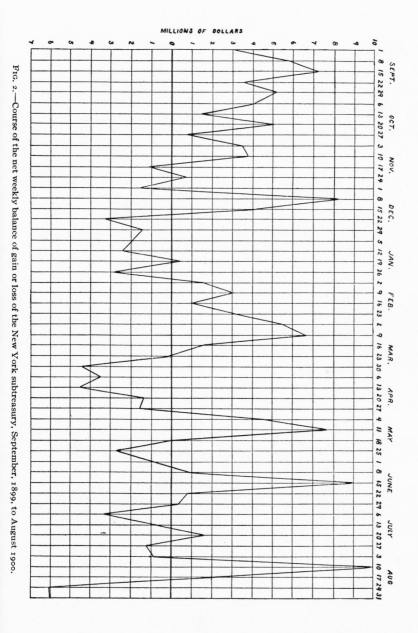

FIG. 2.—Course of the net weekly balance of gain or loss of the New York subtreasury, September, 1899, to August 1900.

TABLE 3.—*Changes in reserve of New York Associated Banks, September 1, 1899, to August 31, 1900.*

[Expressed in thousands of dollars.]

Week ending—	Subtreasury action.	Interior movement.	Net gain (+) or loss (−).	Variation in reserve.
1899.				
Sept. 1......................	− 3,000	−3,387	− 6,387	− 5,272
8......................	− 4,500	−5,156	− 9,656	−10,571
15......................	− 3,100	−4,775	− 7,875	− 5,947
22......................	− 2,000	−3,273	− 5,273	− 2,510
29......................	− 1,000	−2,293	− 3,293	− 4,546
Month..............	−13,600	....	....	....
Oct. 6......................	− 1,500	−2,403	− 3,903	− 2,133
13......................	− 500	−1,612	− 2,112	− 1,019
20......................	+ 2,000	−3,374	− 1,374	− 1,379
27......................	− 200	−1,822	− 2,022	− 88
Month..............	− 200	....	....	....
Nov. 3......................	− 2,000	−2,056	− 4,056	− 4,819
10......................	− 2,600	−1,793	− 4,393	− 5,217
17......................	+ 1,135	− 928	+ 207	+ 486
24......................	+ 6,500	+1,466	+ 7,966	+ 7,244
Month..............	+ 3,035	....	....	....
Dec. 1......................	+ 3,300	− 184	+ 3,116	+ 4,415
8......................	− 3,200	−3,272	− 6,472	− 2,675
15......................	− 3,950	+5,389	+ 1,439	− 970
22......................	− 1,450	−1,318	− 2,768	+ 3,572
29......................	− 4,600	+3,191	− 1,409	+ 697
Month..............	− 9,900	....	....	....
1900.				
Jan. 5......................	− 3,350	+6,393	+ 3,043	+ 2,816
12......................	− 400	+7,188	+ 6,788	+ 5,033
19......................	+ 3,300	+8,071	+11,371	+11,536
26......................	+ 2,300	+7,469	+ 9,769	+ 8,844
Month..............	+ 1,850	....	....	....
Feb. 2......................	+ 500	+4,913	+ 5,413	+ 5,441
9......................	− 700	+2,533	+ 1,833	+ 1,744
16......................	− 1,600	−1,029	− 2,629	− 2,324
23......................	− 2,200	− 845	− 3,045	− 2,875
Month..............	− 4,000	....	....	....

Independent Treasury of the United States

TABLE 3.—*Changes in reserve of New York Associated Banks, September 1, 1899, to August 31, 1900*—Continued.

Week ending—	Subtreasury action.	Interior movement.	Net gain (+) or loss (−).	Variation in reserve.
1900.				
Mar. 2	− 6,000	+1,352	− 4,648	− 5,274
9	− 6,000	−3,826	− 9,826	− 8,088
16	− 4,000	−1,051	− 5,051	− 6,826
23	− 1,200	+2,151	+ 951	− 361
30	+ 1,300	+1,526	+ 2,826	+ 5,944
Month	−15,900			
Apr. 6	+ 4,000	+2,113	+ 6,113	+ 1,738
13	+ 5,900	−2,448	+ 3,452	+ 6,004
20	+ 3,000	+2,639	+ 5,639	+ 6,019
27	+ 1,500	+5,131	+ 6,631	+ 4,538
Month	+14,400			
May 4	− 2,900	+3,483	+ 583	+ 3,177
11	− 2,000	+4,035	+ 2,035	− 1,123
18	− 765	+2,745	+ 1,980	+ 1,566
25	− 300	+4,387	+ 4,087	+ 4,255
Month	− 5,965			
June 1	− 200	+3,065	+ 2,865	+ 4,147
8	− 3,100	+3,192	+ 92	− 301
15	− 4,600	+2,964	− 1,636	− 369
22	− 2,000	+2,685	+ 685	− 3,169
29	− 2,800	+1,554	− 1,246	+ 649
Month	−12,700			
July 6	+ 2,000	+1,657	+ 3,657	− 2,870
13	+ 100	+1,491	+ 1,591	+ 4,781
20	− 1,500	+2,507	+ 1,007	+ 3,793
27	+ 100	+3,113	+ 3,213	+ 4,871
Month	+ 700			
Aug. 3	+ 2,800	+3,191	+ 5,991	+ 3,269
10	− 5,100	+1,481	− 3,619	− 287
17	−10,000	+2,388	− 7,612	− 8,342
24	+ 1,500	+1,418	+ 2,918	+ 5,092
31	+ 2,200	+2,631	+ 4,831	+ 372
Month	− 3,500			

It will be seen from the table that the reserves of the banks fell through September and October; that they rose from the middle of December to the middle of February; fell until the end of March; and at the end of March increased until early in June, during which month they fell and then increased through the summer. During these months the action of the subtreasury was against the bank reserves in September and October; aided them somewhat in November and January; drew them down again in the two following months as well as in May, June, and the following August.

Comparing Tables 2 and 3 it appears that in September, 1899, the net gain of the New York subtreasury was $25,000,000 and the loss of the banks due to subtreasury action nearly $14,000,000. Besides the loss to the bank reserves by subtreasury action there was, therefore, a loss of $11,000,000 or $12,000,000 to the general circulation. Even in the month of November, when the banks gained from the subtreasury, the balance of gain to the subtreasury itself, which was nearly $7,000,000, shows a contraction of the general circulation to the extent of nearly $4,000,000. Other comparisons are unnecessary. The changes of reserve due to the action of the subtreasury alone are represented graphically in figure 3.

Table 4, with its accompanying diagram, gives the weekly receipts and disbursements of the New York subtreasury from April, 1907, to March, 1908. This was a period of violent disturbance in the money market and in business generally. Indeed, it was the severest crisis through which the country has passed since 1893. The rapid variations in the receipts and disbursements of the

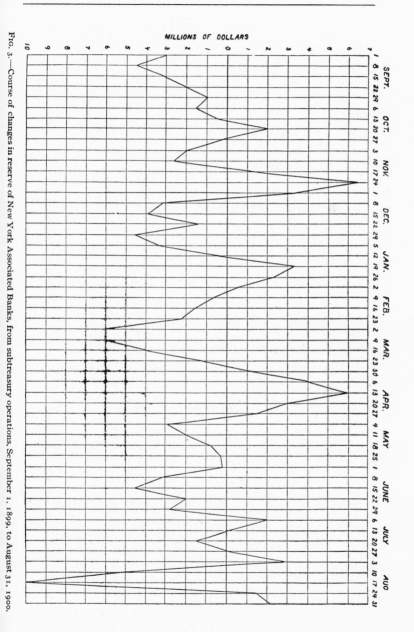

Fig. 3.—Course of changes in reserve of New York Associated Banks, from subtreasury operations, September 1, 1899, to August 31, 1900.

subtreasury, as shown by the diagram, which presents the net balance of gain or loss each week, reflect the great uncertainty of the money market and the close relation of treasury operations and bank reserves, and through them upon loans and discounts and upon business.

In the week beginning April 5, from an excess of receipts of nearly $6,000,000 there was a fall to an excess of disbursements of more than $3,000 000. This excess of disbursements was changed to a net gain of receipts of nearly $3,000,000 two weeks later; which, three weeks afterwards became again an excess of disbursements of nearly $2,000,000. The next two weeks saw a gain in receipts, so that by the 7th of June there was a net excess of receipts over disbursements to the extent of nearly $7,000,000. Similar violent changes are shown from week to week throughout the year. The most striking occurred in the two weeks between the 5th and 19th of July, and the two weeks between October 18 and November 1. In the first two weeks we see a change from a balance of disbursements over expenses of between $6,000,000 and $7,000,000 to an excess of receipts over disbursements in the following week to the extent of nearly $12,000,000, with an immediate fall through the next week to an excess of disbursements over receipts amounting to more than $7,000,000. The change in October was even greater. It was in this period that the most active and radical measures ever taken to counteract the evils of subtreasury influence on the money market were put into operation by the Secretary of the Treasury.

Independent Treasury of the United States

TABLE 4.—*Receipts and disbursements of New York subtreasury, April 5, 1907, to March 27, 1908.*

[Expressed in thousands of dollars.]

Week ending—	Receipts.	Disbursements.	Net gain.	Net loss.	Balance of gain.	Balance of loss.
1907.						
April 5........	43,144	37,460	5,684	....	....	....
April 12.......	28,153	31,353	....	3,200	....	....
April 19.......	30,929	31,551	....	622	....	....
April 26.......	31,682	29,068	2,614	....	....	....
Month ..	....	....	8,298	3,822	4,476	....
May 3.......	33,140	31,429	1,711	....	....	....
May 10........	28,868	27,867	1,001	....	....	....
May 17.......	25,930	27,805	....	1,875	....	....
May 24.......	26,630	26,817	....	187	....	....
May 31.......	25,417	22,951	2,466	....	....	....
Month ..	....	....	5,178	2,062	2,116	....
June 7.......	33,621	26,914	6,707	....	....	....
June 14.......	28,787	27,630	1,157	....	....	....
June 21.......	32,712	28,485	4,227	....	....	....
June 28.......	40,690	37,003	3,687	....	....	....
Month ..	....	....	15,778	....	15,778	....
July 5.......	28,815	35,343	....	6,528	....	....
July 12.......	48,968	37,057	11,911	....	....	....
July 19.......	27,113	34,576	....	7,463	....	....
July 26.......	29,380	33,811	....	4,431	....	....
Month ..	....	....	11,911	18,422	....	6,511
August 2.....	32,380	31,026	1,354	....	....	....
August 9.....	28,063	28,176	....	113	....	....
August 16.....	27,995	29,800	....	1,805	....	....
August 23.....	30,467	27,474	2,993	....	....	....
August 30.....	29,637	28,492	1,145	....	....	....
Month ..	....	....	5,492	1,918	3,574	....
September 6..	22,988	24,358	....	1,370	....	....
September 13..	28,032	29,721	....	1,689	....	....
September 20..	27,958	30,716	....	2,758	....	....
September 27..	30,371	27,490	2,881	....	....	....
Month..	....	....	2,881	5,817	....	2,936

TABLE 4.—*Receipts and disbursements of New York subtreasury, April 5, 1907, to March 27, 1908*—Continued.

Week ending—	Receipts.	Disbursements.	Net gain.	Net loss.	Balance of gain.	Balance of loss.
1907.						
October 4....	30,237	29,503	....	734	....	....
October 11.....	29,715	30,860	....	1,145	....	....
October 18.....	30,437	33,212	....	2,775	....	....
October 25.....	56,264	74,792	....	18,528	....	....
Month ..	....	....	....	23,182	....	23,182
November 1 ..	59,035	49,264	9,771	....	....	....
November 8 ..	47,683	47,549	134	....	....	....
November 15 ..	55,300	52,702	2,598	....	....	....
November 22 ..	42,318	37,292	5,026	....	....	....
November 29 ..	44,166	46,030	....	1,864	....	....
Month ..	....	....	17,529	1,864	15,665	....
December 6...	37,490	41,374	....	3,884	....	....
December 13 ..	33,760	30,375	3,385	....	....	....
December 20...	37,157	38,828	....	1,671	....	....
December 27...	23,475	25,252	....	1,777	....	....
Month ..	....	....	3,385	7,332	....	3,947
1908.						
January 3....	30,931	30,559	372	....	....	....
January 10....	34,703	33,130	1,573	....	....	....
January 17....	53,194	47,620	5,574	....	....	....
January 24....	30,359	45,073	5,386	....	....	....
January 31....	50,791	46,885	3,906	....	....	....
Month ..	....	....	16,711	....	16,711	....
February 7...	36,081	36,931	....	850	....	....
February 14...	30,668	32,010	....	1,342	....	....
February 21...	44,228	37,649	6,579	....	....	....
February 28...	30,198	31,621	....	1,423	....	....
Month ..	....	....	6,579	3,615	2,964	....
March 6......	33,577	35,690	....	2,113	....	....
March 13......	35,072	33,048	2,024	....	....	....
March 20......	33,953	36,996	....	3,043	....	....
March 27......	39,765	36,194	3,571	....	....	....
Month ..	....	....	5,595	5,156	439	....

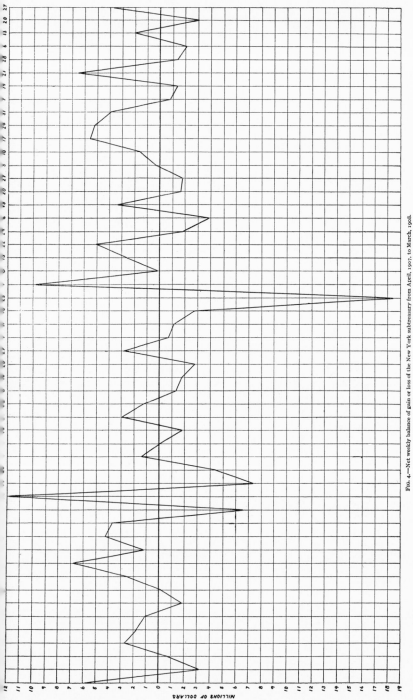

FIG. 4.—Net weekly balance of gain or loss of the New York subtreasury from April, 1907, to March, 1908.

MILLIONS OF DOLLARS

(To face page 166.)

Table 5 with accompanying diagram, shows the changes in the New York Bank reserves for the same period. Perhaps these figures can not be fully relied upon because of the bookkeeping artifices said to have been resorted to by some banks, in the panic, in order to show a proper relation between reserves and deposits. Still they probably show the general tendency correctly.

TABLE 5.—*Changes in the reserves of the clearing-house banks of New York City, April 5, 1907, to March 31, 1908.*

[Expressed in thousands of dollars.]

Week ending—	Subtreasury action.	Interior movement.	Net gain or loss.	Variation in reserve.
1907.				
Apr. 5	+13,600	+ 535	+14,135	+10,534
12	+ 4,500	− 1,317	+ 3,183	+ 7,649
19	+ 4,400	− 992	+ 3,408	+ 2,477
26	− 494	− 2,141	− 2,635	+ 147
Month	+22,006	....	....	....
May 3	+ 900	− 1,913	− 1,013	− 1,918
10	− 2,000	+ 1,529	− 471	− 2,384
17	+ 2,000	+ 4,598	+ 6,598	+ 3,407
24	+ 1,900	+ 2,436	+ 4,336	+ 5,851
31	− 1,000	+ 3,105	+ 2,105	+ 982
Month	+ 4,800	....	....	....
June 7	− 6,400	+ 1,516	− 4,884	− 9,065
14	− 6,900	+ 2,710	− 4,190	− 2,683
21	− 4,000	+ 2,277	− 1,723	− 711
28	−10,500	+ 3,463	− 7,037	− 6,855
Month	−27,800	....	....	....
July 5	− 1,000	+ 2,162	+ 1,162	− 5,026
12	− 9,000	+ 5,896	− 3,104	+ 4,076
19	+ 1,500	+ 3,172	+ 4,672	+ 2,769
26	+ 3,500	+ 4,291	+ 7,791	+ 5,866
Month	− 5,000	....	....	....

TABLE 5.—*Changes in the reserves of the clearing-house banks of New York City, April 5, 1907, to March 31, 1908.*—Continued.

Week ending—	Subtreasury action.	Interior movement.	Net gain or loss.	Variation in reserve.
1907.				
Aug. 2	+ 1,000	+ 2,733	+ 3,733	— 903
9	+ 1,000	— 1,291	— 291	— 5,312
16	— 2,000	+ 1,221	— 779	— 2,828
23	— 2,000	— 4,087	— 6,087	— 2,086
30	— 2,500	+ 1,539	— 961	— 1,652
Month	— 4,500			
Sept. 6	+ 1,000	+ 934	+ 1,934	— 1,427
13	+ 2,500	— 1,412	+ 1,088	— 862
20	+ 3,200	— 1,609	+ 1,501	+ 4,529
27	+ 1,000	— 4,495	— 3,495	— 3,216
Month	+ 7,700			
Oct. 4	— 1,000	— 3,926	— 4,926	— 7,621
11	+ 1,000	— 4,885	— 3,885	— 656
18	+ 4,000	— 4,394	— 394	+ 6,443
25	+21,000	—16,320	+ 4,680	—12,901
Month	+25,000			
Nov. 1	+ 9,500	—17,023	— 7,523	—30,602
8	+15,000	—17,400	— 2,400	— 4,313
15	+15,000	—22,616	— 7,616	— 1,136
22	+13,000	—17,337	— 4,337	— 2,808
29	+15,900	—10,577	+ 5,323	+ 1,980
Month	+68,400			
Dec. 6	+17,300	— 9,024	+ 8,276	+ 4,671
13	+ 6,700	— 6,800	— 100	+ 4,113
20	+ 7,100	— 5,200	+ 1,900	+ 6,507
27	+ 6,511	— 2,169	+ 4,342	+ 9,439
Month	+37,611			
1908.				
Jan. 3	+ 1,000	+ 5,458	+ 6,458	+ 8,046
10	— 1,000	+13,375	+12,375	+18,390
17	+ 3,500	+12,295	+15,795	+26,186
24	+ 1,500	+20,584	+22,084	+23,674
31	+ 3,250	+17,069	+20,326	+ 6,296
Month	+ 8,250			

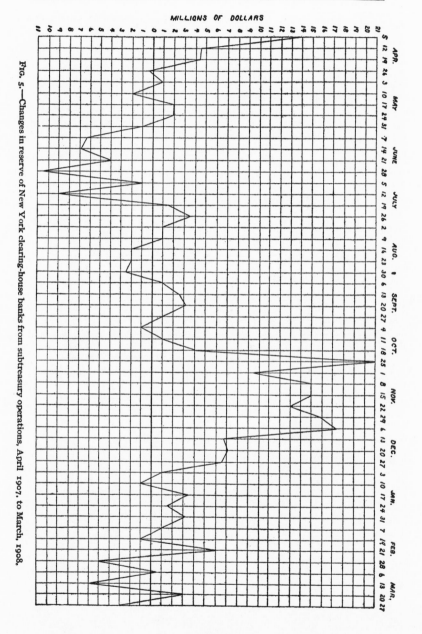

FIG. 5.—Changes in reserve of New York clearing-house banks from subtreasury operations, April 1907, to March, 1908.

TABLE 5.—*Changes in the reserves of the clearing-house banks of New York City, April 5, 1907, to March 31, 1908*—Continued.

Week ending—	Subtreasury action.	Interior movement.	Net gain or loss.	Variation in reserve.
1908.				
Feb. 7	+ 1,000	+ 4,411	+ 5,411	−10,974
14	− 1,000	+ 4,308	+ 3,308	− 251
21	+ 6,011	+ 3,562	+ 9,573	+ 5,114
28	− 5,000	+ 2,949	− 2,051	+ 2,127
Month	+ 1,011			
Mar. 6	+ 500	+ 3,358	+ 3,858	+ 2,893
13	− 5,931	+ 3,079	− 2,852	− 439
20	+ 3,000	+ 4,645	+ 7,645	+ 9,322
27	− 3,011	+ 5,066	+ 2,055	+ 4,178
Month	− 5,431			

These tables furnish a basis for a comparison similar to that made between Tables 2 and 3. In the month of April the bank reserves gained over $22,000,000 from subtreasury operations, yet the subtreasury itself showed a balance of gain of more than $4,000,000, thus showing that it was contracting the circulation, even though it was directly aiding the banks. The same is true of the month of May. In June, however, while the banks lost nearly $28,000,000 through subtreasury action, the subtreasury net gain was nearly $16,000,000. Part of its total gain, therefore, went into general circulation. In July the net loss of the bank reserves through subtreasury action was $5,000,000, yet the subtreasury itself had a net loss of $6,500,000. This shows a great increase of the circulation at a time when it was least needed. Doubtless the plethora of currency had much to do in promoting the speculation which preceded the panic in the fall. It is not necessary to compare the tables more in detail. They again show that no dependence can be put by the banks on the action of the subtreasury. The data of Table 5 are presented graphically in the diagram and reveal the course of procedure more clearly to the eye.

For the sake of showing that the irregularity of action is not peculiar to the New York subtreasury, Table 6 and Diagram 6 are inserted to show the course of the receipts and disbursements of the subtreasury at Chicago for the seven months from September, 1907, through March, 1908.

TABLE 6.—*Receipts and disbursements of the Chicago subtreasury for seven months.a*

Week ending—	Receipts.	Disburse-ments.	Net gain.	Net loss.	Balance of gain.	Balance of loss.
1907.						
Sept. 7	$5,521,429	$5,610,546		$89,117		
14	6,282,169	6,519,416		237,247		
21	5,158,520	6,092,034		933,514		
28	7,040,541	7,109,655		69,114		
Month				1,328,992		$1,328,992
Oct. 5	8,849,424	8,068,617	$780,807			
12	5,860,607	8,267,070		2,406,463		
19	5,860,841	7,468,533		1,607,692		
26	8,830,134	9,330,869		500,735		
Month			780,807	4,514,890		3,734,083
Nov. 2	11,946,612	15,754,518		3,807,906		
9	14,734,100	16,866,872		2,132,772		
16	10,673,226	16,933,146		6,259,920		
23	8,823,177	7,840,526	982,651			
30	10,114,934	9,497,516	617,418			
Month			1,600,069	12,200,598		10,600,529
Dec. 7	8,977,001	9,251,679		274,678		
14	8,826,030	8,670,873	155,157			

Date						
21	8,064,217	8,008,873	55,344			
28	5,571,888	4,461,640	1,110,248			
Month.			1,320,749	274,678	$1,046,071	1,811,987
1908.						
Jan. 4	5,693,655	4,890,198	803,457			
11	11,005,623	11,067,013		61,390		
18	13,866,904	16,914,354		3,047,450		
25	10,752,111	10,258,715	493,396			
Month.			1,296,853	3,108,840		
Feb. 1	13,496,161	11,465,401	2,030,760			
8	9,748,788	9,530,424	218,364			
15	7,827,968	6,011,043	1,816,925			
21	6,627,706	6,590,005	37,701			
29	7,862,201	6,581,174	1,281,027			
Month.			5,384,777		5,384,777	
Mar. 7	9,211,226	7,395,866	1,815,360			
14	9,379,195	8,458,908	920,287			
21	7,060,799	8,213,108		1,152,309		
28	7,503,938	7,898,030		394,092		
Month.			2,735,647	1,546,401	1,189,246	

a The figures were kindly furnished by the assistant treasurer at Chicago.

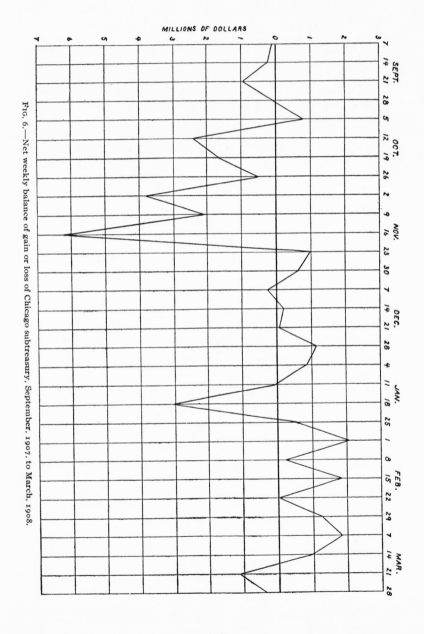

FIG. 6.—Net weekly balance of gain or loss of Chicago subtreasury, September, 1907, to March, 1908.

The data given show a balance of loss to the subtreasury account through the months of September, October, November, and January, and a gain in December, February, and March. Of course the influence of any subtreasury other than that of New York City depends largely on the action of that institution. Hence the figures for Chicago must be considered in their relation to those for New York for the same period. The returns are traced in the diagram following.

To avoid irregularities incidental to the peculiarities of single years, and to show that the lack of coincidence between operations of the independent treasury and the banks are not merely occasional, a series of tables follows. Table 7 shows the average monthly surplus reserve of the New York banks for the four years, 1888–1892. The table shows that the reserves are high in January, February, and through the four summer months, May, June, July, and August. In March, April, and the last four months of the year they fall considerably. Figure 7 presents the data graphically.

TABLE 7.—*Average monthly surplus reserve of New York banks.*[a]

[Expressed in thousands of dollars.]

	1888.	1889.	1890.	1891.	Average for four years.
January.................	18,676	15,784	8,971	18,036	15,367
February................	16,506	14,865	5,855	16,935	13,540
March..................	10,014	7,192	2,253	9,543	7,250
April...................	12,463	8,247	1,638	5,824	7,043
May....................	24,506	14,423	3,002	5,974	11,976
June...................	27,840	9,618	6,172	12,939	14,127
July....................	27,651	6,498	5,496	17,052	14,174
August.................	27,590	5,044	3,530	16,479	13,161
September..............	12,742	4,044	5,172	7,411	7,342
October................	13,612	1,113	3,169	9,500	6,849
November..............	11,384	1,172	962	11,161	6,169
December..............	8,122	2,187	3,815	16,961	8,272

[a] The table is compiled from returns in the Financial Chronicle and the New York Journal of Commerce.

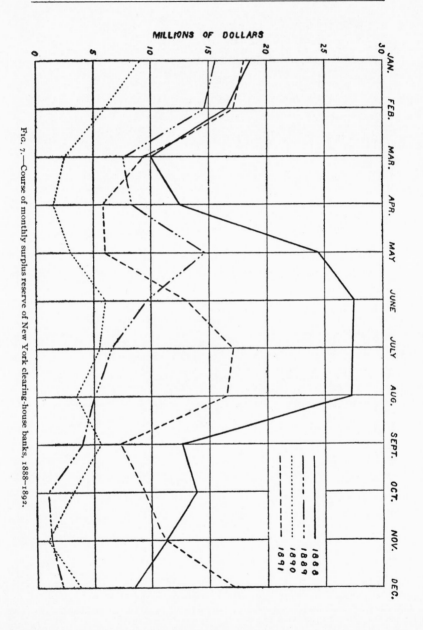

Fig. 7.—Course of monthly surplus reserve of New York clearing-house banks, 1888-1892.

Table 8, in three sections, shows the changes in the reserve of the clearing-house banks of the city of New York on account of the action of the subtreasury, as well as the drain of money to the interior for the three periods: From September 5 to November 28, 1890; from February 4 to December 30, 1898; and from January 5 to December 31, 1906.

TABLE 8.—*Changes in the holdings of the New York associated banks due to the action of the subtreasury and the interior movement of money, and also the changes in the total reserve.*[a]

A. FROM SEPTEMBER 5 TO NOVEMBER 28, 1890.

[Expressed in thousands of dollars.]

Week ending—	Subtreasury action.	Interior movement.	Net gain (+) or loss (−).	Variation in reserve.
Sept. 5	+ 1,600	−3,289	− 1,689	− 52
12	+ 2,600	−3,310	− 710	− 3,193
19	+13,700	−4,411	+ 9,289	+ 6,895
26	+18,500	−3,933	+14,567	+16,384
Oct. 3	+ 4,500	−5,781	− 1,281	+ 1,020
10	− 2,100	−4,752	− 6,852	− 9,924
17	− 2,500	−3,468	− 5,968	− 4,311
24	− 2,300	−2,038	− 4,338	− 964
31	− 700	−2,290	− 2,990	+ 207
Nov. 7	− 900	− 533	− 1,433	− 4,254
14	+ 200	+1,129	+ 1,329	+ 292
21	+ 700	−1,190	− 490	− 300
28	+ 300	− 514	− 214	− 484

B. FROM FEBRUARY 4 TO DECEMBER 30, 1898.

Feb. 4	− 600	+3,111	+ 2,511	+ 2,008
11	− 3,800	+2,245	− 1,555	− 1,131
18	− 2,100	−1,321	− 3,421	− 6,779
25	− 3,000	−4,140	− 7,140	− 5,066
Mar. 4	− 4,000	−2,145	− 6,145	− 7,934
11	+ 800	+2,800	+ 3,600	− 737
18	+ 6,714	−2,097	+ 4,617	+ 3,513
25	+ 7,400	−1,172	+ 6,228	+ 5,160

[a] The tables are compiled from the weekly returns of the Commercial and Financial Chronicle. The (+) sign means gain to the banks, and the (−) sign loss.

TABLE 8.—*Changes in the holdings of the New York associated banks due to the action of the subtreasury and the interior movement of money, and also the changes in the total reserve*—Continued.

B. FROM FEBRUARY 4 TO DECEMBER 30, 1898—Continued.

Week ending—	Subtreasury action.	Interior movement.	Net gain (+) or loss (−).	Variation in reserve.
Apr. 1	+ 5,600	−5,095	+ 505	+ 1,016
8	+11,500	−8,323	+ 3,177	− 3,784
15	+ 5,500	−3,514	+ 1,986	+ 730
22	− 1,506	− 527	− 2,033	+ 5,604
29	+11,500	−4,609	+ 6,891	+ 301
May 6	+ 4,000	−1,717	+ 2,283	− 310
13	+ 4,600	+ 865	+ 5,465	+ 4,857
20	+ 3,200	+3,444	+ 6,644	+ 7,285
27	+ 1,200	+4,755	+ 5,955	+ 6,744
June 3	+ 2,200	+3,312	+ 5,512	+ 1,898
10	+ 1,300	+3,813	+ 5,113	+ 5,289
17	+ 806	+4,388	+ 5,194	+ 7,123
24	+ 1,000	+4,152	+ 5,152	+ 4,576
July 1	+ 100	+4,875	+ 4,975	+ 2,939
8	− 5,700	+3,222	− 2,478	− 6,670
15	−10,000	+2,813	− 7,187	− 4,050
22	−14,000	+2,709	−11,291	−10,468
29	− 3,000	+3,554	+ 554	− 1,020
Aug. 5	− 2,500	+1,903	− 597	+ 1,831
12	− 7,300	+4,446	− 2,854	− 5,855
19	− 6,000	+2,415	− 3,585	− 3,208
26	− 9,000	+2,584	− 6,416	− 8,691
Sept. 2	− 7,500	−1,567	− 9,067	− 8,313
9	−11,000	+1,163	− 9,837	−13,036
16	− 4,000	−1,251	− 5,251	− 7,795
23	+ 500	−1,662	− 1,162	+ 1,184
30	+ 5,800	+2,889	+ 8,689	+ 7,418
Oct. 7	+ 4,500	−2,472	+ 2,028	+ 5,586
14	+ 6,500	−1,771	+ 4,729	+ 5,002
21	+ 7,000	+1,310	+ 8,310	+ 8,413
28	+ 4,000	+3,269	+ 7,269	+ 6,625
Nov. 4	+ 2,250	+1,311	+ 3,561	− 5,190
10	− 1,000	+1,855	+ 855	+ 1,978
18	+ 1,400	+2,093	+ 3,493	+ 4,014
25	− 500	+1,806	+ 1,306	+ 764
Dec. 2	− 1,800	+2,844	+ 1,044	+ 440
9	− 1,600	+1,336	− 264	+ 1,461
16	− 200	+ 662	+ 462	+ 2,761
23	+ 500	+1,184	+ 1,684	+ 4,656
30	− 2,000	+3,934	+ 1,934	+ 1,583

Independent Treasury of the United States

TABLE 8.—*Changes in the holdings of the New York associated banks due to the action of the subtreasury and the interior movement of money, and also the changes in the total reserve*—Continued.

C. FROM JANUARY 5 TO DECEMBER 31, 1906.

Week ending—	Subtreasury action.	Interior movement.	Net gain (+) or loss (−).	Variation in reserve.
Jan. 5	− 4,200	+ 5,351	+ 1,151	− 2,199
12	+ 3,000	+ 6,960	+ 9,960	+15,604
19	+ 4,000	+ 6,170	+10,170	+11,997
26	+ 7,000	+ 4,740	+11,740	+ 3,501
Feb. 2	− 6,000	+ 4,685	− 1,315	− 1,130
9	− 2,000	+ 2,349	+ 349	− 5,297
16	− 3,900	+ 1,880	− 2,020	− 3,233
23	− 1,500	+ 3,494	+ 1,994	− 2,248
Mar. 2	− 3,900	+ 2,838	− 1,062	− 3,305
9	+ 1,000	− 351	+ 649	− 5,448
16	+ 2,000	+ 2,253	+ 4,253	+ 1,136
23	+ 500	+ 1,788	+ 2,288	+ 1,549
30	− 1,216	− 2,777	− 3,993	− 3,428
Apr. 6	− 1,000	− 5,300	− 6,300	− 7,904
13	+ 3,700	+ 3,676	+ 7,376	+ 1,938
20	+10,000	− 4,150	+ 5,850	+17,995
27	+ 6,000	−20,570	−14,570	− 695
May 4	+31,000	−20,914	+10,086	− 4,820
11	+ 7,000	− 2,841	+ 4,159	+ 3,816
18	+ 3,000	− 1,649	+ 1,351	+ 304
25	+ 3,000	− 2,177	+ 823	− 1,960
June 1	+ 4,400	+ 806	+ 5,206	+ 1,127
8	+ 2,400	+ 1,113	+ 3,513	+ 2,942
15	+ 3,000	− 223	+ 2,777	+ 173
22	+ 2,500	+ 1,552	+ 4,052	+ 4,162
29	+ 2,500	+ 3,241	+ 5,741	+ 1,179
July 6	− 3,500	+ 130	+ 3,370	− 8,909
13	− 1,000	+ 2,181	+ 1,181	+ 3,263
20	− 6,000	+ 4,642	− 1,358	+11,762
27	+ 2,500	+ 8,722	+11,222	+ 3,346
Aug. 3	− 2,500	+ 5,191	+ 2,691	− 649
10	− 1,600	− 1,819	− 3,419	− 9,275
17	+ 1,500	− 5,325	− 3,825	− 3,457
24	− 3,000	− 2,517	− 5,517	− 2,788
31	− 1,900	− 2,562	− 4,462	− 4,369
Sept. 7	− 3,500	− 6,235	− 9,735	−16,408
14	+14,000	− 2,070	+11,930	+ 7,933
21	+ 2,000	− 4,560	− 2,560	+12,221
28	− 1,000	− 4,539	− 5,539	+ 3,926

TABLE 8.—*Changes in the holdings of the New York associated banks due to the action of the subtreasury and the interior movement of money, and also the changes in the total reserve*—Continued.

C. FROM JANUARY 5 TO DECEMBER 31, 1906—Continued.

Week ending—	Subtreasury action.	Interior movement.	Net gain (+) or loss (−).	Variation in reserve.
Oct. 5	+ 6,000	− 3,439	+ 2,561	− 3,797
12	+ 1,236	− 5,392	− 4,156	+ 8,461
19	+ 3,500	− 8,279	− 4,779	− 3,934
26	+ 1,000	− 7,495	− 6,495	− 7,436
Nov. 2	− 2,500	− 2,232	− 4,732	− 7,342
9	+ 1,000	− 2,801	− 1,801	− 8,831
16	− 1,000	+ 3,015	+ 2,015	+ 2,817
23	− 1,100	+ 2,156	+ 1,056	+ 2,903
30	− 3,000	− 1,315	− 4,315	− 2,787
Dec. 7	− 2,500	− 1,411	− 3,911	−12,266
14	− 1,000	+ 4,511	+ 3,511	+ 1,224
21	+ 3,600	− 533	+ 3,067	+ 6,127
28	+ 2,101	− 3,879	+ 5,980	+ 4,501

It appears from this table also that the months in which the banks usually gain largely from the subtreasury do not always correspond with the months when it is necessary for them to have the largest reserves. The times of the year when money is least needed, or when it accumulates in the vaults of the banks, are approximately January, the summer months, and the period toward the end of October and the beginning of November.

The accompanying Figure 8 shows the facts graphically.

Table 9, with accompanying diagram in two sections, is presented to show the average monthly surplus reserve of the New York clearing house banks for six years, 1904–1909. The amount of surplus reserve given in the table for each month is the average of the weekly reserve for that month. The diagram 9a represents the course of the reserve through the whole period, while 9b is constructed

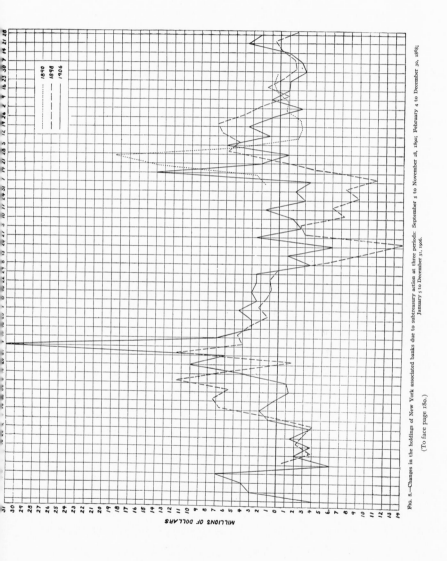

MILLIONS OF DOLLARS

1890
1898
1906

Fig. 8.—Changes in the holdings of New York associated banks due to subtreasury action at three periods: September 5 to November 28, 1890; February 4 to December 30, 1898; January 5 to December 31, 1906.

(To face page 180.)

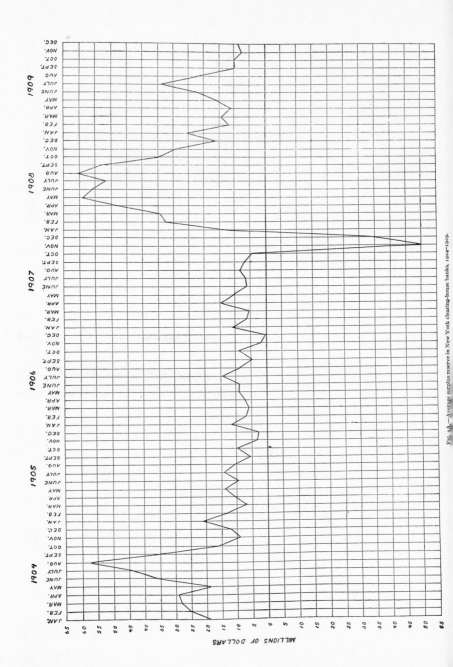

FIG. 9A.—Average surplus reserve in New York clearing-house banks, 1904–1909.

from the averages of the monthly figures for the six years. Therefore it may be regarded as a fair presentation of the usual course of the surplus reserve under conditions such as prevailed in those years.

TABLE 9.—*The average monthly surplus reserve of New York clearing house banks, 1904–1909.*[a]

[Expressed in thousands of dollars.]

	1904.	1905.	1906.	1907.	1908.	1909.	Average.
January............	19,722	21,695	11,468	10,703	13,568	25,464	17,103
February..........	25,469	13,682	6,996	6,180	32,588	11,814	16,121
March............	28,664	7,325	5,766	5,356	34,503	14,230	15,974
April.............	29,064	10,962	7,236	14,836	48,228	11,333	20,277
May..............	19,562	13,781	8,904	10,618	59,047	15,671	21,264
June..............	36,161	9,545	8,804	6,282	56,348	22,221	23,227
July..............	44,657	13,879	14,394	6,520	52,748	33,923	27,687
August...........	57,507	10,836	8,446	8,652	60,886	22,091	28,069
September........	35,386	5,528	4,736	7,085	52,973	9,819	19,255
October..........	16,631	9,877	8,580	4,313	34,987	10,016	14,067
November........	9,244	2,999	2,077	[b]50,304	29,555	7,683	209
December.........	12,276	2,746	339	[b]34,558	16,001	8,890	969

a Figures compiled from the Commercial and Financial Chronicle.
b Deficit.

The table emphasizes the well-known fact that the bank reserves are likely to increase in midsummer and be lowest in spring and fall. The figure 9A further shows that the surplus reserve reached its lowest points in May and December of 1904; March, November, and December of 1905; March and December of 1906; March, June, and November of 1907; July and December of 1908; and April and November of 1909. The period from the late autumn of 1904 until the time of the panic of 1907 was a time of comparative stability. Section B of the diagram, as remarked, brings out the course of the average reserve, according to the preceding data.

Perhaps enough has been said to justify the statement that evil results from a lack of correspondence of government receipts and disbursements with bank needs and seasons of ease. The evidence may be strengthened, however, by a glance at the course of government receipts and disbursements by months. In order to bring this out, Tables 10 and 11 have been prepared. Section A of Table 10 shows the monthly government receipts from

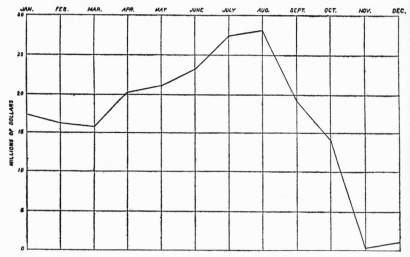

FIG. 9B.—Monthly movement of the average surplus reserve of the New York associated banks for six years, 1904–1909, inclusive.

customs only, for the three years 1888, 1889, and 1891, with the average for each month. Section B of the same table gives the total ordinary receipts of the Government by months for the years 1908 and 1909, with the average for each month. Table 11A shows the disbursements for the three years with the average for each month, and 11B gives the disbursements by months for 1908 and 1909, corresponding with Section B of Table 10. The figures

Independent Treasury of the United States

for the year 1890 have been left out because they were somewhat anomalous.

An inspection of the table of receipts shows that they rise through the summer. This means, of course, that during these months the Treasury is locking up money and contracting the currency. Doubtless the banks must have found relief at times from this situation, for the Treasury absorptions have withdrawn part of the money which would otherwise have lain idle in their vaults. On the other hand, it may at times have weakened them in their efforts to prepare for the autumn demand for money to move the crops. Indeed, there have been years, of which 1890, 1902, and 1903 are, perhaps, good illustrations, in which the necessary ease to the money market has come entirely from government disbursements. One may say that provision for "moving the crops" has become a regular part of the banking business of the Treasury.

TABLE 10.—*Receipts of the Government from customs, by months.*[a]

A.

[Expressed in millions of dollars.]

	1888.	1889.	1891.	Average.
January	18.3	20.7	23.1	20.7
February	16.7	18.8	19.0	18.2
March	17.6	19.2	15.4	17.4
April	17.8	20.0	12.1	16.6
May	15.6	17.2	12.0	14.9
June	18.0	17.6	14.2	16.6
July	19.5	19.0	15.5	18.0
August	22.0	21.5	15.2	19.6
September	19.0	17.8	14.1	16.9
October	18.8	18.8	14.0	17.2
November	15.3	16.7	12.7	14.9
December	16.9	15.9	13.8	15.5

a The figures are from the Commercial and Financial Chronicle.

Ordinary receipts of the Government, by months, for 1908 and 1909.

B.

[Expressed in millions of dollars.]

	1908.	1909.	Average.
January................................	49.4	47.5	48.5
February................................	48.3	46.7	47.5
March................................	44.6	53.4	49.0
April................................	43.9	52.1	48.0
May................................	42.7	53.3	48.0
June................................	53.5	56.9	55.2
July................................	52.2	57.6	54.9
August................................	45.3	51.1	48.2
September................................	48.3	52.3	50.3
October................................	49.3	57.2	53.3
November................................	48.0	51.7	49.8
December................................	50.3	56.9	53.6

TABLE 11.—*Government disbursements, by months.*

A. 1888–1891.

[Expressed in millions of dollars.]

	1888.	1889.	1890.	1891.	Average for the four years.
January................	21.9	26.6	27.9	24.0	25.1
February................	19.9	33.8	25.1	31.7	27.6
March................	15.5	17.0	17.5	31.5	20.4
April................	24.9	22.5	29.9	25.3	25.7
May................	27.5	24.4	27.2	29.8	22.2
June................	16.6	13.8	14.9	35.9	20.3
July................	36.1	42.0	38.1	39.7	39.0
August................	22.2	38.3	33.9	20.7	28.8
September................	19.5	16.5	33.7	23.9	23.4
October................	32.6	28.6	38.0	31.9	32.8
November................	36.6	25.3	42.6	27.9	33.1
December................	15.5	25.9	21.9	31.8	31.7

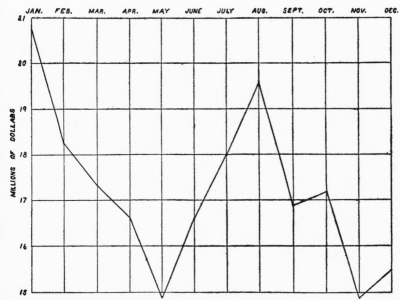

Fig. 10A.—Course of average receipts of the Government from customs for 1888, 1889, 1891.

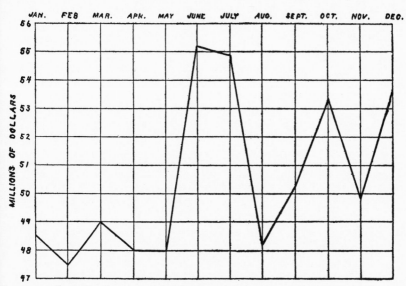

Fig. 10B.—Average course of Government receipts, by months, 1908–1909.

TABLE 11.—*Government disbursements, by months*—Continued

B. 1908–1909.

	1908.	1909	Average.
January	58.8	63.0	60.9
February	56.7	53.2	54.9
March	53.2	56.4	54.8
April	59.9	55.1	57.5
May	54.7	58.8	56.7
June	49.5	49.2	49.4
July	77.1	70.7	73.9
August	49.2	58.5	53.8
September	52.9	52.9	52.9
October	60.0	59.1	59.6
November	57.9	56.3	57.1
December	60.6	53.2	56.9

A study of Table 11, showing the disbursements of the Government, gives us the same kind of information. In Section A the disbursements have been large in October, November, and December, and small in March, April, May, and June. In both sections of the table July is the month when most money was disbursed.

The plethora of currency in the summer is due (1) to the fact that any national bank which receives on deposit notes of another bank may pay them out again in the ordinary course of business, in consequence of which the notes of the country banks are not sent home in the summer; (2) to that provision of the law whereby the deposits in reserve cities count as reserve both for the reserve banks and for the country banks making the deposits; (3) to the payment of interest by the banks on deposits subject to call. No one is benefited by seasons of extreme ease; for, as the money accumulates in New York when it is not wanted in the interior, the producing mercantile classes outside of New York get no benefit from the low rate of discount which the accumulations produce. When a stringency occurs, on the other hand, all parts of the country are likely to be affected. The injury of crises is not compensated by the ease of the money market at the times of great accumulation. Figures 11 A and 11 B show the data of the corresponding tables graphically.

There have been times when the autumnal drain would all have fallen on the banks but for the subtreasury. Two channels were open for the Government to put out its accumulated surplus: The purchase of bonds, which was the usual policy in the autumn for some years before 1890, and making deposits of public money in the banks. With a rising premium on United States bonds, the banks did not always find it profitable to buy them in order to secure government deposits. Relaxation, in recent years, of the law requiring security to be in United States bonds only, together with the provision that customs receipts also may now be deposited in banks, has changed the situation altogether, so that depositing in the banks is now the usual policy. With the changes in the law and in practice, when the Government has a surplus, bond purchases to relieve the market or to "move the crops" will be less necessary.

GENERAL CONCLUSIONS CONCERNING THE INFLUENCE OF THE INDEPENDENT TREASURY SYSTEM.

The two important and striking facts brought out by study of these tables and diagrams are the irregularity of the operations of the subtreasury in absorbing and disbursing currency and, therefore, in contracting and

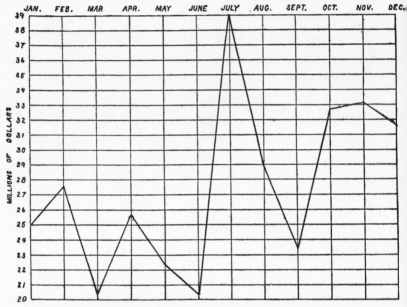

FIG. 11A.—Average course of Government disbursements, by months, 1888–1892.

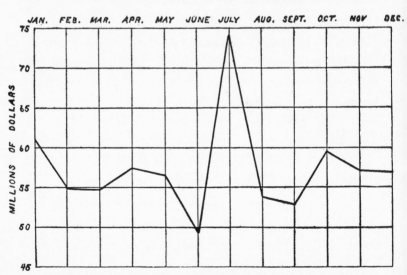

FIG. 11B.—Average course of Government disbursements, by months, 1908–1909.

expanding the currency and the bank reserves; and, second, the lack of correspondence between the periods between subtreasury disbursements and the needs of the banks as well as between subtreasury absorptions and periods of ease on the part of the banks.

It is evident that there is no necessary connection between subtreasury supply and bank need. Sometimes the two movements are in the same direction and sometimes in opposite directions. There is no certainty that the subtreasury movement, whether it coincides with or antagonizes the demand for money from the interior, is in the best direction at any particular time. But we must remember that the subtreasury has often been of great advantage. It is entirely possible that without it the banks might have experienced at times greater difficulty than they did. But the public has a right to insist that the management of banks shall be good enough to enable them to meet all demands upon them. If the banks had not been accustomed so long to rely upon the subtreasury for relief, they might be better able themselves to take measures to meet the regular autumnal drain.

So great an irregularity as the data show can not but have a tendency to make prices irregular too. The effect of the spasmodic variations shows itself first in the price of securities, and some people are inclined to take the view that fluctuations in the market for securities are matters that concern speculators only and need not cause anxiety to the people at large. This, however, is too narrow a view of the situation. Whatever criticism may fairly be made against the merely speculative element of the securities market, it yet is true that the fluctuations of that market have an important and far-reaching influence on the ordinary business of the country. Manufacturers and merchants are interested in the price of securities, although they do not speculate in them. The business man with a surplus of money in a dull season finds it to his advantage to invest it in good securities. When his business becomes brisk again he borrows at his bank and may pledge his securities as collateral. If from any cause the price of his bonds or stocks fluctuates violently he may suffer a loss and may be obliged to provide additional security and thereby strain his resources when he needs them most. Under some conditions the business man who has borrowed may be compelled to reduce his capital or lessen his expenses or sell his goods at a loss. Moreover, we must not forget that the speculation which is so much and so properly criticised may be stimulated, if not caused, by an inopportune disbursement from the sub-treasury itself.

For, as we have already remarked, the influence of the treasury absorptions and disbursements of money on prices is not a direct one. It shows itself through alternate enlargement and lessening of the bank reserves, with consequent changes in the rate of discount. As is well understood, a vast volume of business transactions is based on credit; that is to say, the funds for them are borrowed bank deposits resting directly upon the cash reserves of the banks. It is hardly necessary to lay emphasis on the volume of transactions settled with credit documents supported in one way or another by this reserve. The volume of loans and discounts in the national banks alone, on March 29, 1910, was $5,432,093,194. This great volume of credit transactions rested on a reserve of $661,799,771 in specie and $173,095,815 in legal-tender notes. But this statement does not present the situation completely. The bank reserves of the city of New York and of the other central reserve cities include part of the reserves of banks in other places. Under the national banking law, as is well known, banks in places other than reserve cities are permitted to count as part of their reserve some of their deposits with their correspondent banks in the reserve cities. But the banks in the reserve cities discount on the basis of these deposits. It is evident, therefore, that the reserves of the banks in the central reserve cities support not only the discounts of these banks themselves, but, in large measure, the discounts of the country banks also. But the situation is even more delicate than the facts thus far would show. In practice, not only the national banks outside of the reserve cities, but also other banking institutions, follow this practice of keeping part of their reserves with banks in reserve cities. Doubtless there are many banking institutions which keep practically the whole of their reserves in the reserve city banks. Consequently, the reserves of the banks in these cities, particularly in New York, is, in a real sense, the reserve of all the banks of the country. It is clear, therefore, when we consider the vast superstructure of credit that rests upon the reserves, that any influence exerted upon the reserves in the central reserve cities is likely to have far-reaching immediate consequences upon the business of the country.

The safety and value of the whole credit system depends upon the maintenance of an adequate reserve. The reserve is not adequate unless it is large enough not only to meet all demands upon it but to remove all apprehension that it may not be able so to do. Unless confidence in this respect can be established in the minds of the public, the whole credit system is impaired. Any diminution of the bank reserve, without a corresponding decrease of credit, or any check on its expansion when the needs of business require an enlargement of credit, interferes with operations in every line of business activity. In other words, so small relatively is the bank reserve that a comparatively slight change in its amount may check the whole market. The banks in reserve cities are required by law to keep a minimum reserve of 25 per cent of their deposits in coin and United States notes. This, then, represents the danger line in fluctuations of reserve. Even an approach to it creates anxiety and distress in business.

The amount of reserve necessary depends partly upon the amount of cash deposits, but more upon the volume of discounts. For a borrower at a bank seldom cares to withdraw the actual money. He borrows credit. The amount of the loan is credited to him on the books of the bank, and he draws on it as he needs it. No more money comes into the bank by this transaction; no money at all need pass from the bank to the borrower from the time of the contraction of the debt to that of its liquidation. Yet the transaction is equivalent to an increase of deposits, and necessitates an increase of reserve. If the reserve of the bank is already at the legal minimum, the bank must get more money; if it can not do so, it must contract its loans or refuse further discounts, thus checking the market. Money which is drawn from the banks must come out of the reserve or cash actually on hand. The withdrawal of any sum of money from the banks diminishes the reserve in a ratio larger than that which the amount withdrawn bears to the total deposit account. But if the amount withdrawn is kept in the current of business, where the banks can get at it, they can strengthen their position again immediately. If, however, they can not recover the money let out, every withdrawal brings them nearer to the danger line of the legal minimum reserve. Money withdrawn from the banks for export, or to be locked up in the subtreasury, is put out of reach of the banks for a time at least.

The banks of the central reserve cities are subjected each year to periodical drains from the interior to sow in the spring and to move the crops in the fall. Between times they ordinarily have high surplus reserves and the discount rate is low. Under a good currency and banking system the banks would not be subjected to a strain on their reserves at the times when the demand from the interior is heavy; nor to an influx from the subtreasury at times when money is returning from the interior. That they do undergo these experiences, however, the data in the tables and diagrams presented show very fully.

The diminution of the bank reserves by the subtreasury diminishes the money basis of credit and thereby at times makes credit more difficult to obtain; but at the same time the withdrawal of money from circulation necessitates a larger resort to credit in the attempt to prevent the reduction of business transacted. That is, since one part of the purchasing medium is diminished, the other must enlarge to maintain the same volume of business. Thus the tendency of the action of the subtreasury is to diminish one basis of business activity—the money available for loans—and so to compel a resort to the other basis—credit; while at the same time, and by the same action, it reduces the basis for granting credit. The result is a check on business expansion, perhaps an actual reduction of business activity.

It is sometimes said that if the Government would pay its debts so as to avoid having a surplus on hand, the evil effects of the independent treasury in alternately contracting and expanding the currency would not occur. This statement is hardly correct, because it overlooks the characteristic feature of the system, which is its irregularity of action. The receipts of the Government flow into its vaults in a continuous stream, while payments are periodic. It receives money every day, but the bulk of its payments is made every three months. It must gather beforehand a sufficient amount to meet its payments. That means that for three months money is being withdrawn from circulation, and that at the end of the quarter it is thrown back into circulation and into the banks all, or nearly all, at once. In this irregularity [a] of action on the money market lies the harm of the system. If it be said that the payments made by the Government at the end of every three months amount to a small sum compared with the total circulating medium, and therefore can not have any important effect on business, the argument is conclusively answered by the evidence of experience. It can not be admitted that the disbursements of the Government are so insignificant as the statement seems to assume. To assert that such changes in the available amount of loanable funds as Treasury operations

---

[a] As long ago as 1882, the Secretary of the Treasury, Mr. C. J. Folger, emphasized this point, in his report for that year. He emphasizes too strongly, perhaps, the power of "cliques" in the money market; but these certainly have been at times powerful for evil, and their power has been increased, if not at times made possible, by the influence of the independent treasury on the currency. Secretary Folger wrote:

"From the inequality between daily large receipts and comparatively small daily disbursements there comes an evil effect upon the business of the country. The collections by the Government are taken out of the money market in sums and at dates which have little or no agreement with the natural movement of money, and are returned to it with the same inadaptation to commercial or financial requirements. Occasionally the large disbursements of the Government have created a plethora of money; more frequently its large and continued withdrawals of money have caused such a scarcity of floating capital as to check the proper movement of legitimate business. It is not only that the amount in the Treasury is so much kept from the use of [the] community; the fact becomes an incentive and an aid to men who for their own ends conspire to keep from that use other large sums * * * To-day there are men so rich that by conspiring together, they can at will put and hold hand on near as much money as Government can lay hand to, save by the use of its credit. The power thus had is used from time to time. It results that sudden and violent contractions and expansions afflict the business community, and the Government is an unwilling aider and abettor therein. It has come about that the Treasury Department is looked to as a great, if not a chief cause of recurring stringencies, and the Treasury is called to for relief."

Similar remarks have been made by other Secretaries.

cause will not materially affect business, is to assume that, other things being equal, the rate of interest in the money market will not vary with the amount accessible to borrowers, and that the banks will voluntarily keep idle in their vaults more money than is necessary for conservative banking.

But, to repeat what has already been said, even a small change in the amount of money available for reserves may have an important influence on the market, especially if bank reserves are very near the legal minimum; for contraction then, though apparently insignificant in amount, may produce a most violent reaction in prices, disturbance in settlements, and disorder in almost every part of business activity.

Some years ago the banks of the country took alarm, whether reasonably or not, at some proposed congressional legislation which, in their judgment, would affect the value of United States bonds. Banks generally took measures immediately to recall the bonds deposited with the Treasurer of the United States as security for their circulating notes. To do so they drew on their New York balances for legal-tender notes and ordered them sent to the Treasurer at once. The amount of legal tenders thus withdrawn from the bank reserves in New York City in one week was about $17,000,000, out of a total circulation of all kinds aggregating nearly $1,100,000,000. The demand caused a sudden contraction of the discounts of the New York banks, followed by a fall in the price of securities, which had to be sacrificed by borrowers who could not replace their loans. The result was a loss of fully $200,000,000 in the aggregate value of securities in the New York market within the week.[a]

In addition to the bad influence of the irregularity of the working of the independent treasury, harm arises from the system in connection also with the policy of surplus financiering. By that policy a large amount of money collected in excess of the expenses of the Government is, in effect, withdrawn from circulation. If the Government has a surplus every month, a part of it, at least, must be continuously in the possession of the Government. The effect is the same as if so much money were withdrawn from circulation permanently. The result must be that the country accommodates itself to this new monetary basis by a temporary fall of prices, unless the circulating medium is increasing under the influence of additional coinage with sufficient rapidity to prevent the fall. To be sure, to have a surplus is not a feature of the independent treasury system. The continual holding of a surplus by the Government is a policy, not a system. But if a surplus were by some means kept in circulation, subject to the call of the Government, the evils of hoarding, at least, would be avoided. It is because it makes hoarding in the government vaults possible that the subtreasury system adds to the evils of surplus financiering.

FACTORS WHICH HAVE MODIFIED THE INFLUENCE OF THE INDEPENDENT TREASURY.

The operations which have been described are those which would result under a system of government fiscal

---

[a] See W M. Grosvenor, American Securities, 216ff.

independence, with disbursements made at considerable intervals, and with no reference to the condition of the money market or the demands of business. Such in principle is the independent treasury system of the United States. But the existence of the public debt and the almost constant possession of a surplus revenue have, under wise management by the various Secretaries of the Treasury, made it possible to prevent the occurrence of very serious disturbances from the influence of the system. If this influence had been unchecked, there is no reason to think that the results would have been less evil than the opponents of the system prophesied at its inception. But there have been forces at work that have lessened the evils. The policy of the country in other lines, although these have been followed without any reference to the independent treasury, has been such as to prevent the system from bearing what would be its legitimate fruits if unchecked. The times of largest receipts from customs and of largest payments of interest and pensions, the currency, the silver purchases, and the tariff, have all modified the working of the system of fiscal independence to a greater or less extent. It has happened that some of these influences have prevented or lessened any evils that the subtreasury might have caused.

In the first place, the tariff and the independent treasury have had a certain connection. Until 1907 receipts from customs could not, according to law, be deposited in the banks. When, therefore, imports which are subject to taxation were heavy, considerable money was locked up. This, of course, if continued for a considerable period, and if disbursements did not increase, would diminish the means of paying duties, and might strongly affect the money market and disarrange credit.

The two institutions, tariff and independent treasury, are to a certain extent antagonistic, in so far, at least, as the tariff is for the purpose of raising revenue. For by locking up the customs receipts of one week, and thereby reducing the money within reach for further payments, the subtreasury will tend to check an importation movement sooner than it would cease if our currency varied with the needs of business. So far, however, as the tariff is intended to check importation, so far, that is, as it is purely protective, its purpose harmonizes with the action of the independent treasury.

It has already been observed several times that there is, strictly speaking, no casual connection between the workings of the financial machinery of the Government and the demand of business for money. Yet, strangely enough, the ill effects of the receipts and payments of the Government, in alternately contracting and enlarging the amount of money available for business purposes, have been modified, and to a certain extent diminished, by our peculiar currency system. Bad as that system is in some respects, it must be credited with some good in this direction. The chief defect of our monetary system is its inelasticity. The supply of money in the channels of trade is that which is needed when business is brisk and the demand for money is active and healthy. But there is not what might be called an automatic method of contraction whereby the amount of money in circulation quickly and easily becomes less when business becomes dull for short periods. Our circulating medium is composed of gold and silver coins and certificates, United States notes, and national bank notes. The United States notes, or greenbacks, are by law fixed in amount; the gold would ordinarily diminish only by export for investment or for the settlement of international balances, and is not, therefore, contractible on the occasions under consideration; and the national-bank notes which of late years have considerably increased in volume, grow less only by slow redemption as they wear out,[a] or banks retire them. There is, then, abundant provision for currency expansion, but little for currency contraction. The principal means whereby this process can take place is through the absorption and locking up of money by the Government. Although this mode is purely arbitrary, it sometimes happens that the Government locks up money at a time when there is a plethora in the market. The process can not then do much, if any, injury; in fact, it may be a source of relief to the banks. The inelasticity of the currency implies a social loss, by keeping afloat at times a larger amount of money than is necessary; but, on the other hand, it lessens the severity of contraction by the Treasury.

Between 1880 and 1890 another preventive of stringency in the fall was found in the proper timing of the heavy payments of pensions and interest. Disbursements for these purposes often swelled at times when they could do great good. The pensions and the interest on the 4½ per cent bonds of 1891 were payable in March, June, Sep-

---

[a] Of course the final retirement of the national bank-notes is not a phase of the elasticity of the currency here intended.

tember, and December, and were a source of monetary relief that could be depended on. The interest on the 4 per cents was paid in January, April, July, and October. So far as the influence of these payments was concerned, that of October would continue the relief afforded by the September payments. When the 4½ per cent bonds had been paid there was, of course, no further relief from these interest payments in September. But after the redemption of these bonds it happened that the financial condition of the Government changed. The receipts from customs fell off owing to the high rates of the McKinley tariff law, and the expenditures largely increased, thus reducing the surplus and making income and outgo more nearly equal. The equalization of payments and receipts in the course of a year, however, as we have seen, did not prevent the financial operations of the Government from exerting an influence on the money market. For it was still necessary for the Treasury to accumulate in advance a sufficient amount of money to make payments of interest and pensions quarterly. The irregularities of its operations due to the public debt were not, indeed, as great as before, yet they were sufficient to cause occasional disturbance. The only interest payments of importance were those on the 4 per cent bonds, due in January, April, July, and October of each year. The January payments came at a time when the demand for money slackened, and so money accumulated for a time in the banks, as shown by the increase in their reserves. The April disbursements coincided usually with the demand for money for the spring trade, and thus were a help to the market. The outpour of July fell on a lethargic market and went to swell bank reserves already usually larger than the banks desire at that season of the year. The October payment, as we have already noted, was timely in meeting the usual "fall demand." But this aid was merely a temporary and incidental matter, and had no relation either to permanent fiscal policy, a correct currency system, or sound banking.

A surplus revenue has prevented the independent treasury from exerting the full effect which it would otherwise have had. While the surplus is to a certain extent chargeable with intensifying the contractions which the operation of the Treasury at times tends to produce, it also afforded a means of relief when the acute stage of the demand for money came. Without the public debt and without a surplus to redeem it, the Treasury could not have afforded the help in stringencies which it has so often given. But this very cure of the evils of contraction may be, to a certain extent, its cause. For a surplus can exist only because money is taken out of circulation and locked up for future use, a process which means contraction.

If the bank currency of the country were wholly created by commerce for its own needs, adapted entirely to those needs, and possessing the elasticity which a currency should have, the action of the independent treasury would be more clearly seen. The new coinage made in response to commercial demand, and the export and import of gold and silver, would still have to be allowed for; but the alternate issue and redemption of bank notes under such a currency system as we suppose would respond quickly to the variation in the demand caused by the subtreasury, and so would reflect its action much more clearly.

The independent treasury also enhances the difficulty of the management of the public debt. The Secretary of the Treasury must proceed carefully so as to prevent the withdrawal of too much money for the accumulations from which to pay interest and to purchase bonds for the sinking fund. He must make his withdrawals and disbursements as equable as possible.

The independent treasury, in connection with a surplus revenue, has been responsible for a policy of forced debt payment. When the surplus has grown large the Secretary of the Treasury has been compelled to get rid of some of it by purchasing bonds, even though he had to pay large premiums to do so. This policy has long been followed, especially on the occurrence of the autumn stringencies. The principal occasions will be mentioned in discussing the relation of the independent treasury to crises. One result of such purchases is to raise the price of the bonds so that it may not pay the banks to deposit them as security for circulation; and the consequence not infrequently is a retirement of bank notes and a contraction of the currency, or a prevention of its expansion when needed.

The causes which have modified the action of the subtreasury have prevented the monthly variations in the net government holdings of cash from corresponding necessarily with the gains or loss of money to business from government operations. Hence, one set of changes can not always be learned from the other. The difference between the two sets of changes is often increased by the fact that the disbursements reported as being made in one month may not appear until the following month. The checks issued for pensions, for example, are some time in returning through the banks to the subtreasury for payment. Meantime the money against them remains still in the vaults of the Treasury. The effect of large reported disbursements or absorptions may not appear, therefore, for some little time after they are nominally made.

We see, then, that the evils which the subtreasury might have been expected to produce have often been neutralized by lucky accidents, as it were; for it can hardly be claimed that the various parts of our financial system and policy have been framed with reference to one another so as to offset one another's ill effects and produce a system good on the whole. Irregularities of absorption and disbursement can not be prevented. They occur with all governments. It is not practicable for the Government to pay its bills with sufficient frequency to prevent the locking up of considerable sums for periods long enough to affect the market, especially when it is sensitive. This feature of temporary withdrawals of money is inherent in the "independent" system of government management of its own receipts, and renders impossible the prevention of the evils which arise from contractions and expansions of the currency that are independent of the state of trade.

It may be said that recent legislation whereby the government receipts from customs may be deposited in the banks, in addition to the internal-revenue receipts, sufficiently restores to circulation the money received in taxes, and that the abolition of the independent treasury system is not now necessary. If the Secretary of the Treasury takes full advantage of his discretion in this respect, the evil of Treasury independence would be much lessened, but not wholly removed. For, at present, the Secretary must withdraw his deposits and put the money in a subtreasury in order to use it to pay the creditors of the Government. If, instead of being required to do so, he were permitted to receive checks whenever tendered, and to check against his accounts with the banks, the conditions would be still farther improved.

In defense of the subtreasury system it has been said that there must be a source of supply of specie somewhere in the country, and the Government might as well keep it as the banks.[a] To the first half of this statement no one can object. This reserve of specie is provided for in different countries in different ways. Of course, in all cases the banks provide some of it. Some countries prefer to have a large part of it in active circulation. It has been said that the metallic currency of Great Britain is a reservoir from which the banks are able to replenish their resources to a considerable extent in times of stringency.

Our people pursue the opposite course; we prefer paper money and checks to so great an extent that we have no reserve of this kind when a pinch comes. "If by means of checks and post-office savings banks and small notes and all such methods we diminish the reserve gold circulation in the hands of the people, then we lose security in critical times and we find ourselves in the situation of having our whole coinage system rest on nothing but

---

[a] Bankers' Magazine, November, 1890.

paper."[a] We subject ourselves to this danger. For that reason it is more necessary to provide a store of specie in the banks.

To the second part of the remark, that the supply of gold may as well be kept by the Government as the banks, objection may be made, because there is no relation between the amount that the Government keeps and the amount needed by business. The amount which the Government keeps depends upon its revenue. If the revenue falls off the amount of specie diminishes, unless the Government deliberately makes its Treasury to a greater or less degree a bank of issue. Indeed, no Government can properly keep the specie reserve of a country unless it does this. Moreover, the Government reserve is uncertain, not only in amount, but in time of collection and in disbursement. As we have seen in our study of the subtreasury operations, an independent government reserve may be lacking when it is most needed, and abundant when it is unnecessary. The proper agents to provide the reserve are the banks. They do a commercial business and can protect the specie reserve by changing the rate of discount, a course which is not open to the Government at all.

When the power to receive checks and to check against bank deposits is conferred on the Secretary, then, indeed, the repeal of the independent treasury law will hardly be necessary. For the various amendments, made in recent years, which permit the use of the banks for practically

---

[a] Remark of Doctor Arendt, Rept. of National Monetary Com., German Bank Inquiry of 1908 (stenographic report); Doc. 407, 61st Cong., 2d sess., p. 531.

all the business of the Government, have already virtually abolished the system. It has been repealed piecemeal. The fact that it has been so repealed, that step by step the separation of the Treasury and the banks has been done away with by special legislation, is the best of evidence that this separation was felt to be injurious to the business of the country. The formal repeal of the law now would be largely perfunctory.

METHODS OF RELIEF.

It has become a habit for the business community to
rely on the Treasury for assistance in times of financial
stringency. The practice of the Government to furnish
relief began early in the history of the independent treasury and has been its uniform policy, "when possible, in all
commercial crises from 1846 to the present time."[a] The
methods by which relief to the money market has been
afforded have been, in general, the same on all such occasions; but the extent of the assistance, the seriousness of
the crisis, and the condition of the revenue and the public
debt at different times, make it desirable to study the
period since the adoption of the present national banking
system by itself. But we must first consider the methods
by which the Treasury can give such assistance.

There are several ways in which the power of the Government has been, or may be, brought to bear in a crisis.
In the first place, under some circumstances, a Government whose fiscal operations are independent of banks
may relieve a protracted stringency by requiring dues to
it to be paid in coin. Under the influence of such a requirement specie is likely to be drawn from hoards, or from
abroad, and the Government puts the metal into circulation by its disbursements. Part of the specie so disbursed
is likely to remain in circulation; and even if it should not,
its transitory circulation will accomplish some good.

---

[a] Cf. Secretary Windom: Finance Report, 1890.

Again, the Government may exercise a restraining influence on the banks, retarding discounts and so checking speculation, by absorbing for a time more money than it disburses; it may cheapen domestic exchange by itself doing a transfer business at low rates or even gratuitously, thereby promoting the flow of money from places where it is abundant to places where it is scarce; it may supply money by anticipating payments of interest on its debt, by adapting other payments to the condition of the market, and by the purchase of bonds; it may deposit the public money in banks, and allow the banks to use the deposits as a basis for making loans; and, finally, it may offer to increase the supply of currency by converting interest-bearing bonds into noninterest-bearing treasury notes. This last method has never been used in this country, although something analogous to it was advocated in 1873.[a]

When the country was laboring under a suspension of specie payments by the banks, under the administration of President Van Buren, there is no doubt that the payment of its ordinary obligations in specie enabled the Government to put in motion a small stream of the metals, which "gradually assumed larger dimensions," and furnished a measure of relief. The action of the Government at this time was beneficial in two ways: It relieved the stress, and, by its method of doing this, promoted the restoration of specie payments.

To be sure, the independent treasury was not established at this time, yet it virtually existed; for in the suspension in 1837 only six banks maintained specie payments and so

---

[a] See Adams, H. C., "Public Debts," 214–215.

continued to be government depositaries. Since the Secretary of the Treasury was unable to find banks in which he could legally deposit, he kept part of the public money on special deposit in Washington, while the rest was left in the hands of the collecting officers.[a]

The panic of 1837 was hastened and intensified, in this country, by the great inflation of the currency which was produced by the large number of state banks that sprang up immediately after the downfall of the Second United States Bank. The bank paper in circulation increased from $82,000,000 in January, 1835, to $108,000,000 in January, 1836, and to $120,000,000 in the following December. Within the same period the per capita circulation grew from $7 to nearly $10. The specie in the banks rose only $2,000,000 in the meantime, and that in circulation increased from $18,000,000 to $28,000,000. Thus the currency was almost entirely bank paper; and when the bubble of speculation built on it burst, many of the notes became worthless and most of them very much depreciated. So great was the burden of dishonest credit that resumption would have been exceedingly difficult for the banks had they been unaided. But the Government receipts and payments were by law required to be in specie, or in treasury notes equivalent to specie, and a steady stream of good money was thus kept in circulation, part of which was within reach of the banks and undoubtedly made their task of resumption easier.

The second mode in which the independent treasury may exert a beneficent influence in a crisis, is by exercising a restraining influence on the banks. The theory of this

---

[a] Finance Report, 1837.

action is that by absorbing money the Treasury makes it harder for the banks to get, and that they, in consequence, do not discount so freely. Speculation, therefore, it is argued, is checked and the crisis is retarded. Of course, any effect of this kind can be produced only if the current receipts of the Government exceed its expenditures, that is, if a surplus is accumulating. There is no doubt that under proper conditions the influence exerted by the sub-treasury in this way would be beneficial. If the Government were absorbing money at a time when business was entering on a stage of speculation that was forcing up prices, evidently there would be two sources of drain on the bank reserves: that caused by speculative borrowers, and that caused by locking up money in the Treasury. The operation of the latter would prevent the former from going as far as it otherwise would do; for it would diminish the bank reserves, raise the rate of discount, and make borrowing more difficult. The result would be a diminution of loans to speculative buyers, which would cause them to lessen their demand for the commodities in which they were speculating, and so retard the inflation of prices. Some such influence was exerted in 1854. The bank circulation then was set at $204,689,209, and the gold and silver in the country at $241,000,000.[a]

The restraining influence of government withdrawals of money is what Secretary Guthrie had in mind when, in his report for 1855–56, he wrote: "The independent treasury, when over-trading takes place, gradually fills its vaults, withdraws the deposits, and, pressing the banks, the merchants, and the dealers, exercises that tem-

---

[a] Finance Report, 1854, 15.

perate and timely control, which seems to secure the fortunes of individuals and preserve the general prosperity." While we may readily admit that the action of the independent treasury sometimes produces such results, yet whether it actually does so in any given crisis is a question of fact to be proved, and that it might operate in an opposite way and make the crisis more acute, is a possibility that must be recognized and its conditions defined.

On the face of the matter, it would seem that the simplest way for the Government to give relief in a crisis, is 'for the Treasury to deposit its money in the banks. This does not mean depositing in ordinary times when business is quiet; that is a matter which has been considered in another connection. The deposits here meant are deposits of surplus revenue for the express purpose of relieving the business community in a financial storm. But there are certain objections to such a mode of affording help to business when it is distressed.

Under our present usury law, banks which receive such deposits can not raise their rate of discount above the legal rate in the State in which the bank is located, except in New York where call loans above $5,000 are exempted. Therefore, the banks can not, unless by evasion of the law, apply the well-known rule to discount in the face of a panic, freely, indeed, but at a rate of discount that rises, within certain limits, as the stress increases. Hence the help which the banks could give with the public money deposited with them would be limited by the extent to which they can raise the rate of discount, supposing the law were not evaded. The demand for loans at 6 or 7 per cent, the usual legal limits, would be very large, and all the money to loan would soon be absorbed, a large part of it by those whose financial salvation did not depend on getting it; while others who were on the brink of ruin might be unable to borrow, even though they could and would have paid a higher rate of interest than the law allowed, by outbidding those who were not really in dire need of the money. These remarks apply to all loans throughout the country excepting, of course, those made by banks in New York on call in amounts of $5,000 or more.

Furnishing relief to the money market by depositing the public money in banks can not, then, be very serviceable, under existing conditions, outside of New York, unless by evasion of the law. As a matter of fact, this is what is actually done. Hence this policy of the Treasury condones and encourages evasion of the law. True, the law is an unwise one. But the fact hardly justifies the Government in aiding the evasion of one of its own statutes.

The other methods mentioned as being at the command of the Treasury for influencing the money market are rather methods of direct relief than methods of prevention, palliative rather than deterrent. They partake, indeed, of both characteristics; for aid in transfers, the timing of interest and other payments, and the purchase of bonds, may be utilized in anticipating commercial distress. Until comparatively recent years, however, they have rather been measures of relief when the storm was on.

By the timing of payments is meant simply that a certain latitude is observed in paying public debts. There are generally some debts the payment of which can legitimately be hastened or deferred for a short period. The plan in practice has consisted in throwing the payments of one month into the month following. For example, in the latter part of November, 1889, the Secretary of the Treasury issued a large number of transfer checks so late in the month that they could not well be returned for payment until December.[a] But December is a month in which money is usually in great demand, and the throwing of the November disbursements into December helped to keep the market more equable than it would have been otherwise.

When disbursements have been hastened by the Treasury for the purpose of assisting the money market they have frequently taken the form of prepayments of interest on the public debt. Such prepayments have done some good at times, but for affording relief in a large way they can not be relied on. This plan "must always be a lame method for relieving the Government of its surplus, unless the inducement offered is greater than now, as it interferes with the free sale of bonds."[b] It is unfortunate that the Government should be compelled to resort to such paltry practices because of defective fiscal machinery. It ought not to be necessary. Government payments should be made when they are due. Anticipation and postponement are alike evil; the one is a wrong to the people, the other to the public creditors.

The practice of transferring money for individuals and firms was originally adopted by the Government, not for

---

[a] See New York Commercial and Financial Chronicle, January 5, 1890: 4.
[b] Commercial and Financial Chronicle, September 17, 1887.

the purpose of providing a better distribution of currency, in, order to aid the market, but simply as a measure to force silver into circulation. In 1880 the Government offered to pay silver dollars or certificates free of charge at interior points where there was a subtreasury or United States depositary, in exchange for gold paid in at the sub-treasury in New York.[a] But the practice was evidently available as a means of distributing money to relieve a local stringency. Advantage would be taken of the offer of the Government whenever the demand for money in the places to which free transfers could be made was at least great enough to cause exchange on these places to be at a premium at the points whence the money was to come.

The rationale of the system of currency transfers is found simply in the use by the Government of its power to facilitate exchange, in order to transfer funds rapidly and at nominal cost from places where they are idle or little needed to places where they are urgently needed.

The system was developed in the financial distress of the winter of 1890–91, by the use of the telegraph to make the transfers of money.   In addition to the relief afforded at that time by the actual transfer by telegraph of some $3,000,000 from San Francisco to New York, the situation was doubtless considerably eased by the knowledge that similar action would, if necessary, be taken at other points.

The method of government transfer has merit, especially for moments of special acuteness of strain in the money market, in those cases where a stringency, instead of being

---

a See Taussig, F. W., "The Silver Situation," Public. Amer. Econ. Assoc., vii: 1 (1892).

general in its severity, has a center, or a few centers, of greatest intensity. This was doubtless the case in the winter of 1890. It was in New York City that distress was most severe, and relief consequently most needed. The effect, of course, is simply to relieve the strain by making the distribution of money more equable. But the very strength of the practice is also its source of weakness. Aside from the fact that it trenches on the legitimate business of the banks, it is objectionable also because the relief afforded at one place is afforded at the expense of other places; and its limit, of course, is reached in the transfer of such funds only as will not cause distress at the points whence the money is drawn. As soon as the legal reserves of the banks there are trenched on, or even threatened, the movement has attained the limit of its benefit. The San Francisco banks objected to the telegraphic transfers of 1890–91 on this very ground, that they depleted their reserves.

Moreover, on general principles, the system can not be commended. For unless the amount of money transferred, free of charge, to the community suffering from a stringency, were sufficient to supply all borrowers, there would be danger of intensifying the distress. The free transfer of money in such a case would demoralize exchange on the place where the stringency existed, and make the terms harder for borrowers. In short, the practice is a violation of the oft-quoted principle of good banking, that in a crisis money enough for all necessary purposes should be offered for loan, but on terms so hard that only those in real need will seek to borrow. Finally, if the financial strain were due to the locking up in the subtreasury of money needed to restore the currency to its normal volume,[a] complete relief by the method of currency transfer would be impossible, because the transfers do not add to the volume of money afloat; and the furnishing of only partial relief, of help that stops short of the complete restoration of confidence, may react in a distress more acute than before.

The deposit of public money in the banks for the purpose of relieving a stringency is a method of assistance which could not lawfully be employed in the period we are now considering. It came into use after the resumption of specie payments, and was resorted to in some degree in the twenty following years, but always under considerable criticism. From about 1901 the practice became more usual and reached its fullest development in the panic of 1907. Its advantages and disadvantages will be discussed, therefore, in connection with the study of the later period.

The other mode of affording relief to a straitened market is by the purchase of bonds with money which has accumulated in the Treasury. Evidently if there is no surplus no relief can be furnished in this way. It is on the existence of the policy of surplus financiering, as much as on the existence of the independent treasury, that the efficacy of this mode of relief must depend. If that policy were abandoned, aid could be rendered in this way only from temporary surpluses that happened to accumulate in hard times, and the scope of the influence of this means of assistance would be materially diminished. On the

---

[a] That is, the amount needed for the current volume of commercial transactions.

other hand, the policy of surplus financiering, if there were no independent treasury, would not by itself be a sufficient condition for relief from the Government; for the existence of a surplus, if it were already deposited in the banks, would not make it possible for the Treasury to help the money market. It is the existence of a surplus in the vaults of the independent treasury that confers on the Government the power of easing a panicky market.

OPERATIONS IN 1853 AND 1857.

As already remarked, the policy of giving relief in a stringency by the purchase of bonds is not new. In 1853 there was considerable fear that the accumulation of money in the Treasury would distress the market, and the Secretary was urged to expend the surplus which had accumulated. There was no panic, or even crisis, but only a stringency or pressure for money. Credit was not disturbed. The stringency was intensified by a contraction of the currency due to the disappearance of silver from circulation. To counteract the effect of this contraction the Secretary deposited gold in the mint with which to purchase silver. His own account of the transaction is as follows: " The daily payments at the Treasury, in discharge of the public liabilities and the redemption of said loan,ᵃ did not equal the receipts. A large surplus accumulated in the Treasury, and became a cause of alarm in commercial and financial circles. It was hoped that the accumulation in the Treasury would exercise a beneficial restraint upon importations and speculative credit

ᵃ Of 1843.

enterprises, and bring the business of the country into a safe and wholesome condition; yet, under the apprehension that a panic might arise from a too stringent operation of the Treasury, it was determined to make advances to the mint for the purchase of silver for the new coinage, and to enable the mint to pay promptly and in advance of coinage for gold bullion."[a]   Some $5,000,000 were deposited in the mint to enable "the mint to give gold, which circulated as money, for silver that was out of circulation, because of the premium upon it, and for gold bullion that could not circulate as money until coined."[b]

The relief afforded by this means was not sufficient to make the money market easy, and the purchase of bonds was resorted to. An arrangement was made with brokers in New York and Philadelphia to purchase bonds at the market price, to be paid for on presentation at the Treasury. Even this means failed to allay apprehension, because the surplus still accumulated, and the Secretary increased his offers. In a circular of July 30, 1853, he undertook to redeem before December 1, $5,000,000 of the loans of 1847 and 1848, at a premium of 21 per cent and interest from the 1st of July. On the 22d of August he enlarged his bid by offering to purchase $2,000,000 of the loans due in 1856 and 1862 at a premium of 8½ per cent and of 16 per cent, respectively. "The result," wrote the Secretary, "has been satisfactory." The purchase of bonds was continued through the year.

---

[a] Finance Report, 1853.   [b] Ibid.

The following figures show the specie in the banks and subtreasury at New York in the fall of 1853 to the nearest thousand: [a]

	Bank loans.	Circulation.	Deposits.	Bank specie.	Specie in subtreasury.
August 6	$97,900	$9,510	$60,995	$9,746	$8,406
September 3	91,741	9,554	57,503	11,268	9,079
October 1	90,150	9,522	57,969	11,232	9,726
November 12	82,882	9,288	56,201	12,824	6,147
December 10	86,709	9,076	57,838	12,494	. . . .
December 31	90,162	8,927	58,964	11,058	3,800

The coin in all the subtreasuries and depositaries at the end of the year was $23,951,945. While, in spite of the efforts of the Secretary, the specie in the New York Subtreasury increased through August and September, it did so less rapidly than before, and the banks were benefited.

It would seem from the figures that the disbursements of the subtreasury helped to increase the specie holdings of the banks in November and December, and enabled them to get into a somewhat stronger position toward the end of the year; but, coming when they did, they had little or no effect in curtailing market operations. They seem rather to have given speculation a somewhat freer play.

One effect of the purchase of bonds by the Government is thus recorded by the Bankers' Magazine: [b] "Owing partly to the notice of the Treasury Department the government 6 per cent loans of 1867–68 have advanced from 120½ to 122, and the 5 percents from 108½ to 109."

The next important instance of government relief to the market was in 1857. "The crisis of 1857 was an unu-

---

[a] The figures are from the Bankers' Magazine.   [b] September, 1853.

sually simple case of activity, speculation, overbanking, panic, and depression."[a]

The symptoms of the coming distress were seen early in the year, and to avert disaster, if possible, Secretary Cobb began the purchase of bonds, his purpose being, in his own words, to afford "relief to the commercial and other interests of the country, which were then struggling to ward off the revulsion which finally came upon them."

In the summer months of 1857, the New York banks increased their loans at a rapid rate, the average for June, July, and August being over $8,000,000 larger than the average for the same months in 1856. The banks followed this great expansion with a rapid contraction of loans, the decrease from August 1 to December 5 amounting to over $34,000,000. In the meantime their specie more than doubled, and their notes in circulation decreased over $2,000,000.

The following table shows the state of affairs for 1857, to the nearest thousand:[b]

	Specie in New York subtreasury.	Specie in New York banks.	Loans of New York banks.	Circulation of New York banks.
January 3	$11,430	$11,172	$109,149	$8,602
February 7	13,618	11,144	112,877	8,426
March 7	15,189	11,707	111,900	8,465
April 11	15,175	10,884	115,374	8,787
May 2	14,408	12,100	114,409	9,006
June 6	12,431	13,135	115,338	8,838
July 3	10,317	12,837	115,044	8,901
August 1	12,162	12,918	120,597	8,662
September 5	11,678	10,228	112,221	8,673
October 3	7,748	11,400	105,935	7,916
November 7	5,408	16,492	95,866	6,434
December 5	3,986	26,070	96,526	6,555

a Taussig: "History of the United States Tariff," p. 118.
b The figures are from the Bankers' Magazine, April, 1857.

Between the 1st of August and the first week in December the banks gained a little more than $13,000,000 of specie, while the subtreasury lost about $8,000,000, half of which was paid out in the purchase of bonds. The net imports of gold at New York for the same time were $1,745,000, which, with $8,812,000 from California, made a net total of $10,557,000. It thus appears that a large part of the increased strength of the banks came from the proceeds of the purchases of bonds by the Government. The Secretary of the Treasury continued buying bonds as long as he could, and took the ground that it might be wise to spend the whole of the surplus in that way, so as to relieve the market, even if as a result expenses would have to be met later by new loans.

The influence of the independent treasury in this crisis was not all in one direction. During the years 1855, 1856, and 1857, the customs receipts were unusually large, and the accumulation in government vaults tended to increase. In March, 1857, the Government held in the various branches of the subtreasury over $21,000,000.[a] "At New York the public funds are accumulating at a fearful rate, by means of custom-house duties, the latter being for the current fiscal year, thus far, at the rate of $9,000,000 beyond the extravagant years 1855–56." There is no doubt that the strain in the money market was increased by the accumulations of the Government at this time. In so far as these accumulations restrained the discounts which the banks made for purposes of speculation, their influence must have been to prevent the tide of specula-

---

[a] See Bankers' Magazine, March, 1857.

tion from rising as high as it otherwise would have done, or to bring on the inevitable crash sooner than it would have come of itself. Whatever influence of this nature the absorptions of the subtreasury may have had at this time, was partly counteracted, however, by the early purchase of bonds. The Secretary began to offer help too far in advance of a real crisis, and thus held out hope to speculators that they could rely on further aid. The accumulation of funds in the subtreasury at a "fearful" rate was a good thing so long as the business which caused it was based on overspeculation, because the accumulation was constantly reducing the basis of that speculation. The accumulation should have been permitted to go on until the speculation lessened and the crisis was at hand. Discounting too far in advance of a panic will not prevent it, but rather make it more certain by furnishing fuel, so to speak, on which speculation can feed further. Too early disbursements from the Treasury may intensify rather than mitigate financial distress. At least, disbursements, if made too early, will fail to do as much good as they would if made later. This was the case with Secretary Cobb's early disbursements in 1857.

Although the purchases of bonds did not furnish as much relief as they would have done if they had been held back until later, yet they certainly accomplished much good. The specie paid out strengthened the banks, as the figures show, and made the task of resumption easier and sooner possible; and if the banks had not weakened themselves so much, it is possible that the Government disbursements, especially if they had been delayed a little longer, would have saved them from suspension.

One wholly good result of the existence of the independent treasury at this time was the maintenance of specie payments by the Government. Had the public money been deposited in the banks, or had the receipt of bank notes for public dues been lawful, the Treasury would have been as seriously embarrassed as at the beginning of the panic of 1837. Comparing the situation in 1857 with that in 1837, the Secretary of the Treasury wrote:[a] "The most remarkable feature distinguishing the two periods has reference to the effect upon the commercial and general business interest of the country produced by the present operations of the independent treasury. It is the relief which has been afforded to the money market by the disbursements in specie of the General Government. In 1837 the demand of the Government for its funds with which to meet its obligations weakened the banks or crippled their resources and added to the general panic and pressure. In 1857 the disbursements by the Government of its funds which it kept in its own vaults, supplied the banks with specie, strengthened their hands, and would thus have enabled them to afford relief when it was so much needed if they had been in a condition to do it."

It is worth noticing incidentally that the appearance of the Government on the market to buy bonds forced their prices up once more. Said the Bankers' Magazine of April, 1857: "In government bonds the rates are nominal, few being offered in the market, as the Secretary of the Treasury is preparing to pay a premium of 16 per cent on the bonds due in 1867–68, with the accrued interest of three months, equivalent in all to 117½ per cent."

---

[a] Finance Report, 1857.

Chapter VIII.—Treasury Relief in Crises, 1873 to 1890.

The Panic of 1873.

In the panic of 1873 we have to deal with conditions different from those which prevailed in 1837 or in 1857. The bank paper was as truly inconvertible in 1873, indeed, as it was in the other years mentioned, although it could be exchanged for government notes or greenbacks. For the Government itself was on a depreciated paper basis. Therefore, it could not promote resumption by its disbursements of specie and treasury notes, as it did in 1837 and 1857. At the height of the panic there lay in the vaults of the Treasury "$50,000,000 of gold coin, which could lawfully have been paid out in exchange for government obligations without embarrassing the operations of the Government; but as specie could not be employed to pay private debts without a sacrifice at once of about 12 per cent—the amount of its premium in paper—it was not wanted." [a] The Government was able, however, to lend from its stored-up surplus of the legal-tender currency. Under the national banking law the receipts from internal revenue, as they were collected, could be deposited in the national banks. But this mode of assistance was at the time of comparatively small importance. There were legal tenders in the Treasury, but they could not be transferred to the banks, although an effort was made to induce the Secretary to do so.[b]

---

[a] Upton: "Money in Politics," 139.   [b] See chapter xi.

The proceeds of purchases of bonds, however, could be deposited in the banks, along with internal-revenue receipts, and in the early period of the stringency the legal-tender reserves were increased somewhat by this process.

Like the panic of 1857 that of 1873 was world-wide. In this country it was largely the result of the too rapid transmutation of circulating capital into fixed capital during the few years preceding, under the impetus of a fever of industrial speculation. These years were also years of extensive railroad building. Over 4,000 miles were built in 1873 alone. During the last two months of 1872 the money market was much depressed, the lowest discount rate being 7 per cent. In the middle of the following January the rate sank a little, but soon rose and continued very high until May. The immediate cause of the crash in the money market was due to the fact that some of the largest of these enterprises did not realize profits quickly enough to pay the loans which had been advanced on them. Credit was shaken in consequence, and panic resulted. The panic was not due, properly speaking, to a lack of money, but to a lack, or destruction, of credit.

The forerunner of the coming disaster was a severe money stringency in the fall of 1872, to the occurrence of which the unwise management of the Treasury doubtless contributed. The monthly currency balance of the Treasury averaged fourteen and one-half millions in 1871, and twelve and a half in 1872. The Secretary lessened the money afloat by selling gold to a greater extent than he bought bonds. As the gold could not circulate, the net result was a loss of currency to business. This course of action was the reverse of that followed by Secretary Cobb in 1857.[a] He bought silver, which did not circulate, with gold, which did circulate; Secretary Boutwell, on the other hand, sold noncurrent gold for current greenbacks. So far as this process did not occur in the spring and fall, the seasons at which the interior demand for money is most active, it was not very objectionable under the circumstances which prevailed at the time. For the years 1871, 1872, and 1873 were years of too great speculation, and it is very probable that the absorptions of the Treasury restricted the ability of the banks to loan, and so retarded speculation.[b] But the management of the Treasury was not dictated by conscious adherence to a policy of restriction of speculation. Consequently, what little influence for good the independent treasury may have had in this way, in the three years under consideration, must be regarded as, on the whole, accidental.

The current of speculation was too strong, however, to be stopped by any restrictive influence of the subtreasury. The stringency became severe in the fall of 1872, and the Secretary was again called on to relieve the pressure. In the first week of October he sold $5,000,000 of gold, and deposited the proceeds in designated banks. Then, without previous notice, he bought $5,000,000 worth of five-twenty bonds, so that $10,000,000 of currency were, by the two transactions, made available for business. The bank reserves immediately rose, and the banks enlarged their

[a] See p. 219.
[b] Cf. the New York Independent, January 9, 1873. Monetary article.

discounts.   Following are the figures [a] for the New York
banks:

	Loans and discounts.	Specie in banks.	Legal tenders.
October 5.....................	$269,810,300	$9,943,900	$41,915,700
October 12.....................	268,298,300	12,217,800	45,759,400
October 19.....................	270,557,600	12,625,500	52,586,400
October 26.....................	274,925,000	10,795,300	52,342,100

Under the influence of these changes in the condition of
the banks, call loans, which on the 4th of October had
ranged from 6 per cent in currency to 7 per cent in gold,
with commissions additional in some cases, fell to a range
of from 3 or 4 to 7 per cent in currency, and the market
for such loans became easy, with an average rate of from 5
to 6 per cent.

There was a great difference, however, between the
extent of the relief that came to stockbrokers and that
experienced by commercial borrowers.   The easy rates
accommodated the brokers, but the best indorsed sixty-
day commercial paper could hardly be discounted for less
than 10 per cent.   " It thus appears," said the Chronicle,[b]
"that the Treasury operations have thus far chiefly benefited the borrowers of Wall and Broad streets more than
the commercial community."   This fact would seem
to show that credit was already shaken, and that those
who had money feared to put it where they could not
instantly call it back at need.   As shown at this time,
there is ground for thinking that when a stringency or a

[a] The New York Commercial and Financial Chronicle, October 19, 1872:
519.
[b] Ibid., p. 517.

panic is brought on primarily by a weakening of credit, and not primarily by a lack of money—that is, when the stringency is the result, and not the cause, of unsteadiness of credit—the disbursements of the Government for purposes of relief afford more help to those engaged in speculation than to those in commercial enterprises properly so called. This fact limits very materially the justification of government disbursements for relieving the market under such circumstances.

Although, as we have seen, the Secretary of the Treasury had shaped his policy in aid of the money market early in October, he did not continue to do so for long. The bulk of the money deposited in some of the banks in October was withdrawn later on. During December, a month when money is in demand, the banks lost to the subtreasury about $3,500,000, despite the remonstrances of the mercantile community.[a] The result was that loans on government securities ran up to 7 per cent in gold, while borrowers on other stock collateral were obliged to pay from one-sixteenth to one-quarter per cent per day for their loans.[b]

It is clear that in 1872 the action of the independent treasury, as managed by Secretary Boutwell, favored speculation rather than legitimate business, by the ill-timed contractions and expansions which the Secretary caused, so that its influence must, on the whole, be set down as evil. The same thing is true of the year 1873 for the same injudicious course was followed. No definite, con-

---

[a] See the Bankers' Magazine, January, 1873, and the New York Independent, January 2, 1873.
[b] Ibid.

sistent, and continuous policy was adopted for guiding the relations of the Treasury to the business community.

The stringency of 1872 became the panic of 1873. The money market was in an unsettled condition most of the time through the first nine months of the year. The legal-tender averages of the banks were lower than in 1872. There was a stringency in April, discount rates ran up, and a slight panicky feeling prevailed, especially on the occurrence of the panics in Vienna and Berlin. Between May and August the banks, responding to the speculative demand for money, heedlessly expanded their loans some $20,000,000. On the 17th of September the New York Warehouse and Security Company failed, and the business community was thrown into a state of anxiety. Secretary Richardson took no steps to ease the situation. On the 18th the crash of credit came with the suspension of Jay Cooke & Co. Still the Government took no action, though failure followed failure, until the 19th. Then it was determined to buy $10,000,000 of five-twenty bonds at par in gold on Saturday, the 20th, over the counter of the New York subtreasury. Owing to defective clerical facilities only a little more than $2,500,000 were purchased. Orders were then issued by Secretary Richardson to purchase five-twenty bonds as fast as offered in private sale, at the New York subtreasury, at a price not higher than par in gold. On Monday, the 22d, over $3,000,000 were accordingly paid out in legal tenders for bonds, and over $5,500,000 for legal-tender certificates. Next day $3,000,000 more were put out for bonds and over a million for certificates. On Thursday, the 25th of September, the Treasury stopped buying, having paid out over $24,000,000 of currency for bonds and certificates. During the week the Secretary had bought $12,000,000 of bonds from the savings banks, and on the 29th he prepaid the November interest.

These measures were practically all the help which the Treasury rendered at this time, and, while they were doubtless of some avail, they were utterly futile as a stay to the panic. None of the money disbursed went into the banks. During the week when the Treasury was buying bonds they lost eleven millions of greenbacks; their reserve ran down from $38,000,000 on the 6th of September to $12,000,000 on the 27th, and their deposits decreased some $50,000,000.[a] The figures are:

Date.	Loans.	Specie.	Legal tenders.	Deposits.
August 30...........	$288,883,000	$23,095,200	$44,729,300	$220,390,300
September 6	288,374,200	20,767,000	38,679,900	212,772,700
September 13	284,536,200	20,442,300	36,717,200	207,317,500
September 20........	278,421,700	18,844,600	34,307,900	198,040,100

The figures of the condition of the banks for the ten weeks after September 20 are not available because reports were not published during that time.

The success met by the Government in its efforts to allay the panic is thus shown to have been very small. The Secretary of the Treasury himself evidently felt this, if we may judge from the modest account of his efforts given in his report. He tells us there that bonds were purchased for the sinking fund to the amount of about $13,000,000, "when it became evident that the amount offering for purchase was increasing to an extent beyond

[a] Report of Comptroller of the Currency, 1876; 177 and 251.

the power of the Treasury to accept, and the purchasing was closed. * * * The currency paid out of the Treasury for bonds did much to strengthen many savings banks and to prevent a panic among their numerous depositors, who began to be alarmed; and had there developed an extended run upon those useful institutions, it would inevitably have caused widespread disaster and distress. It also fortified other banks, and checked the general alarm to some extent."

The futility of the efforts of the Government to relieve the distress was shown in the rates of discount also. The rate on call loans went up from 7 per cent in gold, on the 18th of the month, to 1½ per cent a day on the 20th, the day of the first government purchase of bonds; and two or three days later there was no quotable rate. These facts show that the provisions of the Treasury to mitigate the pressure did not inspire confidence, and so could not check the panic. For they prove that the money disbursed by the Government was hoarded. Part of it went into the savings banks. "The savings institutions of New York and Brooklyn hold about thirteen millions of greenbacks," said the Financial Chronicle.[a] "Part of these notes have been drawn from our city banks, but a large amount were obtained from the Treasury last week in payment for United States bonds. These greenbacks are now lying idle in the vaults of the savings banks; and the question is, What ought to be done with them."

It is not to be denied that the aid rendered the savings banks was good and commendable. But this did not

---

[a] October 4, 1873, 447.

help the general situation. There was a time during the panic when, perhaps, it was advisable for the savings banks to increase their stock of greenbacks; but it was not absolutely necessary, because they could have protected themselves from a sudden run by taking advantage of the clause in their charters permitting them to require thirty days' notice of withdrawals. Moreover, the savings banks kept their greenbacks in their vaults after the danger to themselves had passed, and so prevented the use of of them by the mercantile community. By this action the efforts of the Government were so far nullified.

As to the reasons for the complete failure of the Secretary of the Treasury to accomplish his purpose of checking the panic, we must note, in the first place, that his steps were not taken early enough. The Government did not move in the matter until the crash of credit occurred and the market had passed from the stage of crisis to that of panic. The proper time for the purchase of bonds was before that point; the latest time at which it should have begun would have been in time to save Jay Cooke & Co., if that had been possible. That is, it seems that if the Secretary had sold his bonds on Wednesday instead of Saturday, much greater good might have been done; for if there was any time at which confidence could have been restored by easier money, it was then. After the failure of Cooke & Co., the current of suspicion and distrust was altogether too strong to be stopped by the limited aid which the Government could give. Even after the government disbursements of the 20th were supplemented, on the 22d, by the use of $10,000,000 of clearing-house certificates, the feeling of panic did not disappear, and it was thought necessary, two days later, to permit the use of $10,000,000 more certificates.

The measures of the Secretary of the Treasury were also insufficient for the situation at the time they were taken. Indeed, this was felt when the Secretary first announced his intention of buying bonds. There was general disappointment at the narrow scope of his measures. It was felt that more liberal disbursements should have been provided and that the Government should have stood ready to redeem not only the five-twenty bonds, but any issue of its stock. It was announced later, to be sure, that the Treasury would buy bonds indefinitely; but that could be only nominally true, because, as the event showed, the amount of money at the disposal of the Secretary was very limited.

It may be questioned, indeed, whether the action of the Government at this time did not do more harm than good. The money which it spent went, as has been shown, into private hoards and into the savings banks, and so furnished no relief to the market in general. It was just as much out of the reach of the business community as it had been when it lay in the vaults of the Treasury. But the public relied on the Government; they expected that its action would be a great help, and the general tone of affairs immediately after the failure of the measures of the Government seems to show that the reaction of disappointment induced more distrust and added to the panic. Both in 1857 and 1873, then, the ability of the Government to allay the panic was counteracted by the fact that the public knew just about how far the Secretary could go. He could offer only a limited relief, which had little moral effect.

The insufficiency of the Treasury provisions became evident on Saturday, the 20th, and the use of clearing-house certificates became necessary on the next Monday. It is questionable whether a resort to these would have been necessary so early had the events of the 20th not demonstrated the complete inability of the Government to cope with the situation.

We have seen that money put out for bonds was hoarded either by the savings banks or by individuals. This fact implies that they did not get into the hands of those whose need for help was pressing. The reason for this lay in the fact that the government terms were not hard enough. The bonds were paid for in legal tenders, while they were redeemed at their par value in gold. The difference between the premium on the bonds and the premium on gold was less than 2 per cent., a loss altogether too small to prevent those who could have gotten on without the money from selling their bonds and hoarding the proceeds. This is the true meaning of the Secretary's remark that his disbursements aided many savings banks.

Finally, it is worthy of note that, in spite of all efforts, the panic of 1873 ran its course. It can not properly be said to have been checked. The reason is obvious; what was needed was a reestablishment of confidence in the enterprises which had been the primary source of distrust; but no amount of money disbursed by the Government could produce this result.

THE CRISIS OF 1884.

The crisis of 1884 was largely a disturbance of the market for securities. This was the culmination of the period of prosperity which had marked the recovery from the panic of 1873. There had been a decline in prices for some three years and a good deal of speculation in railroad securities. The failure of certain banks and brokers in May brought on the panic. Distress was felt, of course, throughout the country; but, as remarked above, this crisis was rather a panic in the market for securities, especially in the principal cities. The Secretary resorted to some of the usual devices, especially the prepayment of some of the debt which was soon to mature. The crisis presents no features of unusual interest.

THE STRINGENCY OF 1890.

The next important general crisis was that of the autumn of 1890. Various causes had been at work promoting speculation in various parts of the world for some time before. In this country the prospective action of the McKinley tariff had brought about a large increase of imports for speculative holding, and the payment of duties, immediate and prospective, threatened to lock up so great an amount of money as to cause a stringency. Moreover, there was much speculation based on the prospect of inflation, which, it was supposed, would soon be produced by new legislation concerning silver. These sanguine hopes were doomed to disappointment, however. "The silver bill was passed, and the Treasury let out enormous amounts of cash. But the effects were not as

expected. The supplies of currency had only a temporary effect in easing money. Silver certificates [a] rose to
121 in August, but are now down to 103, notwithstanding
the heavy government purchases in the interval. Stock
exchange values, with great pertinacity, declined instead
of advancing, till finally this week the crisis came. Thus
once again has it been demonstrated that legislative edicts
can not arrest the tendency of natural laws, and that something more than a flood of currency is needed to secure
permanent ease in the money market." [b]   In this dubious
state of the public mind the failure of the Barings in England occurred in November, and for a time threatened to
cause a panic. The excitement calmed down, however,
under the prompt and efficient management of the failure
by the Bank of England. But while a panic was averted
the market continued very restricted, and business suffered
from the evils of a crisis. So great was the stringency that
"the banking and currency machinery of the country was
strained to its utmost and worked very unsatisfactorily."
The lack of elasticity in our currency system prevented the
banks from affording the relief that could reasonably have
been expected from them under a better system, so that,
notwithstanding the unusually large.disbursements of the
Government, they were compelled to resort to the use of
clearing-house certificates in the settlement of their balances. As usual, the aid of the Secretary of the Treasury
was invoked, and he responded with the purchase of bonds.
In fact, Secretary Windom had been buying bonds, so as to
prevent a stringency in the fall, as early as July. Under

---

[a] For bar silver on deposit.
[b] New York Commercial and Financial Chronicle, November 15, 1890.

circulars issued in that month the aggregate purchases of 4 per cent and 4½ per cent bonds amounted to $10,358,950. As this disbursement was "inadequate to meet existing conditions," a circular of August 19 announced that 4½ per cent bonds would be redeemed, with interest, through May, 1891. On August 21, $20,000,000 of these bonds were called for, on condition of the prepayment, after September 1, 1890, of all interest on them to September, 1891. Twenty millions more were called for on August 30; and on September 6 the prepayment of interest to the following July was offered to holders of 4 percents and (afterwards) of "currency sixes;" and, finally, on the 13th of September, some $17,000,000 more of 4 percents were redeemed. The transactions are tabulated thus: [a]

	Bonds redeemed.	Disbursements.
Under circular of—		
July 19, 1890...............................	$17,324,850	$21,225,989.46
August 19, 1890...........................	560,050	581,138.12
August 21, 1890...........................	20,060,700	20,964,868.42
August 30, 1890...........................	18,678,100	19,518,176.83
September 6, 1890.........................	(a)	12,009,951.50
September 13, 1890........................	17,071,150	21,617,673.77
	73,694,850	95,917,798.10

a Interest prepaid.

In addition to the heavy payments for bonds the Treasury made large disbursements for other purposes also, during the month of September, and its net available balance was reduced, by the end of October, to a little over $2,000,000, not including fractional currency and the national bank redemption fund. The tremendous amount

a Finance Report, 1890.

of money reported as disbursed in the purchase of bonds was further increased by the ordinary quarterly payments in September, and especially by the very large disbursements for pensions.

It must be borne in mind, however, that not all the money reported as disbursed went into the channels of business immediately. The net gain of currency to commerce, calculated from the monthly reports of the Treasury holdings of money was, for August, $7,479,615, and for September, $57,887,849, allowing for the gain from silver bullion certificates, and for the decrease in national bank circulation.[a] The output of the Treasury in August and September was reflected in an enlargement of the New

---

[a] The figures for September, according to the Chronicle, were as follows:

Net holdings of the United States Treasury.

	September 1.	October 1.
Gold coin and bullion..........................	$185,837,581	$147,981,732
Silver coin and bullion.........................	15,749,535	6,590,212
Treasury notes, act 1890.......................	2,233,100	962,500
Legal-tender notes.............................	10,573,710	5,775,290
National bank notes............................	5,063,227	4,620,511
Fractional silver..............................	22,077,629	20,768,255
	241,534,782	186,698,500

Loss by subtreasury and gain to commerce.............. $54,836,282
Silver bullion certificates issued during the
   month.............................. $4,460,000
National bank notes retired................. 1,408,433
                      3,051,567

   Total net gain to commerce for the month......... 57,887,849

During the month over $10,000,000 were *actually* disbursed for pensions at New York; $24,664,350 of 4½ per cent bonds, and $17,625,600 of 4 percents were actually redeemed; $4,524,190 were paid out in premiums on bonds purchased, and $13,410,001 in interest payments, making a total of $70,000,000.

York bank reserves, as shown in the following table,[a] in the face, too, of a drain of money to the interior:

	Loans.	Specie.	Legal tenders.	Deposits.
August 9	$406,139,500	$73,496,000	$29,766,300	$407,905,200
August 16	402,163,900	70,843,200	28,378,100	399,508,100
August 23	397,672,300	68,621,100	26,254,200	389,553,100
August 30	392,546,400	69,595,600	26,155,100	385,149,500
September 6	394,978,100	70,216,700	25,482,000	388,399,300
September 13	393,160,100	67,842,300	24,663,500	388,250,900
September 20	392,631,600	76,417,200	22,983,700	389,982,800
September 27	394,029,100	93,397,300	22,387,800	406,838,800

The rates on call loans ranged through August and September as follows:[b]

August 4	8– 4
August 11	25– 8
August 18	16– 6
August 25	12– 2
September 6	3–12
September 13	[c] 3– 6
September 20	[d] 2– 6
September 27	2– 6

The rate of discount on call loans fell after the Treasury disbursements, as seen from the table. The net result of the operations of the Treasury was a decided relief of the money market in September. There was, as yet, no serious disturbance of credit; the difficulty was to get enough money to meet the suddenly increased demand, and the government disbursements relieved the pressure.

But the help afforded had only a temporary effect. The stringency recurred in November; and its occurrence, this time, was marked by a failure of confidence and the

---

[a] The figures are from the Financial Chronicle.

[b] The Bankers' Magazine.

[c] One-half of 1 per cent a day commission.

[d] One-fourth of 1 per cent a day commission.

appearance of distrust due to the announcement of some important failures. The reserve of the New York banks began to run down about the middle of October, and continued to do so until the second week of December. The figures for November are:

	Loans.	Specie.	Legal tenders.	Deposits.
November 1	$399,791,900	$77,671,700	$22,101,400	$396,284,500
November 8	398,855,700	74,486,600	21,032,500	392,253,400
November 15	393,277,900	73,995,400	21,816,000	386,574,800
November 22	387,297,200	73,191,200	22,319,800	381,685,000
November 29	384,548,100	71,658,500	23,368,400	378,578,200

The state of the money market for the same month is shown by the rates of discount: [a]

Date.	Discount on—	
	Commercial paper.	Call loans.
November 3	7–8	6– 4
November 10	7–8	186–15
November 17	7–8	186– 6
November 24	8–9	5– 3

These figures show that the panic was in the stock market, and not in business enterprises proper.

So great was the stringency brought on by failure of confidence that the banks of New York, Philadelphia, and Boston issued clearing-house certificates, and there was a renewal of the call on the Government for assistance. But the available surplus of the Treasury had been so heavily drawn on by previous disbursements that Secretary Windom was not able to do much. By a Treasury

[a] Figures from the Bankers' Magazine.

circular of October 9, a standing offer was made to redeem any 4½ per cent bonds, offered at par, with interest to maturity. Nearly $6,000,000 [a] worth were redeemed in October; but these bonds were not presented during the crisis in sufficient amount to prevent the accumulation of a surplus in the Treasury. Accordingly, Secretary Windom issued a circular inviting proposals for the sale of $5,000,000 of 4 per cent bonds, redemption to be made daily beginning with December 8. The worst of the crisis was over by this time, however, and the only influence of these disbursements was to facilitate settlements.

The verdict on the question of the success of the operations of the Treasury to relieve the market in 1890 must be that it was on the whole unsuccessful. The very heavy disbursements in September increased the bank reserves and accomplished considerable good, because the elements of distrust had not widely developed, and the stress of the situation was due simply to the inadequacy of the available supply of money to do a suddenly enlarged volume of business. But the bank reserves soon decreased again by the movement of currency to the interior. This movement, combined with the tendency to export gold under the prevailing high rates of foreign exchange, renewed anxiety in monetary circles. The ability of the Government to furnish help was known to be small, and instability had been revealed in many establishments. All these things together produced distrust; and when failure of confidence in the market occurred, the efforts of the Government proved of little avail.

---

[a] $5,846,150.

Independent Treasury of the United States

The principal cause of the failure of the September disbursements to furnish more than temporary relief to the market was the heavy movement of money to the interior. There was a steady drain from that cause all through the last four months of the year, with the exception of one week. The loss to the banks from this drain aggregated $33,272,000, for September and October. The figures[a] in detail are:

September 5	$3,289,000
September 12	3,310,000
September 19	4,411,000
September 26	3,933,000
October 3	5,781,000
October 10	4,752,000
October 17	3,468,000
October 24	2,038,000
October 31	2,290,000

The main cause of the failure to ease the market in the later stage of the crisis was hoarding, which, at this time, as in 1873, prevented the money paid out of the Treasury from going into the banks, where it would have been of service in easing the market. "A conspicuous feature in the monetary situation," said the Financial Chronicle,[b] "is the unaccountable disappearance of the currency issues made during recent months. Taking September and October together, the official figures of the Treasury Department, which are no doubt correct, show that the currency afloat in the country—that is, in circulation—increased during these two months $62,934,675 net, and yet our New York City banks held on November 1 only $99,773,100 of different kinds of currency, against a total of $95,750,700 on August 30." The returns of the banks in the interior of

---

[a] From the Financial Chronicle.   [b] November, 1892.

the country showed that the money was not in their vaults, and we are forced to conclude, therefore, that it was hoarded.[a] The inference is supported by the fact that in the first week of the new year the banks showed an increase of reserve, although they lost money both to the interior and to the subtreasury.[b]

[a] It is possible that the money was in slow circulation, in the hands of merchants who were increasing their stocks in anticipation of higher prices under the new tariff law; the effect on the money market would be the same.

[b] The reserve increased from $103,237,500 on December 26 to $105,234,900 on January 3, a gain of almost $2,000,000. The net loss of the banks to the subtreasury for the week was $100,000 and to the interior $1,500,000.

THE PANIC OF 1893.

In the panics of 1873, 1884, and 1890 the Treasury had been looked to for assistance to the money market. In the panic of 1893 conditions were reversed and the Treasury was obliged to rely upon the banks for aid. It is true that bonds were issued by the Government in this crisis, but they were issued rather for the purpose of meeting a deficit in the revenue than for easing the money market. The latter was a secondary purpose. For at the other times mentioned there was a surplus in the Treasury. In 1893 the revenue had fallen off so that the Treasury was confronted with a deficit. Moreover, the Treasury was at the mercy of the public in the matter of the loss of its gold. A heavy demand for the redemption of notes in gold began in December, 1892, and continued to the close of the fiscal year. More than ten times as many United States notes were redeemed in the fiscal year 1893 as in the preceding year, and more than fifteen times as many treasury notes of 1890.

In another respect, also, the situation was different from that at previous times. Our currency legislation, always vicious from the time of the civil war, was peculiarly so in the early nineties. In 1890 the silver-purchase act was put upon the statute books, whereby the Secretary of the Treasury was required to purchase

4,500,000 ounces of silver each month, or so much of that amount as should be offered. The law had previously required the purchase of between $2,000,000 and $4,000,000 worth of silver bullion per month, to be paid for in legal-tender notes. Under this law the treasury notes increased for the next two years about $50,000,000 annually. The amount of silver and its representatives in the country's circulation had risen from 8.9 per cent in 1882 to 28.9 per cent in 1892. Nearly the entire increase in the currency in twelve years was in silver.[a] The inflation of the currency, with other forces then at work, soon brought the country to the verge of disaster.

The great surplus revenues of the later eighties had been used in redeeming bonds. As early as 1887, with increasing revenue, the bonds which the Treasurer could purchase at par were exhausted and redemptions at a premium were begun. Within a year the Treasury held an amount of money in its cash surplus equal to nearly one-fourth the total outside circulation. In that year the Secretary purchased more than $50,000,000 worth of 4 per cent bonds at premiums ranging between 23 and 29, and also $33,000,000 of 4½ percents at a premium of between 6 and 9 per cent. Indeed, within four years, from 1888 to 1892, the Government expended about $235,000,000 for bond redemption above the amount which was expended for purchases for the sinking fund.

One consequence of this policy was to reduce the number and raise the price of the bonds available as a basis of national-bank circulation, and consequently the circula-

---

[a] Bankers' Magazine, February, 1893, 573.

tion of the national banks began to decrease. In 1892, however, the replacement of the surplus with a deficit led to the abandonment of bond purchases, thus checking the retirement of national bank notes. At the same time the silver legal-tender issues were rapidly increasing. These processes gradually produced an inflated currency. As usual, gold began to be exported, as much as $70,000,-000 going abroad in the first six months of 1891. Among other occurrences, the gold reserve rapidly fell during the latter half of the year. In the first six months of the following year, 1892, $41,500,000 of gold went abroad, followed by the export of from $2,000,000 to $7,000,000 a week through the months of July and August. As early as May of this year the gold reserve, whose minimum was the traditional $100,000,000, fell to $114,-000,000. The gold receipts of the Treasury from customs payments had rapidly diminished, for the silver paper had driven it out of the country, so that more and more legal tender appeared in the bank reserves and in the receipts of the Government. In the aggregate the bank reserves were largely changed. For many years the banks had supplied practically all the gold needed for export; now their reserves consisted so largely of legal-tender paper that they were obliged to turn this into the Treasury for gold, to satisfy their customers who needed the metal to send abroad. At the same time the gold receipts of the Treasury itself were falling off. The extent to which this process was going on is strikingly shown by the fact that, while in the twenty-two years following 1879 only $34,000,000 of United States legal-tender notes had been presented to the Treasury for redemption,[a] in the last month of 1892 and the first month of 1893 the Treasury was called upon to supply more than $25,000,000 in gold, in return for legal tenders, for the purpose of export. At the end of the latter month the gold reserve had fallen to $108,000,000.[b]

So acute did the situation become that the Secretary of the Treasury requested the New York banks to supply gold in exchange for legal tenders, and they did so to the extent of nearly $8,000,000.[c] In the two following months the banks gave up about $25,000,000 more, while almost the same amount was taken out of the Treasury by the redemption of legal tenders for export. In April the reserve fell to the legal minimum, and for the first time the issue of gold certificates ceased.

When Secretary Carlisle took up the Treasury portfolio, succeeding Mr. Foster, in March, the gold reserve stood at $100,982,410, and the other money in the Treasury amounted to $25,000,000.[d] Public apprehension as to the decrease in the gold reserve was becoming acute. The Treasury was in the position of a bank which had issued more notes than it had reserves to redeem. The situation was made more difficult by a statement from the Secretary of the Treasury in April, which raised doubt in the public mind as to the continuance of the policy of redeeming silver notes with gold, and it was necessary for President Cleveland to reassure the public on this point.

[a] Finance Report, 1893, 13.
[b] Ibid, 12 and 96.
[c] Commercial and Financial Chronicle, February 11, 1893.
[d] Finance Report, 1893, 96.

Increased congressional appropriations had destroyed the surplus and left the Treasury with a deficit for ordinary expenses. Moreover, its income, as has been remarked, was very largely in paper. The deficit drove the Secretary to draw on the gold reserve to meet ordinary expenses. Thus there was a double drain upon the reserve, to meet current expense and to redeem legal tenders. By February the crash had come in the business world with the bankruptcy of the Philadelphia and Reading Railway Company on the 26th of the month. The failure of the National Cordage Company followed in May, the public began to hoard, and the banks began to totter. The severest panic came in midsummer. The banks had liquidated their balances heavily in June and July and the reserve of the New York banks decreased more than $40,000,000. Call loans went to 74, and money could not be borrowed on time at all. The banks were forced to resort to the use of clearing-house certificates and some of them refused to cash the checks of their own depositors. During the year about 578 banks, trust and mortgage companies throughout the country failed, 158 of them being national banks. On account of its deficit, the Treasury was unable to aid the banks, and as a bank of issue it was not strong enough to maintain its own credit.

The breakdown of credit made the importation of gold impossible for a time, and in August a premium appeared not only on the metal, but on currency. This in turn made importation possible, and the tide began to turn. Meantime Congress met in special session in August, and the public demanded the repeal of the silver purchase act. This was done, and the reassuring effect on the public mind, together with some importation of gold to take advantage of the premium, in a measure restored confidence. After the crisis had passed the hoarded currency came into circulation again, gold began to appear in government receipts, and the reserve rose in August to a little over $103,000,000. By October it had fallen again, however, to $81,501,385.[a] This was due mainly to the deficit in revenue.

In December the reserve was $80,000,000;[b] in January of the following year it had fallen below $68,000,000.[c]

BOND SALES, 1894 TO 1898.

It was necessary, therefore, to resort to a bond issue and $50,000,000 of 5 per cent bonds were offered to the public at the price of 117.223, which was equivalent to a 3 per cent bond at par. The loan was not subscribed for by the public, and a few days before the time for closing the books the banks were appealed to, as they had been before, and they took up the issue, the banks of New York City alone taking 80 per cent of them. The sale netted the Treasury $58,660,000 of gold; but of this amount the Treasury had itself supplied $24,000,000 in the redemption of greenbacks, so that by the sale of bonds it made a net gain of only $34,000,000. Still the reserve rose to $107,000,000 in the first week in March, but exportation of gold began the following month, the "endless chain" of redemption of legal tenders again was put in motion, and the reserve fell, in August, to $52,189,500.[d] Again the

---

a Finance Report, 1893: lxxiii.   c Finance Report, 1894: lxviii.
b Finance Report, 1894: 55.   d Finance Report, 1894: lxix.

banks were appealed to for gold in exchange for notes and surrendered $15,000,000. Another bond sale was resorted to in November, and again was a failure in replenishing the gold supply of the Treasury, because most of the gold used in the purchase of the bonds was obtained, either in the beginning or later, from the Treasury itself in exchange for legal tenders.

"The first loan of 1894 had failed of its purpose within ten months; the second had failed within ten weeks, and, outside the loan market, no recourse was left to the Government."[a]

In January, 1895, the "endless chain" was again operating, and the Treasury lost in exchange for legal tenders $45,000,000 in gold. The following month the reserve fell to $41,340,181 and throughout the month fell off in the neighborhood of $2,000,000 a day.

In the face of these conditions it became imperative for the Government to take some measures to save itself not only from bankruptcy, but from the utter destruction of its credit. The banks of the country had supplied all the gold they could spare. The state of credit and foreign trade made importation of the yellow metal out of the question. After tying its fortunes to those of the banks and nearly wrecking their credit with its own, until they could no longer respond to the stimulus of public opinion by supplying gold, the Government turned to the international bankers. Thoroughly convinced that the situation was desperate and that no usual remedy would avail, President Cleveland made arrangements with the famous bond syndicate of 1895 to pull the Government out of its

---

[a] Noyes, A. D., Forty Years of American Finance: 232.

difficulties. An arrangement was made with J. P. Morgan & Co., and H. P. Belmont & Co., whereby they should take $50,000,000 of 4 per cent thirty-year bonds at 104½. The terms of the loan were severe. Yet it must be conceded that the risk which the purchasers ran of failing in their attempt to supply the Treasury with gold was so great that they were justified in making hard terms. The policy of the country whose credit they were seeking to save was hostile to them and their attempt. The syndicate agreed to supply at least half of the gold to be paid for bonds from Europe, and further agreed not to withdraw gold from the Treasury nor, so far as they could prevent it, to permit others to do so, for the purchase of these bonds. In accordance with their agreement, the syndicate delivered 300,000 ounces of gold each month for the next six months. In consequence the gold reserve rose until, in July, it was $107,571,230. The first effort of the syndicate was successful, because a speculative fever happened to break out in England which caused a demand for United States securities. Their purchase of course promoted the importation of gold. Later speculation became active among ourselves. As a consequence there was a rise in the price of our securities which led foreign holders to sell what they had bought a little while before, and thereby reversed the conditions of the gold market. This result was furthered also by the foreign exchange rate which had been fixed by the syndicate, for nonbanking corporations and individuals could go into the foreign exchange market and sell drafts below the syndicate's figure. They covered these drafts by drawing gold from the Treasury with legal tenders.

During the five months following July $65,000,000 of gold were thus withdrawn, and the reserve fell to $63,000,000 in December.[a]   The syndicate was unable to control the situation toward the end of its contract, but did what it could to aid the Treasury by exchanging gold for notes.   It was found necessary in January of the following year, 1896, to go into the money market again. The Secretary offered for sale the large sum of $100,000,000 4 per cent bonds to be paid for in gold.   The loan proved popular, 4,640 individual bids being received, aggregating $568,000,000.   It was high time, for in February the gold reserve reached the low point of $44,563,493.   The proceeds of the loan raised it in the following month to $128,713,709, and the crisis was passed.   There was no further trouble for the next two or three years, and the reserve reached the great sum of $245,000,000 by the middle of 1898.

The lesson of these extremely trying times, for our purpose, is significant.   We have seen the Treasury aiding the banks in the other crises described; here the Treasury was dependent upon the banks.   Its difficulties arose partly from the insufficiency of the current revenue and partly from the fact that it was engaged in note issue.   The insufficiency of the revenue made it necessary for the Secretary of the Treasury, illegally as some thought, to draw on the gold reserve for ordinary expenses. At the same time he needed the gold to redeem legal tenders.   They were forced upon him for redemption because their number was so largely increased under the operation of the silver-purchase act.   Since the only

---

[a] Treasury Report, 1895: 51.

ways at the command of the Government for obtaining gold are in receipts of revenues or by borrowing, as soon as the revenues fell off, resort was had to the latter method. It is to be noticed, however, that in trying to place its loans the Treasury found it impossible to disassociate itself from the banks. Several times it was obliged to take the humiliating position of appealing to the banks to favor it with an exchange of gold for notes. At other times it was obliged to act through the banks in placing its loans. At the time of greatest distress and hardship it was forced to appeal to a group of bankers outside the usual circle of its dealings, not merely to place its bonds, but to furnish it with revenue to save its credit.

We see, therefore, that in this crisis the Treasury disturbed the money market, not, however, in the usual way by pouring in its surplus revenue, but by drawing on the reserves of the banks at a time when the banks themselves sorely needed them, making drafts upon the banks necessary by the Government's own vicious policy. As a banking institution the Treasury was a failure.

In conclusion, we may say that in the crisis of 1893 the Treasury failed (1) to maintain its own credit; (2) to keep the gold reserve intact; (3) to protect itself against attacks of money brokers; (4) to place its own loans directly. Incidentally, attention might be called not inappropriately to the mischief done by Secretary Carlisle's ill-advised personal views and statements of policy. It is an illustration of the danger of leaving the domination of the money market so largely in the hands of the Secretary.

CHAPTER X.—TREASURY RELIEF IN THE PANIC OF 1907.

The next important disturbance of the money market was the panic of 1907. Following the slight disturbance of 1903, there sprung up in 1905–6 a world-wide speculation and inflation of credit. The year 1906 saw panics in Egypt, Japan, Hamburg, and Chile, before the storm broke upon ourselves. It is not the purpose of this essay to write a financial history of the time and, therefore, it is not necessary to give a history of the panic. Our present concern is with the relation of the Treasury to crises. Accordingly, we pass over very rapidly and lightly the details of the panic.

While cautious observers had earlier seen signs of a coming storm in the midst of general confidence, the public at large saw but little out of the way until the failure of one of the large iron manufacturing houses of the country, in the month of June, with liabilities of $8,000,000. A few weeks afterwards two New York City loans which were offered on the market failed, showing that the investing public was exceedingly cautious and that credit was strained. In the early fall the New York City street railway combination went into the hands of a receiver, as, a little later, did the Westinghouse Electric Company.

During the process of credit inflation which went on for a year or two before 1907, an occurrence had taken place in banking circles which was fraught with great danger. This was the organization of chain banking, as it has been called. Some men interested in speculation in industrial and mining securities obtained control of one bank. With the stock of this in their possession they borrowed upon it as collateral and with the proceeds of the loan bought stock of another bank. They repeated this process until six or more banks were under their control. The funds of these banks were of course used for the promotion of industrial speculation in which those in control of them were interested. This use of commercial banks, it may be said, is the most vicious feature of our recent American banking practice. The confidence of the public in banking management has been more severely shaken, perhaps, by the practice of using commercial banks, not for commercial purposes, but for the promotion of industrial and financial enterprises, than by any other evil in our banking practice.

In due time one of these chain banks found itself in difficulty in meeting its obligations, under its condition of expanded discounts. Therefore it applied to the clearing house for help. Of course, this event, which occurred on October 16, aroused uneasiness. On the 21st of the same month the great failure of the Knickerbocker Trust Company occurred, with liabilities of $35,000,000 owing to 17,000 depositors. In a few days the Lincoln Trust Company and the Trust Company of North America were also in trouble and the feeling of public uneasiness became a panic.

When Mr. George B. Cortelyou became Secretary of the Treasury in March, 1907, he soon became aware that the money market was unsettled and he was duly called upon to interfere with Treasury reserves for the relief of the market. In the latter part of August the Secretary offered to make weekly deposits in the national banks "with a view of facilitating the movement of the crops in various sections of the country." At the end of July the national banks had $156,990,204 of the public money. Beginning, therefore, on August 28 and continuing until October 14, the Secretary's plan of making weekly deposits was followed until a total of about $28,000,000 had been allotted to banks in each of the forty-six States, in the Territories, and in the District of Columbia. "Every endeavor was made, from information and requests at hand, so to distribute this fund that it would meet the actual needs in sections where the business activity was at a maximum and currency was most urgently required."[a]

On the 24th of October a panic broke upon the stock exchange and the rate on demand loans rose to 125. Through the efforts of individual financiers, the banks of the city, which naturally were holding tightly to their funds, decided to release $25,000,000. On the 26th the clearing-house banks resorted to the familiar device of issuing loan certificates, with the result that cash payments were practically suspended. Meantime the interior banks were calling for their balances, and the net loss of the New York banks on this account, between October 26 and December 7, was $106,921,700.

During the ten days from October 21 to 31 the Treasury transferred to the national banks of the city $37,597,000, which the banks immediately advanced to the trust companies to meet the run on them. In order to aid the banks in meeting the demand of the interior for currency, the Treasury Department in three days furnished the

---

[a] Response of the Secretary of the Treasury calling for certain information in regard to Treasury operations, etc., S. Doc. 208, 60th Cong., 1st sess.

New York banks about $36,000,000 in small bills. "As the stringency progressed the Treasurer gave relief in every important locality where assistance seemed to be required."[a] Meantime hoarding set in to such an extent that it is estimated that in the neighborhood of $296,000,000 disappeared from circulation during the panic. To meet the difficulties, besides the usual clearing-house certificates, emergency currency was issued by the clearing-house banks and by individual manufacturers and corporations. So severe became the crisis that there even was a demand, which, strange to say, received some support from respectable quarters, for a Government issue of fiat money, so accustomed had the money market become to relying upon the Treasury. By the middle of November the Treasury had deposited in the banks all the money it could spare; indeed, it had reduced its working surplus to about $5,000,000. Meantime, as the Secretary tells us,[b] considerable difficulty was experienced in bringing from the subtreasuries to the New York office money actually collected and the public revenue was falling off.

Further to relieve the situation, therefore, Secretary Cortelyou notified the national banks that they might substitute "bonds suitable for savings-banks investments for government bonds which were held as securities against public deposits."[b] The Secretary's purpose in doing this was the same as that of Secretary Shaw in resorting to the same device four years previously. He

---

[a] Response of the Secretary of the Treasury calling for certain information in regard to Treasury operations, etc., S. Doc. 208, 60th Cong., 1st sess., 7.

[b] Ibid., 10.

wished to increase the volume of United States bonds available for circulation. Under this stimulus the circulation of the national banks increased by December 31, 1907, to $83,012,153. Still the difficulty of obtaining bonds and the awkward machinery of administration in issuing national-bank notes had the usual result of making the increase of circulation virtually ineffective until after the need for it had passed away. The volume of national-bank currency increased by $24,000,000 between October 15 and November 15, but at the close of the year, as we have seen, it had risen much more. The circulation continued to increase, however, although the demand for it no longer existed, until, about the middle of January, it became $695,927,806.

Of course the usual effect on the price of bonds followed. The increased demand drove up the 2 per cent bonds as high as 110, and even at that price the amount available was regarded as too small. Accordingly the Secretary thought it necessary to adopt additional means to relieve the situation, and on November 17 he offered a loan of $50,000,000 in Panama Canal bonds under authority of the act of June 28, 1902, and $100,000,000 of 3 per cent certificates of indebtedness under the act of June 30, 1898. Of the bonds only $24,631,980 were taken by the public and $15,436,500 of the loan certificates. It is a little difficult to understand the reason for this action unless the Secretary hoped to sell the bonds and securities to people who were hoarding money. Of course the purchase of these securities by the banks, or by people who were not hoarding, simply reduced the circulation and would have made the situation worse. In order to avoid this, however, the Secretary transferred part of the purchase money to the banks. Therefore, with one hand he was withdrawing money from circulation in payment of his bonds and with the other was restoring it by depositing it in the banks. The banks which purchased these securities were allowed to retain 90 per cent of the purchase price of the Panama bonds as a deposit and 75 per cent of that of the certificates.

In addition to these positive means of assistance undertaken by the Secretary of the Treasury, the Comptroller of the Currency, fearing that a revelation of their condition would add to the panic in a measure, however, postponed the call on the national banks for a report in November. This action operated favorably, because the banks were putting themselves in shape to meet the call. The delay made them more cautious in making discounts and lowering their reserves. Evidence that this was the case is found in a statement of the Secretary himself that "the fact that a call had been made and a report submitted contributed another favorable factor to the situation immediately afterwards by enabling the banks to release a part of this accumulated cash to meet the pressing needs of their clients, with the knowledge that they would probably be able fully to reinstate their reserves before another call was made by the comptroller."[a]

But the tide had turned before the latter measures of the Secretary were taken. Early in December, therefore, the Secretary called upon the banks to return part of the

---

[a] Response of the Secretary of the Treasury calling for certain information in regard to Treasury operations, etc., S. Doc. 208, 60th Cong., 1st sess., 12.

money deposited with them. In that month $6,000,000 were returned, and toward the end of January $10,000,000 more were called in.

Of course during the occurrence of these events the gold movement had contributed not a little to the ultimate solution of the difficulties. Toward the end of October gold began to come from Europe, and by the end of November more than $100,000,000 of the metal had been received. All of this, together with about $25,000,000 additional, went from the New York banks to other parts of the country.

In explaining his active interference with the situation, the Secretary tells us [a] that he was influenced by the belief that it was advisable to take a strong and resolute step which would convince the public, both at home and abroad, that the Government was thoroughly alive to the situation and determined to give its aid in every possible legal and proper form. This is a plain intimation that the public and the banks, as well as the government officers themselves, have reached a point where they regard the Treasury Department as a proper and necessary safety valve in monetary stringencies. The fact that the Treasury had a surplus made it possible for the Secretary to intervene with more success than was the case in 1893. At that time, as we have seen, the Treasury with a deficit in the revenue was appealing to the banks to save it. In this case it was intervening to save the banks, as was supposed. The lesson of 1893, that the banks were able

---

[a] Response of the Secretary of the Treasury calling for certain information in regard to Treasury operations, etc., S. Doc. 208, 60th Cong., 1st sess.

to take care not only of themselves, but of the Treasury also, seems not to have made any impression either on the public or on government officers. The Secretary himself was of the opinion that the offer of Panama bonds and Treasury certificates restored confidence. The facts seem to be that the corner had been turned and confidence restored before these measures were taken.

Secretary Cortelyou was subjected to much the same criticism for issuing these bonds as Secretary Carlisle had been fourteen years before, though with much better reason. With a nominal cash balance in the neighborhood of $200,000,000, it seems difficult to believe that the Treasury was justified in issuing one-year certificates which, by the law permitting them, could be put out only when necessary to meet the expenses of the Treasury. To take the other view, is to admit that government funds on deposit in the banks were not available; but this is a confession of insolvency on the part of the banks. The fact is that the Treasury did not need the money to be obtained from the sale of loan certificates. In any case, even if the most favorable view be taken, and it be held that the Secretary's construction of the law was correct, we must admit that it is a power of extreme danger that is thus conferred upon him.

Before passing from this subject attention may well be called to the method of allotment of the new issues of securities. The 2 per cent bonds are much sought after by the national banks as a basis for note issue; consequently the award of the loan was limited in the first instance to national banks in order to encourage them to do this. The Secretary took the position that he could have limited the whole award to this class of bidders if he so chose. In order, therefore, to promote additional note issue and check withdrawals by individual depositors from the banks to pay for the securities, it was decided, as has been said, to make the allotment first to national banks, in the case of the Panama bonds, and to make no awards to individuals in excess of $10,000.

On December 7, public deposits aggregating $222,352,252 were distributed in different parts of the country as follows: In New York City, 26.8 per cent of their capital and surplus; in New England and the eastern and middle western banks, including New York, a little more than 15 per cent; and in the banks of the Southern and Western Pacific States, about 18 per cent. These percentages, be it noted, are the percentages of deposits of public money to capital and surplus. Putting the matter in another way, the banks of the New England States on December 7, 1907, held $13,358,544, which was 8 per cent of their capital and surplus. The banks of the Eastern States held $110,793,758, or 18.3 per cent of their capital and surplus. Those of the Southern States had $31,813,914, or 16.8 per cent of their capital and surplus. In the Middle Western States the banks had $47,047,800, or 13.7 per cent of their capital and surplus. The Western States had $11,790,864, and those of the Pacific coast had $16,939,419, the former being 14.7 and the latter 24.3 per cent of capital and surplus. The total number of banks holding deposits at this time was 1,421. The Secretary made a specific effort to make a geographical distribution "equitably." In doing so, however, he did not ignore the particular trade movements which in certain sections of the country created special demands for currency.

In this panic we find for the first time a deliberate and general application of the section of the law of March 4, 1907, providing that the Secretary of the Treasury, in depositing public money in the banks, shall make the distribution as equitable as possible. As has been pointed out in another connection, the meaning of this term is difficult to determine. The only considerations which should govern the Secretary in depositing public funds in national banks are convenience and safety. The claims of political friends, geographical distribution, and other similar reasons should have no influence whatever. It is conceivable that the interests of the country would be best subserved, under some conditions, by depositing the whole available amount of public money in the banks of a single place. It is a well-known fact that money gravitates to money centers. From the small places, the outposts of the business world, it simply returns to the business centers. It saves time and expense, to say nothing of other advantages, to put it in the centers in the first place. In other words, in carrying out this provision of the law, the Secretary of the Treasury is virtually made the judge of the need for the money supply in different sections of the country as based upon their location, their industrial condition, and the particular trade movements at the time. This is a tremendous responsibility. The law, moreover, subjects him to great political and sectional pressure and exposes the interests of the country at such times to influences that can be only injurious.

Indeed, so keenly did Secretary Cortelyou feel the difficulties, that he appointed a commission in April, 1907, to consider the whole matter of dealing with public deposits.[a] In commenting on the matter the Secretary tells us that the policy of gradual distribution of funds to places where they were most needed, which was inaugurated in the spring of the year and carried through the summer, was continued by the banks in October. He adds: "It then became necessary to mass the funds in large amounts where they would be most effective, and the figures of the Government show that from the financial centers they were distributed almost automatically to the points most seriously threatened." This remark is simply saying in another way that all that is necessary in making government deposits to secure the most effective distribution is to put them in the banks in the financial centers.

The Secretary also attempted to "broaden the basis upon which public deposits might be made" by adding to the list of acceptable bonds some new ones. State, railway, and municipal bonds, within the provisions of the savings banks laws of Massachusetts and New York were accepted as security at 90 per cent of their market value. These became scarce in October, and the Secretary accepted bonds which came within the laws of Connecticut and New Jersey. In addition, he accepted, as he says, a few bonds not strictly coming in either of these classes, but of good market value. Deposits were made against these to 75 per cent of their market value. Here, again, we have a discretion which opens up the possibility of great

[a] See p. 127.

danger from possible pressure on the Secretary to accept bonds for security. It should be added that when the market price of the bonds accepted was above par they were accepted for only 90 per cent of their par value.

It is easier to deposit public money in the banks without causing disturbance, in such times as we have described, than it is to get it back again without causing further disturbance. The only method whereby money once deposited in the banks can be recovered is by its actual transfer. The Treasury may not check against its account with the banks. The recall of public deposits means, therefore, a reduction of the reserve and a possible contraction of discounts. The Secretary, therefore, must exercise considerable caution in recalling his deposits. On the whole the Secretary managed his part of the work very well. Of course in a crisis money accumulates in the banks, discount rates fall, and it is less difficult to recall deposits than it otherwise would be.

The manipulation of the money market by the Treasury has gone so far that the Secretary seems obliged now to exercise guardianship over the money market, not only in times of crises, but at other times. He feels that he must relieve the money market by depositing the public money in the banks in the fall to meet the autumnal drain from the interior, and taking it out after that drain has passed.

All these are matters of great responsibility, and most of the Secretaries in the past twenty years have felt the responsibility very heavily. Their feeling is very well put by ex-Secretary Cortelyou in a report to the Senate already referred to:

"In every measure taken the Secretary felt that he was bound, under our existing fiscal and monetary system, to have regard not simply to the operations of the Treasury, but to their effect upon the financial condition of the country. The present head of the department has not assumed this obligation willingly and would be glad to be relieved of it at least in part by suitable legislation, but under a fiscal and monetary system which results in large accumulations of actual currency in the Treasury at times when it may be most needed in the markets, and which affords inadequate means of adapting the circulation to the demands of business, it would, in his opinion, be a narrow view of his functions which should limit him to keeping his own balance sheet favorable, while ignoring the effect of Treasury operations upon the condition of the country. If recent events should lead to intelligent legislation, tending to adapt the movement of currency more nearly automatically to the requirements of business, it would be a source of gratification to the Secretary and would greatly diminish the sense of responsibility which must weigh heavily upon any occupant of the office under conditions such as those of the recent crisis."[a]   These are wise words.

---

[a] Response of the Secretary of the Treasury calling for certain information in regard to Treasury operations, etc., S. Doc. 208, 60th Cong., 1st sess., 32.

GENERAL CONCLUSIONS.

As shown by the history of the periods of great business disturbance which we have briefly sketched, the effects of the utilization of the independent treasury to afford relief to the money market, evidently depend on the character of the crisis, the methods of relief adopted, and the wisdom shown in applying it.   We have seen the system producing stringency when [a] ease in the market was needed for legitimate business, and also when [a] speculation was rife and had its course checked by the subtreasury absorptions.   We have seen that the output of money to relieve a distressed market may result in promoting speculation,[b] or in yielding some needed help to business men,[b] or partly or altogether neutralized by hoarding [c] from lack of public confidence in the immediate future of business.   This variety of action clearly shows that the independent-treasury system does not have such an automatic connection, so to speak, with business, as to make its operation responsive to the exigencies of the mercantile community.   So far as the history we have examined shows, the independent treasury has been useful in monetary stringencies and crisis, when its absorptions have coincided with a rise of prices caused by speculation, because it then retarded speculation; and when its disbursements have coincided with a demand for money

---

[a] In 1857.   [b] In 1853, 1890, and 1902.   [c] In 1873, 1890, and 1907.

for a legitimate temporary expansion of business its action has been beneficial. When it has disbursed during speculation, or absorbed during a healthy business expansion, it has done mischief. It has failed altogether when credit was suspended, and has sometimes made the situation worse by promoting hoarding.

Of the various methods mentioned whereby the independent treasury has had, or may have, a calming influence on a troubled market, three are of importance at present— namely, the restraining influence on banks, which Secretary Guthrie claimed the system exercises on a rising market by locking up money opportunely; the redemption of the public debt, including the purchase of bonds and the prepayment of interest; and depositing the public money in the banks. The first of these processes retards speculation, and, if used at all, should be applied on a rising speculative market. The other two methods are measures of relief when the stress is on.

To begin with, objection is sometimes made that all government interference in the money market is out of place. But while *laissez-faire* as a doctrine is more or less discredited, in the absence of any better principle, government interference must justify itself in each new field it enters. Experience, both in England and in this country, has shown that judicious action on the part of the Government may do much to prevent a panic, and success in one instance is all that is logically necessary to establish a case for future interference under similar conditions.

The danger of relying on the Government for aid in times of monetary distress lies less in the promotion of speculation, or in the diminution of caution in the usual conduct of business, than in the possibility that the action of the Government will be pushed by public clamor, or by pressure from banking interests, to a point where it may be more injurious than inaction would have been. That this danger is not merely fanciful is shown by the experience of 1873 and 1890, and, perhaps, 1907. In the first of these years "great pressure was brought to bear upon the Treasury Department" to loan its notes on secured clearing-house certificates as collateral, or to use the money on hand in the purchase of exchange, or to issue notes on the deposit of gold in the Bank of England, or to pay "at once" the $20,000,000 loan of 1858, or to deposit money at designated places to be used in the purchase of exchange on New York. There were even many persons "who insisted with great earnestness that it was the duty of the Executive to disregard any and all laws which stood in the way of affording the relief suggested by them."[a] In 1890 some people demanded the use of the $100,000,000 of gold kept for redemption of the greenbacks. In 1893 and 1907, there were voices heard for the issue of more government paper.

To be most effective, the help of the Government must in every case be timely, certain, and sufficient completely to remove the danger. But it is not always so. In the panic of 1873 the support of the public purse was tardy, timid, and insufficient. The Secretary of the Treasury did not undertake to purchase bonds until the market had reached its breaking point, and the panicky feeling could not be checked, as fully at least as it might have

[a] Finance Report for 1873. Also Upton's "Money in Politics," 140.

been by earlier action. In 1907, too, after the surplus was deposited in the banks, the Treasury could afford no more relief.

Of course, it is true that some one or some group of men must use their judgment to determine whether at a particular time stringency in the money market should be anticipated, or relief should be furnished when the crisis is on. While no candid student of our Treasury can have other than praise for the good judgment which, on the whole, has been shown by successive secretaries in their relations to the money market, nevertheless, the Secretary of the Treasury is not the proper person to determine these points. He is not in immediate touch with business matters. He must get his information of the situation largely at second hand from bankers and others. He is likely to be less experienced in judging of such matters than men whose business it is constantly to watch them and care for them.

The success of the effort of the Government to relieve a panic depends, then, largely on the good judgment of the officers of the Government. The first important method of relief consists in what Secretary Guthrie called "restraining the banks." That is, the subtreasury locks up government receipts from circulation. If this takes place at a time when business is slack, reserves large, and discount rates low, it will very likely be of assistance to the banks and the money market. As we have seen, however, the fatal defect of the subtreasury action is that there is no correspondence between its output and intake on the one hand, and the periods of stress and ease of the banks on the other. If the independent treasury were by its nature and organization a suitable means of relief it should be available in every crisis. To be so its accumulations of money should depend, in some measure, upon the conditions which make money dear. But this is not the case. It accumulates and disburses independently of the state of the money market. While it presses the banks, to use an old term, it is never pressed by them in turn. That is, its action can never be restrained by them. Its vaults may not be full when its help is needed most, as was the case in 1873, 1890, and 1893.

RELIEF BY BOND PURCHASES.

The objections to the relief of the money market by the purchase of bonds are these:

1. The fact that the timeliness of the relief thus offered is uncertain.

2. The loss due to the purchase of the bonds at a premium before they are due.

3. The loss due to the curtailment of bank circulation by lessening the amount of the bonds available for security of note issue.

4. The loss that arises from forcing up the market price.

5. The possibility of cornering the treasury.

The purchase of bonds for the relief of the market depends, like the depositing of public money in banks, on the judgment of the Secretary of the Treasury. If he purchases at the right time the transaction does good. If he purchases at proper prices the transaction may do good. Aside from the danger of untimeliness of relief in purchase of bonds from bad judgment on the part of the Secretary, there is also danger that the money thus disbursed is paid out on too easy terms. The purchase of bonds at the market rate, or the full repayment of interest, makes the money too easy to get. Under such terms the Treasury would need an amount of money large enough to supply not only those who were in real need of it, and ready to make a large sacrifice to obtain it, but also those who might want it, not for immediate use, but for hoarding. To obviate this difficulty the bonds should be purchased at a sufficiently large discount from the market value. But if, on the other hand, the Secretary of the Treasury makes the money hard to get, banks which need money and try to obtain it by selling public securities are put in a more difficult position, and their ability to aid in easing the stringency is curtailed. This last consideration is of great importance in view of the fact that the direct relief afforded by government disbursements is measured by the money paid out of the Treasury, whereas the same money deposited in the banks would enable them to discount to two or three times the amount, thus affording a large measure of relief.

Another objection that might be urged is the loss to the people in the forced purchase of bonds at a high premium. Secretary Fairchild, in his report for 1888, writes: "Ninety-four millions of dollars of bonds have been secured under this circular, and a premium paid for the privilege of buying them of about $18,000,000; . . . the saving in the total amount of interest which would have been paid had the bonds been allowed to run to maturity, is about $27,000,000. Had taxation been reduced so as to leave this money with the people, and if it is worth in their business 6 per cent per annum, the total value of the money to them during the term which these bonds had to run would be about $83,000,000; thus, there is a resulting loss to the people of $56,000,000 upon this transaction alone." This is not strictly accurate. It is impossible to state exactly the loss to the people on such a transaction; first, because it can not be fairly assumed that the money left with the people would all "fructify" at the rate of 6 per cent; and secondly, because the amount of money disbursed by the Government in purchasing bonds is, it may be reasonably assumed, largely restored to the channels of business. The total social loss, then, is composed of two elements—that which arises from the nonemployment of the money while it is in the government vaults, and that which is caused by the fact that, while the money is indeed returned to business by the government payments, it is likely to reach persons other than those from whom it was taken by taxation. Such a transfer will involve a social loss, especially if those to whom the money is paid do not employ it so productively as those from whom it was taken by taxation. One of Secretary Windom's transactions in 1890 will serve as an illustration. Under the circular of September 13 of that year, $17,071,150 of 4 per cent bonds were redeemed at a cost of $21,617,673.77, which represents a premium of 26.6 per cent. The reduction of interest charge from the transaction was $682,846 per annum. The bonds were due in 1907, and had, therefore, about seventeen years to run. The amount of the premium paid was $4,546,523.77. If the $21,617,673 had been kept by the Government, and put out at interest at 4 per cent, compounded annually, for seventeen years, and the amount of the interest, $682,846, is paid every year from the proceeds, the amount which the Government would have at the end of the seventeen years for the payment of the principal would be $25,927,322. This would leave a surplus of $8,856,172, the present value of which would be the loss to the Government. That value is, of course, the premium actually paid.

But it is hardly fair to assume that the Government would, or should, invest in this way. Another way to look at the matter is this: If the Government waited until the bonds were due, it would in the meantime pay $682,846 each year as interest; and at the end of the seventeen years it would pay the par value of the bonds. But in the meantime it would have the use of $682,846 for seventeen years, sixteen years, and so on, down to one year. The gain or loss will be the difference between the amount paid and the present worth of a seventeen years' annuity of $682,846, at 4 per cent, plus the present worth of the par value of the bonds. From this standpoint, also, the loss was the amount of the premium. It must be borne in mind that no one of these amounts represents the social loss or the loss to the nation as a social unit. The loss spoken of is the loss which the Government, or the whole people as a debtor, sustains to part of the people as creditor.[a] Moreover, all such computations are, at best, only guesses.

---

[a] The transaction mentioned was equivalent to buying bonds at par, at about 2.1 per cent; evidently since the Government could not have floated a new issue of bonds at so low a rate as that, there must have been a loss on the purchase actually made.

The direct loss from the forced purchase of bonds at a premium is not the only one to be considered. The purchase may do harm in addition by curtailing bank circulation. "It is difficult to estimate the full effect of bond purchases by the Secretary of the Treasury upon the volume of circulation of the national banks, for while $24,117,400 of bonds were withdrawn and directly transferred for purchase, about $8,000,000 being substituted, the total withdrawals amounted to more than $40,000,000; but undoubtedly the larger part of the $16,000,000 not withdrawn for transfer were either placed on the market or were purchased by the Secretary directly from the banks after withdrawal."[a] If the purchase of bonds forces the price up, it may be more profitable for the banks to sell bonds, contract their issues, and take advantage of prevailing high rates of discounts to enlarge their loans.

That the Treasury purchases of bonds may force their price up there is no doubt. Speaking of a Treasury offer to purchase bonds, in 1887, the Financial Chronicle[b] said: "Early in the week when it was represented that there would be no change in the Treasury policy prices sharply declined, and at times the market verged close on a panic. On Wednesday, after it was known that the offerings of 4½ percents to the Government had been very small, a recovery took place. This may seem paradoxical, but the theory was that it would lead the Government to extend the offer to purchase bonds so as to include the 4 percents. As this proved to be the case the very next day, the

---

[a] Rept. Comptroller of the Currency, 1890, Cf. Ibid., 1888, p. 453.
[b] September 24, 1887.

market further advanced, and it has been quite strong since."

"An illustration of almost weekly occurrence, during several years when the Government was rapidly reducing its indebtedness, will serve to show the effect of an inflation of the currency. On certain days each week, about 12 o'clock, messengers from many establishments in Wall street were waiting at the subtreasury. An official brought out and posted a written notice, announcing that the Government would redeem on a certain date bonds amounting to $10,000,000. * * * Within five minutes orders began to pour into the exchange for the purchase of stocks. At the same time those who had stocks to sell were warned by their messengers to hold them at high prices. A sudden upward rush in prices occurred."[a]

But even this is not the whole case. Under cover of the excitement of a panic, influences may be set at work to "corner the Treasury" and compel the Secretary to purchase bonds; that is, public excitement, worked up for the purpose, may exercise a coercive power. This was undoubtedly one element in the crisis of 1890. Under cover of the panic a combination of speculators, "'short' of the stock market and 'long' of government bonds," operated to force down railroad shares and force up government bonds. Of course the purpose was that the "shorts" might "cover" at a profit, and that the others, in the apprehension created, might compel the Secretary of the Treasury to relieve the market and enable them to sell their bonds. That there was some such combination seems probable from the fact that, although the Treasury

[a] Grosvenor, Wm. M., American Securities, 220.

purchased heavily up to the 17th of September, the bulk of the money went outside of New York, but that all paid out on that day—on the consummation of the plan—remained in the city.[a]

RELIEF BY DEPOSITS IN BANKS.

The other important method now available for anticipating a stringency in the market, or furnishing a relief when the stringency has come, is to transfer the public money from the Treasury to the banks. By depositing is here meant, however, not the continuous, regular, deposit of government funds, but the occasional transfer of them to the banks from the subtreasuries, in order to strengthen the banks or relieve them in distress. It is deposit for the purpose of relief, therefore, that we are considering.

The objections which have been made to the method of relieving the money market by the purchase of bonds, apply in the main to the method of relief through bank deposits. The whole process depends, of course, upon the existence of a surplus and, like premature debt payment, is involved with the policy of surplus financiering. If there is not a constant surplus the opportunity to give relief will be purely accidental. The advantage, if any, which comes, must depend upon the good judgment of the Secretary. If he anticipates a stringency he must show good judgment in the timeliness of his deposits. If his action is too early it will promote speculation. If it is too late he will fail to accomplish the good he aims at.

However, if the Treasury is to be looked to as the proper source of relief in crises, the deposit of its receipts

---

[a] See Bankers' Magazine, October, 1890.

in the banks is the best method of accomplishing the purpose; but, under our system of banking, the present practice concerning deposits is open to some serious objections. We have a system of scattered banks whose interests are likely to clash in times of difficulty. There is some truth in the statement that has been often made that in a crisis the banks of the country are likely to seek their respective individual interests instead of uniting their forces to overcome the difficulty. Of course this statement is made with due regard to the cooperation of the clearing-house banks in all money centers. There certainly is lack of unity of purpose and action, and therefore a certain waste or lack of full utilization of power in time of distress. This is a consequence of our system of independent banking.

To be most effective in affording relief to the strained market government deposits should be placed in the banks of the principal money centers, or possibly in the principal money center. The provision of the present law requiring an equitable distribution is vicious. It is true, to be sure, that the law is so worded that the Secretary has large discretion, but he should not be limited by any such condition. In times of stress the best place for the money to be deposited, as has just been remarked, is in the money centers. It is needed most there. It is in these places that the credit pyramid has been built highest. It is in these in which credit payments fall off more and money is more in demand for settlement when a crisis comes. In these places the deposits should be put both to enlarge reserves and to furnish the supply of money needed for the unusual cash settlement. If ease is established in these centers, other places are not likely to suffer.

If the deposits of public money are to be relied on as a source of relief in times of trouble, they should not be made at other times. That is to say, reliance upon the Treasury for relief through the deposit of public money in crises is unavailable if the Treasury deposits its receipts currently with the banks, for obviously there will be no surplus in the Treasury to deposit when trouble comes. This happened in 1907. The surplus was all deposited in the banks. The Treasury could do nothing more either in the way of enlarging its deposits or of enlarging the circulation by bond purchases. Hence the Secretary resorted to the extraordinary plan of selling bonds, with the expectation, apparently, that hoarded money would be drawn out, or that the banks would buy them as a basis of new circulation.

From the foregoing considerations it appears that the use of the independent treasury for affording relief in a panic by means of the money accumulated in the course of its operations is not a satisfactory mode of accomplishing that purpose. Its aid is arbitrary in method, very likely to be misdirected, generally insufficient as rendered, and actually promotive of injury by stimulating speculation and by making it more difficult for the banks to replenish and keep intact their reserves. Even when it is helpful, the aid which the independent treasury can render is measured by the amount of its disbursements, and the maximum effect of this aid must be lessened by the easy conditions under which it is offered; or else, if these conditions are made harder, the aid which the banks could otherwise render is diminished and counteracts to a certain extent the good effect of the Treasury operations. Moreover, the good done by the subtreasury expansions is less in a delicate condition of the market than the evil done by its contractions, for contraction of the currency then is quicker to produce distrust than expansion is to restore confidence.

LIMITATIONS OF SUBTREASURY RELIEF IN CRISES.

The limitations of the usefulness of the independent treasury for the relief of business when distressed are, then, very great. The helpfulness of an expansion of the currency in calming the disturbance, whether by the Treasury or by banks, will depend in part on the nature of the crisis and its degree of severity. The independent treasury has all the limitations of banks in an attempt to relieve a crisis, besides many of its own, for even the banks are limited in such cases by the fact that under certain circumstances something more than an expansion of the currency is needed to give relief. A short examination of the character of crises will bring out more clearly the limitations common to both the banks and the independent treasury.

If the disturbance is due simply to a lack of money, while business is in an otherwise healthy condition, an expansion of the currency, whether by an increase of bank discounts or notes or by an outpour of a Treasury surplus, will relieve the crisis and prevent a panic. But if the expansion is due to the independent treasury, this result will be attained, as we have seen, with more or less success, according to the skill of the Secretary of the Treasury. Even if a crisis becomes a panic, and is accompanied by a complete breakdown of the circulating medium, as in 1857, an independent treasury could, under certain conditions, do much to ease the situation.

If, however, the crisis is an industrial one, an expansion of the currency, whatever its source, can be of little avail. A difficulty of this kind is due to a falling off of demand for goods in some line, or lines, of production. This lessening of demand may be caused either by some change of custom or mode of life, or by cheaper production elsewhere, or by the too rapid transmutation of circulating capital into fixed capital. In this case the difficulty is likely to be lasting, and any increase of the amount of money afloat can have but little effect unless it is great enough and prolonged enough to enable debtors to "hold on" until the new fixed capital begins to make a return on the investment. But this is usually a matter of many months, or even years, and is too long a period to be influenced by temporary inflations or contractions of the currency. Hence, even if there had been money enough in the Treasury to satisfy all demands for it in that fatal third week of September, 1873, for example, the crash would not have been avoided, but only postponed. It might not have been so great, for many of the enterprises that had been undertaken proved sound ultimately; but many others were incapable of repaying the outlay on them, at least for a long time, and some not at all. These had to collapse.

The immediate cause of the culmination of an industrial crisis into a panic is loss of confidence. This is also the ultimate cause of commercial panics, and may be due to some slight accident that throws suspicion on firms pre-

viously supposed to be perfectly "sound," or to a wise
conclusion on the part of traders that speculation has gone
too far. Whatever its cause, a breakdown of confidence
puts a crisis beyond the influence of Treasury disbursements, as we saw was the case in 1873. What is needed at
such a time is a restoration of confidence, and confidence
can be restored only by a period of quiet. Time must be
allowed for the events of the crisis to pass from men's
minds. "The track must be cleared of the wreck. The
places left vacant by the casualties of the great crash must
be filled by new men." The sting of failure must cease to
be felt, the memory of dishonored credit must be allowed
to grow dim, new grounds of confidence must be seen,
sound conditions of business must be reestablished. With
all of this the temporary absorptions and disbursements
of money by the Treasury have nothing directly to do.
There can be no restoration of business and no rehabili-
tation of prices until credit is restored. For prices are
affected by the variations in the compound purchasing
medium of credit *and* money, and credit is relatively the
more important of the two.[a] Indeed, at such times money
may be plentiful, as indicated by the prevailing rates of
discount. But "cheap money does not necessarily mean
active speculation and high prices. We have had our
lowest prices and most stagnant markets when bank vaults
were phenomenally overloaded."[b] A further outpour of
money would therefore prove useless. And, indeed, it is
extremely doubtful whether it is wise, in a so-called capi-

[a] Cf. Taussig's "The Silver Situation." Publ Amer. Econ. Assoc., vii;
1: 63.

[b] E. B. Andrew's "An Honest Dollar." Ibid., iv : 6 : 8.

tal[a] panic, to try to devise means whereby all the enterprises endangered by shaken credit may be reserved. Many of them are of such a character that the interests of society will be better served by their destruction. The difficulty is that their undertakers usually involve others in their downfall, and the saving of these others is a legitimate and desirable object, even although its accomplishment involves some support of the unsound.

Finally, the questions must be considered whether the independent treasury may not have an influence in creating stringencies which it afterwards undertakes to relieve, and at what period of a crisis its help is most efficacious. As we have already seen,[b] Secretary Guthrie praised the independent treasury in 1856, on the ground that it exercises a restrictive influence on the banks when "overtrading" takes place, and so preserves "the general prosperity."

As the rise in prices under such circumstances is supposed to be due wholly or mainly to speculation, evidently any influence that opposes the speculative spirit will retard, perhaps stop, the rise of prices, and may prevent their reaching a point of danger. The retarding influence usually operative in such cases is the export of the metals; but any cause tending to contract the currency will have a similarly beneficial effect. The absorption of money by the independent treasury is such a cause, and may, therefore, be regarded as herein beneficial. It not only diminishes the amount of money, but, as it draws mostly from the banks, it at the same time

[a] A too rapid transmutation of circulating to fixed capital.
[b] See p. 70.

diminishes their power to lend. Hence it may exercise a powerful restraining influence on speculation, because it will arrest speculative extensions of credit at an earlier stage, with a less drain of gold. As the amount of their own notes which banks have to loan is limited, deposits are their chief means of discount. Hence the rate of interest must rise immediately when the demand for loans drives the reserve below a certain proportion, loans become more difficult to get, and speculation is checked. This process is made to begin earlier if the Treasury is absorbing money at the same time. Its restriction of the banks under these circumstances "is a real impediment to their making those advances which arrest the tide at its turn and make it rush like a torrent afterwards." The independent treasury can exert such an influence, however, only when its absorption of money coincides with this stage of the stringency. A kind of guaranty that such coincidence will occur is found in the fact that, under the circumstances described, the export of the metals generally implies import of commodities and consequent payment of custom dues. But such coincidence can be regarded as certain only when the speculation affects commodities which are imported subject to duty. Under our inclusive tariff system such articles will generally be thus affected, however; and we may, therefore, regard the effect of our independent treasury as usually beneficial in this phase of the inflation of prices.

There are still other sets of conditions in a speculative market. Exchange may be in favor of this country, prices may be rising, and yet there may be a drain of gold. This was the case in 1890.   Under such circumstances, in so far as the gold we lose belongs to foreign creditors, no action we can take will prevent our losing it if its owners are in great need, as seems to have been the case at the time mentioned.   Its loss, of course, may injure us by contracting the currency, and obviously any further contraction by the locking up of money in the Treasury vaults must then be an additional injury.   But if the gold is going abroad, attracted by higher rates of interest, as when the Bank of England by arbitrarily raising its rate of discount tends to raise the rate generally in the Kingdom, then the Treasury action will tend to keep the gold here, by making it temporarily scarcer.   The export will not stop until the scarcity of money here raises the rate of discount to a point where the home rate, plus cost of carriage, will be about equal to the foreign rate.   But nothing is gained by this.   Money becomes scarcer just the same.   What we would have lost by export is locked up by the Government.

When, however, speculation has attained its culmination, when the point of danger is reached, and a collapse of prices is threatened, the situation is different.   The need is for free discounting at high rates; but the amount of loans that the banks can give is limited, because a large amount of money that would otherwise be at their disposal is locked in the vaults of the Treasury.   Now the influence of the system is evil.   The evil is lessened, indeed, if the money is at once disbursed; but, as already pointed out, the money usually comes out, if it comes at all, under conditions that lessen its usefulness in calming a panic or relieving a stringency.

If, however, the monetary stress is caused not by an advance of prices under the stimulus of speculation, but by some cause withdrawing capital from the market, the whole case is different. Such are times when, for example, heavy foreign payments have to be made, or when there is a rapid transmutation of circulating into fixed capital. Such drafts are met either by the withdrawal of deposits from the banks or by the sale of property as securities, or by the contraction of loans. In any case the source of loans is curtailed, the rate of discount rises, loans are made only on prime security, and shaky houses go down, probably involving in their ruin some that are virtually solvent. The cause of the evil in this series of phenomena is the reduction of loanable funds. Any influence contributing to that reduction intensifies the evil. The locking up of money in the vaults of the independent treasury is such an influence, and that action is therefore bad. The results will come about if the absorption by the independent treasury coincides with the withdrawal of money from the market for any of the purposes indicated. When the money comes out of the Treasury again, if the need still exists for drafting it for any of the objects mentioned, the disbursement will be good, unless it is made in a way to encourage hoarding. If, however, the disbursement is delayed until the market has turned and prices have adjusted themselves to a lower level, it can do little or no good.

It is very obvious, however, that, so far as monetary stringencies and crises are caused by excessive stock speculation or intensified thereby, any efforts made by the Treasurer to relieve the tension of the money market simply condone this speculation, if indeed they do not encourage its continuance and increase. This effect can be traced in several instances in our history. For instance, in 1901 occurred the agitation contingent upon the Northern Pacific corner. It was a time of great industrial and financial speculation. This and the following year, 1902, will be remembered as a time of general prolonged stringency, which became more acute toward the end of the year. "It was essentially an artificial situation. * * * Approximately there was locked up in connection with syndicate operations not less than $400,000,000, while during the upward march of securities and prices an enormous amount of borrowing occurred in speculative operations. At the time there appeared the customary withdrawal of funds by western and southern banks. * * * The drain on New York was also larger in connection with industrial functions. * * * Borrowing abroad was also indulged in to excess. Owing to Wall street operations associated banks were put into a bad position, loans rising well above deposits and surplus reserves falling to an uncomfortably low point. Call money reached its highest point at 35 per cent, just half the top record of 1901; but instead of being caused by a temporary panic in the street there was a more lasting financial stringency that threatened to produce disaster in the stock market, making tight money the cause rather than the effect. An abnormal situation such as that called for heroic measures or a disastrous panic would have resulted. Secretary Shaw was equal to the occasion, however, and suggested two measures that were so unique as to arouse some criticism. The most radical was the acceptance of other than government bonds as security for public deposits. * * * It was also provided that the associated banks were not required to hold a reserve against public deposits. * * * The former proposition was * * * criticised. * * * It established a precedent for some less conservative officer. The stock market avoided a severe panic."[a]

The above facts recited by a leading financial journal show by another instance that it is possible for stock speculators to force up the market, relying on the Treasury disbursements when the pinch comes. Therefore, Treasury regulation of the money market may promote speculation and profit speculators. There is little reason to doubt that public deposits in the banks have been made at times the basis of a speculative fever. When the stringency became acute, the Treasury was looked to to save the situation on the ground of the public interest.

The substance of this analysis, then, is that, so far as crises are concerned, the independent treasury exercises a beneficial influence only in the early stages of a crisis caused by a speculative advance of prices; that in the later stages of such an occurrence its influence is evil to a greater or less degree, according as its receipts happen to exceed or to be less than its disbursements; that in a stringency caused by a rapid but healthy increase of busi-

---

[a] Dun's Review, 1903, 2 : 11

ness its absorptive influence is wholly bad, but that in the later stage of such a crisis its disbursements are promotive of good, unless mismanaged or too long delayed.

Hence we see that the coincidence of a particular phase, or stage, of the progress of a crisis is necessary in order that the influence of the subtreasury may be beneficial. But such a coincidence is purely fortuitous, and this fact deprives the system of all value as a scientific mode of relief in crises.

Chapter XII.—The Independent Treasury as a Fiscal Agent.

In the Mexican War.

Thus far we have examined the effects of the independence of the treasury system in its relation to business in ordinary times and in crises. It remains to inquire into the advantages of its independence when the Government finds it necessary to negotiate loans, especially in a time of war.

The Mexican war, the civil war, and the war with Spain have occurred since the adoption of the independent treasury system. The financing of the first of these was comparatively easy and the necessary fiscal machinery correspondingly simple. The country was prosperous, the finances in good condition, and the war was short. In this war, therefore, the subtreasury system appeared to advantage. A net indebtedness of $49,000,000 was created, all the loans being placed at par or above. The subscriptions for one of the loans amounted to more than three times the amount asked for, and were paid in specie. Nevertheless some difficulty was experienced. In October, 1846, Secretary Walker advertised for the exchange of $3,000,000 of treasury notes at par for specie, but got only a few responses. Concerning the operations the Secretary wrote: [a] "On the 22d October, 1846, the department advertised for the exchange of $3,000,000 of treasury notes at par for deposits of specie with the

---

[a] H. Ex. Doc., 30th Cong., 1st sess.; 6 : 17.

assistant treasurers. For a considerable time but very few of such deposits were made, or treasury notes thus taken; and from this long delay and continued reluctance upon the part of the community in taking these treasury notes at par, although at any time after the 28th of January last they were convertible into the twenty-year 6 per cent stock at par, many of the notes heretofore offered at par not having been taken at the date of my advertisement of the 9th of February last, serious doubts were entertained whether the whole of the new loan could be taken at or above par. It had been usual heretofore with my predecessors, in advertising for loans, to emit no sum to any individual under $25,000; but, with a view to insure the largest possible subscription, and at the best rates, and to diffuse the loan as far as practicable throughout all classes of the community, bids were authorized to be received by the advertisement as low as the lowest denomination of treasury notes permitted by law—namely, $50. It was the duty of the department to accept noting but specie—being the first loan ever negotiated in specie from the foundation of the Government down to that date, and the first loan, except that of last fall, ever thus negotiated at or above par during a period of war. The magnitude of the loan, the fluctuations below par of the previous stock and notes, the untried and, to many, alarming restraining operation of the constitutional treasury, the heavy expenditures of the war, and the requirement of all the payments from time to time in specie, were deemed by many as insuperable obstacles to the negotiation of the whole of the loan at or above par. But, under the salutary provisions of the constitutional treasury, the credit of the Government was in truth enhanced by receiving and disbursing nothing but coin; thus placing all its transactions upon a basis more sound and entitled to higher credit than when it held no specie, had no money in its own possession, and none even in the banks to pay its creditors but bank paper."

The contracting influence of the subtreasury was evident even at that early day, and this, together with the refusal to accept anything but specie, interfered with the placing of loans. Yet, in the opinion of the Secretary of the Treasury, the refusal of the Government to receive or pay out anything but specie in its transactions enhanced its credit and so made its efforts to place loans more successful than they would otherwise have been. Doubtless this opinion was to some extent correct.

The Treasury succeeded, in its position of fiscal agent of the Government, in placing loans, and under the conditions of that time the subtreasury system was a success. But whatever good was accomplished by the independence of the Treasury, acting as its own fiscal agent, was more or less offset by the result of its independence in locking up the money with which the bonds were paid. "By emissions of this kind [treasury notes] and his 'war warrants' Secretary Walker supplied in some sense the want of a national currency and relieved local banks of deposit from the heavy strain which was made by the metallic hoard the Government gathered under the new subtreasury act." [a] Even so, there is good reason for thinking that if our exports had not been so large at the

---

[a] Schouler, James, History of the United States, 4 : 541.

time the loan of $23,000,000, authorized January 28, 1847, would not have been so successful. In the fiscal year 1846–47 our imports of specie were $24,121,289. [a]

IN THE CIVIL WAR.

The civil war furnishes more adequate opportunities than the Mexican for studying the effects of fiscal independence of banks. Its lessons are, therefore, more valuable.

The struggle opened with the country in a good industrial condition, but with a revenue altogether inadequate to the prosecution of a great war, and with a system of taxation which could not easily be so adjusted as to produce such a revenue. The Government was thus compelled to rely on its credit for immediate resources, and the policy of carrying on the war largely by borrowing was practically adopted. It was in the attempts to place the large loans suddenly made necessary by the tremendous increase in its expenses that the Treasury Department first found the machinery of the subtreasury inadequate to perform the services demanded by the exigencies of the new situation.

A complete separation from banks made it necessary for the Treasury to be its own broker.

The financial operations of the Mexican war were trifles compared with the transactions which the Treasury was called upon to undertake when confronted with the civil war. The amount borrowed in the single year ending December, 1861, was over $300,000,000, while the loans contracted during the whole Mexican war summed up only

---

[a] H. Ex. Doc., 30th Cong., 1st sess., 6 : 12.

$49,000,000. It was not easy for the Treasury to constitute itself a broker's office on so large a scale, and the process would have been too slow to meet the needs of the financial situation.

Secretary Chase was early impressed with the fact that "the safest, surest, and most beneficial plan would be to engage the banking institutions of the three chief commercial cities of the seaboard to advance the amounts needed for disbursement."[a] Accordingly he conferred with their representatives, and on their agreeing to advance the money he asked for, undertook "to issue three-year 7.30 bonds or Treasury notes, bearing even date with the subscription and of equal amount; to cause books of subscription to the national loan to be immediately opened; to reimburse the advances of the banks as far as practicable from this national subscription; and to deliver to them 7.30 bonds, or Treasury notes, for the amount not thus reimbursed." The object of turning to the banks was to secure the needed money speedily; but the Secretary wished to give the public an equal opportunity with the banks to subscribe for the loan, while yet avoiding competition with them in the disposal of the bonds. The direct popular subscriptions amounted to a little more than half the $50,000,000 advanced by the banks. The second loan of $50,000,000 seems to have been advanced wholly by the banks; and "as no reasonable prospect appeared of obtaining terms equally advantageous by advertisement, * * * the Secretary * * * arranged this third loan also (of Nov. 16, 1861) with the associates"[b]—that is, with the banks.

---

[a] Finance Report, 1861, p. 8.   [b] Finance Report, 1861, p. 9.

Secretary Chase did attempt to place loans directly—
that is, to make the Government its own agent—and at
the same time he tried to diffuse the loans. One of the
objects which, in his report for 1863 he tells us, he kept
steadily in view, "in the creation of debt by the negotiation of loans or otherwise," was "general distribution."
The finance report for 1863 records a certain amount of
success in the attempt to place some of the later loans by
popular subscription. "The general distribution of the
debt into the hands of the greatest possible number of
holders," wrote Secretary Chase, " * * * has been
accomplished * * * by arrangements to popularize
the loans by giving to the people everywhere opportunities
to subscribe for bonds. These subscription arrangements
have been especially useful and successful. They have
been adopted as yet with reference to only two descrip-
tions of bonds—the two commonly known as seven-
thirties and five-twenties * * * The plan of distributing the seven-thirties was that of employing a large
number of agents in many places and directing their
action from the department. It worked well for a time,
but was soon found inadequate to the financial necessities
of the Government." Accordingly this plan had to be
abandoned and the work intrusted to an agent—that is,
a banker or broker was employed. In June, 1864, Secretary Fessenden, who had succeeded Mr. Chase, found it
necessary to get more money. Accordingly, he advertised a loan, which he was compelled to withdraw within
a few days, as the public would not subscribe on the terms
offered. . He turned to the banks, but they insisted on
terms to which he would not agree, and so he issued

greenbacks. Thus, from the beginning of the war, as early as 1861, the Secretary had been compelled to rely on the banks for aid, and his report for 1862 gives full acknowledgment of their assistance.

The final breakdown of the government independence of the banks in raising loans was emphasized by the establishment of the national banks. In fact, the primary purpose of creating the national banking system was to make a market for government bonds. Secretary Chase, in his report for 1862, said that "among the advantages which would arise from the establishment of a national banking system would be the fact that the bonds of the Government would be required for banking purposes; a steady market would be established, and their negotiation greatly facilitated; a uniformity of price for the bonds would be maintained at a rate above that of funds of equal credit but not available as security for circulation."[a]

The causes which made it necessary for the Government to depend on the banks during the war are obvious enough. In the first place, even if the Government had established a network of agencies over the country for the purpose of receiving subscriptions to its loans, the plan could not have been successful in meeting its financial needs, for the money was needed immediately. The loans had to be placed quickly, and their collection in driblets, so to speak, even if possible in course of time, would not have filled the coffers of the Treasury with sufficient rapidity for its needs. The vaults of the banks were the only place where large amounts of money could be immediately

---

[a] Report of the Comptroller of the Currency, 1879: 113.

and directly obtained, because it was in them only that sufficiently large amounts were already collected. This necessity for rapidity in getting the money would of itself suffice to render almost useless, at the beginning of a war, a system of agencies for popular subscription.

Still another explanation of the resort of the Government to the banks for loans is the fact that the arousing of confidence is an essential element in the floating of a loan, and for the Government to have established confidence directly in the minds of thousands of individual subscribers would have been, under the existing circumstances, a very difficult task. But when the banks showed sufficient trust in the Government to loan it their funds the establishment of public confidence received a powerful impulse. For the banks are institutions which are supposed to know the trustworthiness of those to whom they lend, and individual capitalists will follow where they lead.

The lack of confidence in the Government was manifest on several occasions. "The prospect of negotiating a loan in the ordinary way," the Secretary tells us in 1864, "was by no means flattering, as the notice for a loan of $33,000,000, advertised on the 25th day of June, had been withdrawn on the 2d of July. * * * The Secretary thought it advisable to borrow * * * $50,000,000 of the banks." [a] The negotiations fell through, however, and the Secretary again advertised for a loan, incurring considerable expense, and offering "liberal inducements to stimulate the effort of corporations and individuals to

[a] Finance Report, 1864, p. 20.

dispose of their notes." But the effort was only partly successful.

The partial success, in 1863, of the attempt to place by popular subscription may perhaps be ascribed to the change that the Government made at the time in its financial policy for the management of the war. The inadequacy of the loan policy was seen and steps taken to increase the revenue from taxation.[a]

The Government may be dependent on banks and bankers for the success of its financial measures, even although it does not employ them as agents to sell its bonds. The Secretary of the Treasury may be his own broker, may be administratively independent of the banks, and yet virtually dependent on them. For he may be compelled to turn to them as the only available purchasers of bonds, and if so he must adjust the terms of his loan more or less to their conditions. This happened in the civil war, and it was this necessity that led to the national banking law, which was an effort to force the banks to sustain the public credit. The law was a confession of the inability of the Government to get on without the help of the banks.

The amount of bonds held by private citizens may be fairly regarded as a measure of the success of the effort to diffuse the loans by popular subscriptions. The figures for the years immediately after the war are not available; but there is no reason to think that the analysis of the holdings of the public debt made in the census of 1880

[a] See H. C. Adams's "Public Debts," 127–131. A table is given there showing the course of the government credit during the war; its uniformly downward course was temporarily checked toward the end of 1863.

represents a state of affairs very different from that which originally prevailed. Prof. H. C. Adams summarizes that investigation by saying: "It thus appears that out of a total of over $1,000,000,000 of registered debt, private citizens of the United States were proprietors of the comparatively small sum of $417,538,850.[a]

The dependence of the Government on the banks during the civil war, then, was real, even in the instances in which it acted as its own broker, because it had to turn to the banks as customers for its issues of stock; but even this amount of dependence was contrary to the spirit, if not the letter, of the act of August 6, 1846. For the whole tenor of the arguments of the advocates of the independent treasury was that the Government should have nothing whatever to do with the banks.

The linking of the affairs of the Government with those of the banks may be shown to exist in other ways than in mere dependence on them as customers, or as agents for the sale of bonds; although, to be sure, this close connection can be fairly considered as only an incident of the banking system which was adopted. Even if the Government had not sold any bonds to the banks, those institutions must have bought them from private holders, in order to deposit them with the United States Treasurer as security for their notes. This deposit, as is well known, makes the Government the guarantor of the bank notes; and a connection of this kind is unquestionably foreign to the purpose of the framers of the independent treasury law.

---

[a] " Public Debts," p. 45.

Thus, by the exigencies of the war, the independence of the Government with reference to banks was set aside, both formally and virtually, in the matter of negotiation of loans: formally, in those instances in which the Government employed them as its agents; and virtually, even in those cases in which, though acting as its own agent or broker, it still had to rely on the banks as the immediate source of the money which it borrowed.

It may be said that the necessity for relying on the banks as a source of loans was a mere consequence of the conditions of the war and not a defect of the independent treasury system. But it must be insisted in reply, first, that these conditions are similar to those which we must expect to recur if we should be unfortunate enough to be involved in another great war; and, second, that the lack of adaptability of the fiscal system to these vitiates the system and renders it unsuitable in a great war.

The use of the banks, directly or indirectly, for floating loans, was the first step in the abandonment of the principle of fiscal independence adopted fifteen years before. The second step followed necessarily, and consisted in once more making the banks, to a certain extent, depositaries of public money. Indeed, the circumstances of the situation made them so by the very fact of their receiving subscriptions to the government loans. And it was not long before the general suspension of specie payments cut away the foundation of the act of 1846, so far also as it relates to the use of "hard money" in government payments. For the suspension of specie payments by the banks made a similar step a matter of necessity for the

Government. The receipts from taxation were not large enough to enable the Treasury to pay all its debts in coin, and the banks were drained of their gold by their advances to the Government, which the Secretary of the Treasury required should be in specie. As the Secretary could not borrow fast enough to meet his needs, and as he could not use bank notes, government paper—the well-known "greenbacks"—had to be resorted to.

The separation of the Government from the banks could not prevent a suspension of specie payments by the Government, when it needed money in very large amounts, although the authors of the law of 1846 thought it could. They made provision, indeed, for Treasury notes, but these were always to be equivalent to coin. But with the greenbacks even the pretence of specie payments was soon abandoned. Could the greenbacks have taken the place of the bank notes in circulation, instead of being added to them, the inflation and depreciation would probably have been less; but owing to existing laws, and to the state of public and congressional opinion, they could not do so, and hence they constituted a clear addition to the circulating medium of the country.

During the civil war, then, the independent treasury law was really inoperative. It was entirely so, practically, except for the maintenance of specie payments in customs receipts and for interest on the public debt; and it was partly so even according to law, because it was deemed necessary to suspend certain sections of the subtreasury act, by making the national banks depositaries of public money. The purposes for which the subtreasury system was created, separation from banks and maintenance of specie payments, were both abandoned, owing to a stress of circumstances some of which, at least, were brought about by the very system that was created to prevent them.

The experience of the civil war would seem to show then that even if it be considered best for the Public Treasury to negotiate its loans directly with individual subscribers, the machinery of the subtreasury is entirely inadequate to enable it to do so successfully under the stress of a war, and that the system is not a guaranty, as it was supposed by some of its authors to be, that the Government would, under all circumstances, be freed from the evils of depreciated paper.

For the depositing and safe-keeping of internal-revenue receipts also in time of war the subtreasury system is unwieldy, if not inadequate. The collection of the great receipts at such a time, by means of a complex and greatly ramified system of taxation, from many different sources, and from points often remote from a subtreasury or a United States depositary, was found inconvenient and expensive, and also dangerous, because the money had to be intrusted to inexperienced collectors often hastily appointed. These difficulties were so strongly felt that when the national banks were established they were made depositaries of money received in payment of internal-revenue taxes. The fiscal growth of the country was far beyond the confines set for it by the independent treasury act. The channels provided by the system were neither sufficiently large nor sufficiently ramified to carry the increased streams of revenue with the rapidity necessary for the needs of the Government.

The only important service of the independent treasury during the war and immediately afterwards was to keep the supply of gold received in payment of customs dues wherewith to pay the interest on the public debt during the period of paper inflation. In supplying the needs of the Government in this respect the independent treasury performed a real service. But this service was as much an accident of the unsound financial management of the war as a result of independence of the Treasury; that is, if the financial management of the war had been such as to render unnecessary the use of a depreciated paper currency there would have been no call for this service from the independent treasury. Moreover, in so far as it absorbed gold beyond what the Government required for such payments as had to be made in specie, it promoted gold speculation, and so caused injury to legitimate business.

IN REFUNDING OPERATIONS.

More can be said, however, in favor of the independent treasury as an engine for the performance of refunding operations, although even for that purpose it is not wholly efficient, at least for operations on so gigantic a scale as that which, soon after the war, began to testify to the growing credit of the Government and the industrial development of the country. Here, again, as in the placing of loans and the collection of revenue, there is needed a great network of agencies all over the country, and this network can be well supplied only by the banks. Secretary Sherman wrote in 1880:[a] "Without the aid of the

---

[a] Letter to the Convention of American Bankers, 1880.

national banks the unprecedented refunding operations of last year would have been almost, if not quite, impossible."

The need which the Government felt for depending on the banks in measures of refunding is of a somewhat different kind from that which made them indispensable in the financial operations of the war. In selling bonds for refunding purposes the Treasury often can be, to advantage, its own broker. The experience of Secretary Sherman shows that the Government itself could place bonds on the market at less expense than if it sold them through syndicates of bankers. "Previous to the summer of 1877 all operations in refunding were carried on by syndicates, the commission allowed being the total amount[a] appropriated by the law to cover the expense of conversion. * * * But when Secretary Sherman took the Treasury portfolio the plan of placing bonds by syndicates was abandoned for sale upon public advertisements, or, as it was termed, 'under circulars.' This plan was followed for the entire amount of 4 percents, with the exception of about $15,000,000, which were secured on a foreign contract. * * * The success of the policy of sale by circulars may be seen from the following facts: The total sale of 4 per cent bonds amounted to $740,847,800; the cost of this sale, according to the plan followed by the other Secretaries, would have been $3,704,239; by the method adopted by Mr. Sherman it was effected at a cost of $2,645,802.60. The teaching of this experiment is * * * that in matters of administration it is wise

---

[a] The usual rate allowed syndicates for placing loans during the war was 1 per cent. In 1870 it was reduced to one-half of 1 per cent.

for the Government to keep itself independent of the agencies of the banks. Popular enthusiasm brings banking support, but banking enthusiasm can not arouse popular interest."[a] But that Secretary Sherman did not abandon the use of banks in his future operations is shown by the fact that on the 1st of August, 1878, he issued a circular in which he said: "All national banks are now invited to become financial agents of the Government and depositaries of public moneys received on the sale of these bonds upon complying with section 5153, Revised Statutes of the United States. All banks, bankers, postmasters, and other public officers, and all other persons, are invited to aid in placing these bonds. They can make their arrangements through national banks for the deposit of the purchase money of the bonds."[b]

But could the national debt have been so easily and so soon refunded at lower rates of interest if the national banks had not furnished a ready-made market for the new bonds as a basis for their circulation? There is at least some doubt whether it could have been. The forced market created by the banks for the bonds enhanced the credit of the Government, and enabled it sooner to command better terms for its loans. The difficulty experienced in 1891, in the attempt to refund the 3½ per cent bonds at 1½ per cent, is an illustration of the point under consideration. The banks refused to exchange the bonds they held for others at less than 2 per cent, and the Secretary had finally to adopt that rate. If in so small an

---

[a] H. C. Adams's "Public Debts," 235–238. Although banking support may not arouse popular interest, it may inspire confidence.

[b] Specie Resumption and Refunding of National Debt, H. Ex. Doc. 46th Cong., 2d sess., No. 9: 356.

operation as this one was the Treasury had to accede to the demands of the banks, certainly it was much more dependent on them in the refunding operations which were so large that if the banks had not had their own terms they would have presented their bonds for payment and seriously embarrassed the Government.

Of course, if the refunding operations consisted in the mere direct exchange of bonds between holders and the Government—that is, if present holders were willing to give up their stock in exchange for a new issue at a lower rate of interest, the transaction might be regarded as one of mere bookkeeping, and the government offices could do the work without interfering with business. But when, as was the usual method, new bonds must be sold for cash to redeem the old ones, great injury might be done, by contracting the currency, if the money paid in for new bonds had to lie idle in the vaults of the sub-treasury, to await the maturity of the bonds called in under the three months' notice of redemption required by law. This evil could be obviated under the independent method of placing loans, only if money received for new bonds were paid out for old ones as fast as it came in. When, however, the bonds are placed through the banks the money paid for them is not taken from the channels of commerce at all for any considerable length of time. Moreover, here again, as in time of war, the large stock of money is held by the banks, or can be most easily brought out through regular banking channels.

As illustrations of the aid rendered by the banks and bankers in refunding, we may cite some of the operations between 1870 and 1879. In August, 1871, over

$65,000,000 worth of 5 per cent bonds were subscribed for, "chiefly by the national banks." In the same month the firm of Jay Cooke & Co. contracted for $200,000,000 worth of the same bonds. In 1876–77 August Belmont & Co. purchased 4½ per cent bonds to the amount of $200,000,000. During the first four months of 1879, $497,247,750 worth of 4 per cents were sold, $121,000,000 being taken by the First National Bank of New York and associates, and the remainder by other national banks.[a] It is needless to mention the unprecedented operations in debt conversion in still more recent years. In all of them the assistance of the banks was indispensable.

Thus, again, during and after the civil war, as after the Revolutionary War and that of 1812, the nation was driven to avail itself of the aid of the banks. "The first Bank of the United States absorbed nearly one-fifth of the public debt in 1797. The second Bank of the United States carried about the same proportion of the debt of 1816. When the civil war closed, in April, 1865, the newly organized national banks had aided the Treasury in placing and carrying the immense loans required to maintain the armies and fleets in active service for four years, and held themselves government paper to the amount of $390,000,000."[b]

A breakdown of the subtreasury system at still another point became manifest when the country came to face the question of resumption of specie payments. The facts show that if the Treasury had been left to its own

---

a Report of the Comptroller of the Currency, 1879, p. 108.
b Richardson, H. W., "The National Banks" p. 112.

resources—that is, if it had been "independent"—
resumption probably could not have taken place when it
did.[a] "In the resumption of specie payments, and in the
funding of the national debt, * * * the cooperation
of the national banks has been of essential service to the
Government. The banks, in the aggregate, have constantly kept on hand, as reserve, nearly one-fourth of
the entire amount of legal-tender notes outstanding,
which, together with the coin, is much in excess of the
amount of the reserve required by law."[b] The connection made with the banks through the New York Clearing
House practically relieved the Treasury of the necessity
of making coin payments to any large extent, because the
clearing house agreed to accept legal-tender notes in
payment of all dues from the Government. Moreover,
the banks, although holders of more than one-third of the
amount of government notes outstanding, refrained from
presenting them for redemption.[c] If the banks had
demanded the redemption of these notes, the attempt at
resumption would have been gravely imperiled. At this
time again, as in the case of the bonds sold to carry on
the war, the banks were the only source whence it was
practicable to draw large sums; they had large accumulations of gold, and were the channels through which more
could readily be obtained by means of subscriptions.
For "the inconvenience of obtaining coin outside of the

---

[a] For an account of the operations of refunding and resumption, see
Report of the Secretary of the Treasury on "Specie Resumption and
Refunding of the National Debt," H. Ex. Docs. 46th Cong., 2d sess., vol.
xvii, 1879–80.

[b] Finance Report, 1879, p. 20.

[c] Ibid., 1879, p. 114.

large cities forbade any direct appeal to the great body of the people.''

But in still another way was the aid of the banks rendered, a way which made them an essential part of the resumption machinery. They were the agents of the Government in negotiating the loans necessary to secure gold for specie payments and the depositaries of the money received from the sale of bonds. As Secretary Sherman pointed out in the letter mentioned before,[a] but for the use of the banks as depositaries the money received for bonds would have been withdrawn from circulation for deposit in the Treasury vaults to await the maturity of the bonds called in. The banks bought during the first four months of 1879 nearly $500,000,000 worth of 4 per cent bonds. The absorption by the Treasury of all the money thus paid in would have contracted the currency of the country over 50 per cent. Distress was caused by the gradual contraction that went on for the five years preceding resumption, and raised an outcry against the attempt to resume; such a contraction as would have taken place had all the money paid in for the new bonds been kept in the Treasury would undoubtedly have caused suffering sufficient to arouse against resumption such opposition as would have rendered its success at least problematical. The aid of the banks here was absolutely indispensable. This view of the case is not weakened by the fact, sometimes brought forward to belittle the aid rendered by the banks at this juncture, that although for them to have sent in their treasury

---

[a] See p. 304.

notes for redemption would have been to destroy the credit
of the Government, it would have involved themselves
also in ruin. For the dependence of their safety on that
of the Government was a condition for which the Government, and not the banks themselves, was responsible.

THE LOANS OF 1893–1896.

Although the loans of 1893 and the three following
years were not war loans, they strengthen the conclusions reached from a study of the operations of the subtreasury system before that time. We have seen that in
the panic of 1893 the Treasury was not only unable to help
the banks, but even to help itself. The many difficulties
in which the country was plunged by the silver purchase
law, added to other mischievous features of our currency
system, conjoined with the fact that the receipts of the
Treasury for ordinary expenses showed a deficit, made it
impossible for the Secretary to lend any aid in the crisis.
The banks, as we have seen, were appealed to on several
occasions to exchange gold for notes. In 1894 it was
decided to place a loan of $50,000,000 of 5 per cent ten-
year bonds. The situation was difficult. "Judged by
executive precedent and tradition, there was need, in the
face of this dubious situation, to promote negotiations
with the larger financial interests. That such solicita-
tion is not only prudent business policy, but the legitimate
office of the national finance minister, has been tested in
nearly all issues of public loans, here and abroad, during
the century."[a] Secretary Carlisle, however, heeded the

---

[a] Noyes, A. D.: Forty Years of American Finance, 213.

prejudice of his party against a relationship with the banks, and therefore kept aloof from them. The banks were not in a position to be interested in a new loan, and therefore the loan did not take with the public. It became evident, a few days before the time for closing the subscription books, that the loan would fail, and Mr. Carlisle appealed to the New York banks to prevent this. A syndicate of them immediately responded and took up four-fifths of the entire issue. Thus we see that the Treasury was unable independently to float its bonds, under the circumstances that then obtained. Nor could any other result have been expected. The country had just passed through a crisis, money had been hoarded, and confidence had been shaken. There was no ground for patriotic enthusiasm, one of the conditions under which a popular loan is likely to succeed, and every indication pointed to the necessity of lending to banks and bankers. The condition of the Treasury made it necessary to place a further loan in November of the same year, to the amount of $50,000,000. Mr. Carlisle had learned by experience and again appealed to the banks. A syndicate was gotten together which took up virtually the whole issue.

The same experience was passed through in 1895, when the Belmont-Morgan syndicate was created to carry the country through a crisis. As we have seen, they insisted on a thirty-year 4 per cent bond as the price of their services. The amount sold was $62,315,400 and the amount received by the Government therefrom was $65,116,214.

In January of the following year, it was necessary to borrow once more, and a new 4 per cent loan of $100,000,000, to be subscribed for in gold was offered to the public. It was to be a popular loan—that is, it was offered for popular subscription. The country was well on the road to business recovery; confidence had been in large measure restored, and the loan was successful. Indeed, it was subscribed for nearly six times over. There were 4,640 subscribers, and the amount of their subscriptions aggregated $568,000,000. The Secretary was able, therefore, to place the loan on exceedingly advantageous terms and selected bids which ranged from 110.5 to 120. Yet it appears that many bids were made in behalf of the banks, many more were made for the purpose of selling immediately and getting any premium that might accrue, and it was only a short time before virtually the whole issue was owned by banks and bankers.

THE SPANISH WAR LOAN.

In July, 1898, came the Spanish war loan. This is no place to point out the financial mistakes that were made in placing this loan. Its management, however, throws a good deal of light on the relation of the independent treasury to popular loans. By act of Congress the Government offered $200,000,000 3 per cent bonds at par. The subscriptions were widely distributed and large in number. According to the report of the Secretary,[a] there were 320,000 subscribers who offered $1,500,000,000, or more than seven times the amount of the loan. The loan was therefore hailed as a tremendous success. Again we must notice, however, that many of the bids were made by individual representatives of banking houses and a great many more were made by people who bought

---

[a] Treasury Report, 1898.

to sell soon after and found their way into the hands of banks, so that after three or four months the distribution of the loan had materially changed. The popularity of the loan, in the sense that it was a widely distributed loan, was less in evidence, however, when we remember that the subscribers for amounts of $500 or less of the loan numbered 230,000 out of the whole 320,000. It is significant, moreover, that the Secretary of the Treasury had arranged with a New York banking syndicate beforehand to take up the bonds if the people did not subscribe for them. The Assistant Secretary of the Treasury at the time tells us that it was the guaranty of the syndicate of banks which "put spirit into the loan from the first moment."[a] A loan can hardly be called popular in which interest has to be stimulated by a syndicate guaranty and a large speculative premium. The bonds were sold at par, although there were bids for them as high as 105. This can hardly be regarded as sound financiering. The expense of management was also much greater than if the loan had been placed in the usual way through a banking syndicate. It succeeded, moreover, because the war was popular. We may therefore summarize the causes of its success as the popularity of the Spanish war, the previous arrangement with the syndicate, and the low price.

As a result of this review it is very evident that the Treasury felt itself unable to manage the loan successfully, for it appealed to the banks to boom it. The Government lost the premium which it might have had, the method of placing the loan added to the expense of management,

---

[a] The Forum, September, 1898.

and as a matter of fact the bonds soon got into the hands of the banks, and the Government was obliged to leave the money in the banks to prevent contraction of the currency. From no point of view can any advantage be found in the direct independent management of the loan by the Treasury itself.

CONCLUSIONS.

As an agent for the fiscal operations during and consequent on a great war, it is evident, then, that the independent treasury can have but a limited scope, namely, that of keeping the gold wherewith the Government may make its specie payments. But it can have even this limited scope only on the supposition that the country is on a paper basis. To be sure, that is a condition of affairs which has very frequently occurred in countries carrying on great and prolonged wars; but its necessity, in the case of a wealthy country, is by no means self-evident. It rather seems possible for such a nation to maintain specie payments even under so great a stress as we endured in the civil war.

If better financial management in the case of future wars should prevent a degeneration to the use of irredeemable paper, even the present restricted possibilities for usefulness in war would be taken from the independent treasury. A state of war is, indeed, exceptional; and the fiscal machinery needed under its conditions must, as a matter of course, be exceptional also. But the unusualness should not lie so much in the nature of the machinery as in the extent of its operations. The creation of a new system for the collection and disbursement of revenue, difficult under any circumstances, is doubly so under the strain of war, and should be unnecessary then. If, as was the case in the civil war, specie payments be suspended, and if the suspension continue after the restoration of peace, the independent treasury, as already pointed out, absorbs gold. The Government, under such circumstances, receives the gold in payment of duties, and as no one wants it to pay debts that can be legally paid in depreciated paper, the gold tends to accumulate. The result must be a tendency to enhance the price of gold, or, what amounts to the same thing, further to depreciate paper. This tendency, of course, reacts on prices, and introduces an element of uncertainty into business. But, in addition, such locking up of gold causes speculation in gold itself, varying its price more rapidly and largely than would probably otherwise be the case. The operations of the New York gold board furnish an illustration. With an excellent *raison d'être*, a legitimate field for its operations, it became at times a tool which, assisted by foolish legislation, exerted a baneful influence on the business of the country. All these considerations, in connection with the fact that of the four great wars in which the country has engaged, beginning with the Revolution, in only one, and that the least important financially, have we been able to do without the aid of banks and bankers, demonstrate the inadequacy of the "independent" system of financiering for war purposes.

Chapter XIII.—Proposals for Replacement of the Subtreasury System.

CONDITIONS TO BE MET.

The trend of the conclusions drawn from the working of the subtreasury system to-day is that the harm done by it is greater than the good, which is the opposite of what was true when the system was established. At present the advantages of the system are its occasional accidental restriction of the expansion of bank loans under the influence of speculation, the certainty that the Government can get its money for use promptly without disturbing the market, and its occasional assistance in stringencies and crises. But of even these advantages the first and third are uncertain, and the system is a continued source of disturbance to the money market and the banks.

The primary purpose of the adoption of the independent treasury was the safety of the public money. To have continued to intrust the public money to the banks, as they were then constituted, would have been to invite frequent embarrassment and often positive loss to the Government. It may be said, indeed, that the deposits of the nation would have been safe enough if the life of the second United States Bank had been prolonged, and that the political strife that brought about its destruction was the cause which made the creation of the subtreasury system necessary. It is true that up to a certain time the public deposits in that bank were safe, and that the reasons

for its overthrow were political rather than economic.   But
whatever view one may take of the political motives and
measures that caused its downfall, there is good reason for
thinking that its preservation as a semipublic institution
would have been impossible in any event; and certainly
there was no likelihood at all of permanent safety for the
public deposits in the banks that succeeded the national
institution.   Therefore some means had to be devised to
secure safety, and under the prevailing public opinion, no
better means could have been found than that which provides that the Government should keep its money in its
own vaults.   This plan had its peculiar dangers, to be sure.
It exposed the public money to risk of loss from accident
and from peculation at the hands of inexperienced officials
who were necessary under the new system.   But there is
no reason to think that these were personally less honest
than the officers and employees of the banks; and they
were probably fewer in number and less exposed to the
temptation of using the public money for their personal
ends, because they had not the facilities for using it which
were open to those employed in the banks.

A second purpose of the establishment of the independent treasury was to furnish a safe currency to the Government.   This was one of the purposes for which the second
national bank had been chartered; and it was claimed,
with some show of reason, that the purpose had not been
fulfilled by that institution.   After the fall of the national
bank there was no method available for the provision of
a safe currency and for its regulation, except for the Government to undertake the matter itself.   This plan, again,
to be sure, had objections peculiar to itself.   Treasury

notes as well as bank notes would depreciate under certain circumstances, and the Government could not always make all its payments in specie. When the country committed itself to the policy of fiat paper money, it attempted to preserve the independence of the Treasury at the expense of the safety of the currency; and its entry into the field of note issue made continued independence of the banks impossible.

In providing for the safety of the public funds and, at first, for a safe currency, the independent treasury did not provide, at least sufficiently, for elasticity in the circulating medium; nor did it insure business against disturbances due to the alternate and arbitrary contractions and expansions of the currency which its operations caused. These evils, indeed, were of less moment in its early days, because, as we have seen, the financial operations of the Government were not sufficiently large to do much harm. To-day the situation is different. The need of elasticity and the necessity for the prevention of disturbance by the treasury operations have become of greater importance as the business of the country has expanded. While in 1846 the Treasury was comparatively isolated from the business of the country, the influence of its operations now is felt in every direction; there is scarcely an industry in the country that is not more or less affected by its operations. "The annual and daily transactions of the Treasury have become so large, its financial operations and movements touch the interests of the people at so many points, that great care should be taken to avoid any unnecessary friction. As the country increases in wealth and population, with the consequent increase of its revenues and disbursements, it will be found impossible to continue the system in its present form."[a]

As the national debt is reduced it becomes more difficult so to adjust the purchase of bonds as to furnish relief to the money market at times when it is strained. "As these derangements happen almost invariably at the time of the moving of the crops of the country, this statement is equivalent to saying that every productive interest in the country must pay toll to foreign buyers through the lower range of prices which obtain at such times, because of the fact that our arrangements for collecting and disbursing our revenue are so defective as to need an artificial and violent remedy in order to place in active circulation the moneys withdrawn from the business of the country."[b]

Of course, safety for the public money is as necessary now as it ever was; but it can be secured in other ways. The public money on deposit in banks is in far less danger of loss to-day than at any previous period of our history. Since the safety of the public money can be secured as well in some other way as by the independent treasury; and since that system under present conditions produces effects that are of great injury to business, the question naturally arises whether some method can not be found whereby the evils of the system can be largely or wholly obviated, while yet its good points shall be conserved; some method which shall continue the insurance of safety, but shall provide for greater and more automatic elasticity of the currency; shall put an end to the disturbance of business

---

[a] Report U. S. Treasurer, 1886: 67–68.   [b] Ibid.

by arbitrary absorptions and disbursements; shall prevent the occurrences of stringencies in the money market from government operations, but shall yet furnish a means of affording relief in crises to as great an extent, at least, as the independent treasury does now. Safety, of course, is the prime requisite. Its loss could not be offset by any other advantage that could be secured. That the Treasury shall get its money when it needs it, in full, freely and promptly, is the most important consideration, and no proposal that does not provide for that end should be considered for a moment.

But with safety and instantaneous availability secured, there are some secondary advantages at which every government should aim in its system of keeping the public funds. The most important of these is, that the receipts of the Government shall not be locked away from use in the trade of the country. A second is that the system shall be elastic enough to conform to changes in the fiscal policy of the Government. For example, it must be able to prevent the evils that must follow from surplus financiering, and be ready to furnish the means necessary for the Government to carry on its operations through periods of deficits.

Again, whatever system prevails, any profits that come from the use of the money of the Government on deposit should accrue, in part at least, to the Government. The method which prevailed for some years, of depositing the money of the people in banks without interest, was merely a means of permitting private interests to profit at the expense of the people.

CLASSIFICATION OF PROPOSALS.

All the proposals that have been made for the replacement of the independent treasury may be roughly classified as follows:

1. Enlarge the present national bank depositary system by putting the receipts of the Government immediately into the banks when collected, without a deposit of bonds as security, the banks to pay a reasonable rate of interest to the Government on its balances, and the government officers to check against accounts like other depositors. Deposit in banks throughout the country, as now; or only in reserve city banks.

2. Modify the first proposal by dividing the country into clearing-house or bank depositary districts. Establish a clearing house for each district, and enlarge the functions of the clearing house so as to make it the agent for all the banks of the district, with which the government officers may deal directly. Under this system all government moneys will be deposited with the clearing house or district bank, which will be responsible to the Government, and it may redeposit with the banks of its district under arrangements to be provided.

3. Establish a central bank independent of the Government and of existing banks, which shall be the depositary and fiscal agent of the Government.

4. Establish a federated bank to include all national banks. This, of course, is a form of central bank. Instead of being independent of the existing banks, it would be a federation of them.

5. Make the Treasury itself a government bank by enlarging its present banking functions and giving the Secretary a staff of expert business and banking advisers.

Chapter XIV.—Summary.

(A) as to history.

Our study of the history and effects of the methods by which the United States Government has kept the public money may be briefly summarized as follows:

1. The policy of the Government has been changeable. In the first few years after the adoption of the Constitution, before the subject attracted serious public attention, there were no specific places for the custody of the public money, and it was left largely in the hands of collecting and disbursing officers.

2. During the existence of the first and second United States Banks, that is from 1796 to 1811, and from 1816 to 1833, the date of the "removal of the deposits," the public money was kept mainly in these institutions and their branches. Nevertheless, even during these periods some state banks were employed.

3. In the interim between the closing of the first United States Bank and the opening of the second, the public money was kept mainly in the state-chartered banks. These banks were also used after the Government ceased to employ the second United States Bank in 1833, and also after the expiration of the charter of that bank until the establishment of the independent treasury in 1846.

4. Beginning with 1847, immediately after the establishment of the independent treasury, the public money was kept in the Treasury and subtreasuries, and no banks were used until after the establishment of the present

national banking system, in 1863. Since that time the depositary banks have supplemented the use of the subtreasuries as places for the keeping of the public money.

5. In the past one hundred and twenty years, therefore, there are only seventeen, 1847–1864, in which the Government did not use depositary banks for keeping the public money.

6. The evidence therefore shows that there has been, uniformly, a strong tendency for the Government, throughout its history, to use banks.

7. The causes of this tendency are shown to have been the greater convenience in the management of the public money, the desire of the Secretary and the public that government fiscal operations should interfere as little as possible with the monetary circulation and with business conditions, the necessities of the Government and pressure from banking and other interests.

8. Under the influence and pressure described, first the Secretary of the Treasury, and later Congress, have given way, and virtually abandoned the policy of independence in the keeping and management of public money which was established by the act of August, 1846. Congress authorized the use of national banks in which to deposit receipts from internal revenue. With some vacillations, the extent of the use of the banks as depositaries for these receipts has steadily increased. By recent legislation receipts from customs may also be deposited in the banks. Under the first interpretation of the law permitting these deposits, they could accrue only as the collecting officers placed the money received by them in the banks and not

from the transfer of government receipts once deposited in the treasuries. By later practice the latter method of deposit has also been adopted and is claimed by some to be legal. Under present practice and legislation, therefore, the Secretary of the Treasury has a free hand to put any and all receipts of public money in the depositary banks. The independence of the Treasury depends entirely upon the will of the Secretary.

9. A further departure from the policy of independence is shown by the course of opinion and legislation concerning security for deposits. Under the law as passed, public deposits were to be secured by United States bonds and otherwise. This was understood to mean United States bonds in addition to a personal bond. Eight years ago the phrase was differently interpreted, and banks were permitted to secure deposits on the basis of other than United States bonds as security. The practice thus established was legalized between two and three years ago.

10. At first the banks which obtained public money on deposit were expected to keep a reserve against it, as provided by the law of their being. Some seven or eight years ago this practice was broken and the banks allowed to hold public deposits without protecting them by a reserve. The practice thus initiated was also later made legal.

11. Finally, with all these changes, the amount of public money deposited with the banks has steadily increased, until at one time in recent years, only a comparatively small working balance was kept in hand by the Treasury itself.

(B) AS TO OPERATION AND INFLUENCE.

Our study of the operation of the independent treasury during the period of its independence, that is, during the period of the smallest use of depositary banks since 1864, has led us to the following conclusions:

1. The subtreasury system disturbs the money market in ordinary times by its irregular intake and output of money.

2. If the intake happens to occur on a rising speculative market it may do some good by restricting speculation.

3. If the intake happens to occur at a time when business operations call for an easier market, the influence is likely to be harmful.

4. Corresponding results flow from the relative times of occurrence of the output.

5. These results occur when government receipts and expenditures are approximately equal. Their influences are intensified at times when government receipts for considerable periods exceed expenditures.

6. On the whole, the evil done by the independence of the Treasury, both in ordinary times and in times of surplus financiering, exceeds the good.

7. In times of crises, or panic, the independent treasury may aid the money market by depositing a surplus revenue in the banks and thus restoring the money to circulation; by prepaying interest on the public debt when business needs a larger volume of currency, by "timing" interest, pension, and other payments; and by buying bonds.

8. All of these methods do restore to circulation the money collected in taxes. The first method is open to the objection that pressure from the banks for a general distribution may defeat the purpose of the deposits, by preventing them from being made in sufficient measure where they are most needed. The charge of favoritism has also been made in the selection of banks. If such deposits are to be made, there is no good reason for requiring security; and there is also no good reason for not insisting that the banks shall take such precaution in the way of maintaining a proper reserve against these deposits as they do in the case of other deposits. Moreover, if deposits are to be made in banks, the Secretary of the Treasury should be allowed to check against them instead of being compelled to use the present compressed method of withdrawal.

9. The prepayment of interest and the "timing" of other payments are too trivial to be worthy of a great government. Resort to such practices should not be necessary. Moreover, the proper time for the Government, like any other debtor, to pay interest is when it is due.

10. Attempts made to relieve the money market by buying bonds are open to the objection that there is a loss involved in prepaying the debt. The Government should not have a revenue larger than it needs. Apparent saving of interest is at the expense of the productive employment of capital by individuals and corporations.

11. All the modes of relieving the money market are open to the three general objections that the process puts too great power in the hands of the Secretary; that how-

ever well he discharges his responsibility, he is likely to make mistakes which will make the situation worse; and that any such interference must be, from its nature, arbitrary.

12. Objections may be made against the independent treasury in the fiscal operations of the Government in time of war. Although by means of the system the Treasury succeeded in placing its loans during the Mexican war, it failed to do so in the civil war. It also failed during the time following 1890, although this was not a period of war. It succeeded, in a way, in placing the Spanish war loan directly, but ventured to make the experiment only after securing the assurance of the banks that they would sustain it. In all important loan negotiations in the past fifty years the Treasury has been obliged, in one way or another, to rely upon the banks for aid.

13. The main advantage claimed for the direct placing of loans by the independent treasury is that the loans are more widely distributed or more popular. Experience shows that this is not the case. Even though the loan be widely distributed at first, the securities soon become concentrated in the hands of a few holders, principally the banks. There is reason to think, too, that in time of war a loan can be placed at less expense through banks and banking syndicates.

ADVANTAGES OF THE INDEPENDENT TREASURY.

1. The money may be regarded as absolutely safe. Experience shows, however, that defalcations and thefts may occur under the system.

2. The system has had the support of popular opinion. This support arises from the fact that the system worked well for some time after it was established, thus forming a striking contrast with the evil operation of the state bank depositaries. Moreoever, there is a popular distrust of banks, especially large ones.

3. The absorptions and disbursements of money by the Government do good when they happen to coincide with the needs of the money market.

PROPOSALS FOR REPLACEMENT.

1. The deposit of all government receipts in the national banks at the places of collection, the Secretary to check against these deposits as he needs the money. Whether this would remove the evils of the irregular action of the subtreasury system would depend mainly upon the way in which the banks were managed. Unless they assumed the responsibility of making proper provision for the seasonal demands for money, no great advantage would be gained. Moreover their exclusive use would not altogether do away with alternate pressure and relaxation in the money market due to the government operations. For the Government must collect its revenue and make its payments. At times when its income is heavy, its deposits would be heavy and cause great temporary withdrawals of money from circulation. The condition of the London money market in the latter part of April, 1910, illustrates this. There was unsteadiness in the market in anticipation of the withdrawal of a large amount of money to pay the income tax. "Nearly $120,000,000 were due on this

account. The money will go into the Bank of England, of course, but it can not be let out excepting in the ordinary course of business. These large payments will occasion a large sale of securities with a depreciation of their price."[a]

2. The bank district, or clearing-house district, system. This has the advantage of not being too centralized and, therefore, possibly less objectionable to the public. It amounts virtually to a central cooperative banking association, the controlling board being the representatives of the clearing-house districts elected by the banks of the districts. The autonomy of the individual banks would not be interfered with, nor would it be necessary to interfere with the issue of notes by the individual banks.

3. An independent central bank, located in the country's money center.

4. A federated bank or a bank of banks.

---

[a] Daily paper.

APPENDICES.

I.

REFERENCES.

ADAMS, H. C.: Public Debts. New York, 1887.

AMERICAN STATE PAPERS: Finance.

ANDREW, A. PIATT: The Partial Responsibility of Secretaries Gage and Shaw for the crisis of 1907. Bankers' Mag., 76 : 493.

————: The United States Treasury and the Money Market. Publ. Amer. Econ. Assoc., 3d ser. 9 : 1 : 218.

————: The Treasury and the Banks under Secretary Shaw. Quarterly Journal of Economics, 21 : 519–568.

BANCROFT, GEORGE: Literary and Historical Miscellanies.

BANKERS' MAGAZINE. New York.

BANKERS' ASSOCIATION, Proceedings of American. New York.

BENTON, THOS. H.: Abridgment of Debates of Congress from 1789 to 1856. 16 v. New York, 1857–1861.

————: Thirty Years' View; or A History of the Working of the American Government for Thirty Years, from 1820 to 1850. New York, 1854–1856.

BOLLES, A. S.: Financial History of the United States. 2d ed. New York, 1884–1886.

BOURNE, E. G.: History of the Surplus Revenue of 1837. New York, 1885.

BRADSTREET'S. New York.

BURGESS, JOHN W.: The Middle Period, 1817–1858. New York, 1897.

CALHOUN, JOHN C.: Works of, ed. by R. K. Crallé, Columbia, S. C. and New York, 1853–1857.

CATTERAL, R. C. H.: The Second Bank of the United States. Chicago, 1903.

CLAY, HENRY: Works of; ed. by Calvin Colton, 7 v. New York, 1897.

CLEVELAND, F. A.: The Bank and the Treasury. New York, 1905.

COLTON, C. C.: Public Economy for the United States. New York, 1853.

CONANT, C. A.: A History of Modern Banks of Issue. New York, 1897.

COMMERCIAL AND FINANCIAL CHRONICLE. New York.

DEMOCRATIC REVIEW, XVII. New York.

DEWEY, D. R.: The Financial History of the United States. New York, 3d ed., 1907.

DUANE, W. J.: Narrative and Correspondence concerning the Removal of the Deposits and Occurrences connected therewith. Philadelphia, 1838.

DUNBAR, C. F.: Laws of the United States relating to Currency, Finance, and Banking from 1789 to 1891. Boston, 1891.

————: Chapters on the Theory and History of Banking. 2d ed. New York, 1904.

DUNN'S WEEKLY REVIEW. New York.

AEGIS, THE. Students' Paper, University of Wisconsin. Report of Debate on Independent Treasury. March 8, 1895.

FERRIS, J. A.: Financial Economy of the United States. San Francisco, New York, 1867.

FORUM, THE. New York.

GALLATIN, ALBERT: Writings of; ed. by Henry Adams, Philadelphia, 1879.

GAUSS, H. C.: The American Government. New York, 1908.

GIBBONS, J. S.: Public Debt of the United States. New York, 1867.

GILBART, J. W.: History of Banking in America. - London, 1837.

GILLETT, R. H.: Life and Times of Silas Wright. Albany, 1874.

GOUGE, W. M.: An Inquiry into the Expediency of Dispensing with Bank Agency and with Bank Paper in the Fiscal Concerns of the United States. Philadelphia, 1837.

GOVERNMENT PUBLICATIONS: Executive Documents; House and Senate Documents and Reports; Finance Reports; Congressional Record, etc.

GROSVENOR, W. M.: American Securities. New York, 1885.

HAMILTON, ALEXANDER, WORKS OF: Ed. by J. C. Hamilton, New York, 1850–51. Also ed. by Henry Cabot Lodge, 9 v., New York, 1885–86.

HAMMOND, J. D.: Life and Times of Silas Wright. Syracuse, 1852.

HARPER'S MAGAZINE, New York, xliv. 481.

HOCK, CARL F. VON: Die Finanzen der Vereinigten Staaten, Stuttgart, 1867.

HOLST, H. VON: Constitutional History of the United States. Chicago, 1877–1892.

HUNT'S MERCHANT'S MAGAZINE. New York.

INDEPENDENT, THE. New York, 1872–3.

JUGLAR, C.: A Brief History of Panics in the United States. Ed. by DeC. W. Thomas. New York, 1893.

KINLEY, DAVID: The Independent Treasury of the United States. New York, 1893.

————: The Relation of the United States Treasury to the Money Market. Publ. Amer. Econ. Assoc., 3d ser. 9:1:199.

KNOX, J. J.: United States Notes. 3d ed. New York, 1894.

LALOR, J. J.: Cyclopedia of Political Science, etc. Chicago, 1882–1884.

LAMPHERE, G. N.: United States Government. Philadelphia, 1880.

LAUCK, W. J.: Causes of the Panic of 1893. New York, 1907.

LAUGHLIN, J. LAURENCE: See North American Review as quoted.

LIPPINCOTT'S MAGAZINE. Philadelphia, December, 1873.

LODGE, H. C.: Life of Daniel Webster. Boston, 1883 and 1899.

MACKENZIE, W. L.: Life and Times of Martin Van Buren. Boston, 1846.

MUHLEMAN, M. A.: Monetary and Banking Systems. New York, 1908.

NILES, HEZEKIAH: Weekly Register, 1811–1848.

NORTH AMERICAN REVIEW. New York, 137: 552–564.

NOYES, A. D.: Forty Years of American Finance, New York. 1909.

PENN MONTHLY MAGAZINE. Philadelphia, July, 1882.

PHILLIPS, J. B.: Methods of Keeping the Public Money of the United States. Publ. Mich. Pol. Sci. Assoc. 4: 3.

PRATT, A. S. & SONS: Digest of the National Bank Act. Washington, 1870.

———: Pratts' Digest. Washington, 1908.

RAGUET, CONDY: A Treatise on Currency and Banking. Philadelphia, 1839.

RHODES JOURNAL OF BANKING. (Now combined with Bankers' Magazine.)

RICHARDSON, H. W.: The National Banks. New York, 1880.

SARGENT, NATHAN: Public Men and Events. Philadelphia, 1875.

SCHURZ, CARL: The Life of Henry Clay. Boston, 1887.

SHEPARD, E. M.: Martin Van Buren. Boston, 1888.

STORY, JOSEPH: Commentaries on the Constitution. Boston, 1873.

SUMNER, W. G.: Andrew Jackson. 11th ed. New York, 1888.

———: History of American Currency. New York, 1876.

———: History of Banking in the United States. New York, 1896.

TAUSSIG, F. W.: The Tariff History of the United States. 4th ed. New York, 1898.

———: The Silver Situation in the United States. Am. Econ. Assoc. Public. 7: 1. New York, 1893.

UPTON, J. K.: Money in Politics. Boston, 1884.

UNITED STATES SUPREME COURT REPORTS.

WALKER, FRANCIS A.: Political Economy. New York, 1883.

———: Money, Trade, and Industry. New York, 1889.

WALKER, J. H.: Money, Trade, and Banking. Boston, 1894.

WEBSTER, DANIEL: Writings and Speeches. Boston, 1903.

WIRTH, M. W. G.: Geschichte der Handelskrisen. Frankfurt, 1890.

WORLD'S CONGRESS OF BANKERS AND FINANCIERS. Chicago, 1893.

YOUNG, A. W.: American Statesman. 1856. New ed. 1888.

Subtreasury Law and Amendments.

AN ACT To provide for the better organization of the Treasury, and for the collection, safe-keeping, transfer, and disbursement of the public revenue.

Whereas by the fourth section of the act entitled "An act to establish the Treasury Department," approved September second, seventeen hundred and eighty-nine, it was provided that it should be the duty of the Treasurer to receive and keep the moneys of the United States, and to disburse the same upon warrants drawn by the Secretary of the Treasury, countersigned by the Comptroller, and recorded by the Register, and not otherwise; and whereas it is found necessary to make further provisions to enable the Treasurer the better to carry into effect the intent of the said section in relation to the receiving and disbursing the moneys of the United States. Therefore:

SECTION 1. *Be it enacted by the Senate and House of Representatives of the United States of America in Congress assembled,* That the rooms prepared and provided in the new Treasury building at the seat of government for the use of the Treasurer of the United States, his assistants and clerks, and occupied by them, and also the fireproof vaults and safes erected in said rooms for the keeping of the public moneys in the possession and under the immediate control of said Treasurer, and such other apartments as are provided for by this act as places of deposit of the public money, are hereby constituted, and declared to be, the Treasury of the United States. And all moneys paid into the same shall be subject to the draft of the Treasurer, drawn agreeably to appropriations made by law.

SEC. 2. *And be it further enacted*, That the mint of the United States, in the city of Philadelphia, in the State of Pennsylvania, and the branch mint in the city of New Orleans, in the State of Louisiana, and the vaults and safes thereof, respectively, shall be places of deposit and safe-keeping of the public moneys at these points respectively; and the treasurers of the said mint and branch mint, respectively, for the time being, shall be assistant treasurers under the provisions of this act, and shall have the custody and care of all public moneys deposited within the same, and shall perform all the duties required to be performed by them in reference to the receipt, safe-keeping, transfer, and disbursement of all such moneys, according to the provisions hereinafter contained.

SEC. 3. *And be it further enacted*, That the rooms which were directed to be prepared and provided within the custom-houses in the city of New York, in the State of New York, and in the city of Boston, in the State of Massachusetts, for the use of receivers-general of public moneys, under the provisions of the act entitled "An act to provide for the collection, safe-keeping, transfer, and disbursement of the public revenue," approved July fourth, eighteen hundred and forty, shall be for the use of the assistant treasurers hereinafter directed to be appointed at those places, respectively; as shall be also the fireproof vaults and safes prepared and provided within said rooms for the keeping of the public moneys collected and deposited with them, respectively; and the assistant treasurers from time to time appointed at those points, shall have the custody and care of the said rooms, vaults, and safes, respectively, and of all the public moneys deposited within the same, and shall perform all the duties required to be performed by them in reference to the receipt, safe-keeping, transfer, and disbursement of all such moneys, according to the provisions of this act.

SEC. 4. *And be it further enacted,* That the officers, with suitable and convenient rooms, which were directed to be erected, prepared, and provided for the use of receivers-general of public money, at the expense of the United States, at the city of Charleston, in the State of South Carolina, and at the city of St. Louis, in the State of Missouri, under the act entitled "An act to provide for the collection, safe-keeping, transfer, and disbursement of the public revenue," approved July fourth, eighteen hundred and forty, shall be for the use of the assistant treasurers hereinafter directed to be appointed at the places above named; as shall be also the fireproof vaults and safes erected within the said offices and rooms for the keeping of the public money collected and deposited at those points, respectively; and the said assistant treasurers from time to time appointed at those places shall have the custody and care of the said offices, vaults, and safes, erected, prepared, and provided as aforesaid, and of all the public moneys deposited within the same, and shall perform all the duties required to be performed by them in reference to the receipt, safe-keeping, transfer, and disbursement of all such moneys, according to the provisions hereinafter contained.

SEC. 5. *And be it further enacted,* That the President shall nominate, and, by and with the advice and consent of the Senate, appoint four officers, to be denominated "assistant treasurers of the United States," which said officers shall hold their respective offices for the term of four years, unless sooner removed therefrom; one of which shall be located at the city of New York, in the State of New York; one other of which shall be located at the city of Boston, in the State of Massachusetts; one other of which shall be located at the city of Charleston, in the State of South Carolina; and one other at St. Louis, in the State of Missouri; and all of which said officers shall give bonds to the United States, with security according to the provisions hereinafter contained, for the faithful discharge of the duties of their respective offices.

SEC. 6. *And be it further enacted,* That the Treasurer of the United States, the treasurer of the mint of the United States, the treasurers, and those acting as such, of the various branch mints, all collectors of the customs, all surveyors of the customs acting also as collectors, all assistant treasurers, all receivers of public moneys at the several land offices, all postmasters, and all public officers of whatsoever character be, and they are hereby, required to keep safely, without loaning, using, depositing in banks, or exchanging for other funds than as allowed by this act, all the public money collected by them, or otherwise at any time placed in their possession and custody, till the same is ordered by the proper department or officer of the Government to be transferred or paid out; and when such orders for transfer or payment are received, faithfully and promptly to make the same as directed, and to do and perform all other duties as fiscal agents of the Government which may be imposed by this or any other acts of Congress, or by any regulation of the Treasury Department made in conformity to law; and, also, to do and perform all acts and duties required by law, or by direction of any of the Executive Departments of the Government, as agents for paying pensions, or for making any other disbursements which either of the heads of those departments may be required by law to make, and which are of a character to be made by the depositaries hereby constituted, consistently with the official duties imposed upon them.

SEC. 7. *And be it further enacted*, That the Treasurer of the United States, the treasurer of the mint of the United States, the treasurer of the branch mint at New Orleans, and all the assistant treasurers hereinbefore directed to be appointed, shall respectively give bonds to the United States faithfully to discharge the duties of their respective offices according to law and for such amounts as shall be directed by the Secretary of the Treasury, with sureties to the satisfaction of the Solicitor of the Treasury; and shall, from time to time, renew, strengthen, and increase their official bonds, as the Secretary of the Treasury may direct, any law in reference to any of the official bonds of any of the said officers to the contrary notwithstanding.

SEC. 8. *And be it further enacted*, That it shall be the duty of the Secretary of the Treasury, at as early a date as possible after the passage of this act, to require the several depositaries hereby constituted, and whose official bonds are not hereinbefore provided for, to execute bonds, new and suitable in their terms, to meet the new and increased duties imposed upon them, respectively, by this act, and with sureties and in sums such as shall seem reasonable and safe to the Solicitor of the Treasury; and, from time to time, to require such bonds to be renewed and increased in amount, and strengthened by new sureties, to meet any increasing responsibility which may grow out of accumulations of money in the hands of the depositary, or out of any other duty or responsibility arising under this or any other law of Congress.

SEC. 9. *And be it further enacted,* That all collectors and receivers of public money, of every character and description, within the District of Columbia, shall, as frequently as they may be directed by the Secretary of the Treasury or the Postmaster-General so to do, pay over to the Treasurer of the United States, at the Treasury, all the public moneys collected by them or in their hands; that all such collectors and receivers of public moneys within the cities of Philadelphia and New Orleans shall, upon the same direction, pay over to the treasurers of the mints in their respective cities, at the said mints, all public moneys collected by them or in their hands; and that all such collectors and receivers of public moneys within the cities of New York, Boston, Charleston, and St. Louis shall, upon the same direction, pay over to the assistant treasurers in their respective cities, at their offices, respectively, all the public moneys collected by them or in their hands, to be safely kept by the said respective depositaries until otherwise disposed of according to law; and it shall be the duty of said Secretary and Postmaster-General, respectively, to direct such payments by the said collectors and receivers at all the said places at least as often as once in each week, and as much more frequently, and in all cases, as they in their discretion may think proper.

SEC. 10. *And be it further enacted,* That it shall be lawful for the Secretary of the Treasury to transfer the moneys in the hands of any depositary hereby constituted to the Treasury of the United States, to be there safely kept, to the credit of the Treasurer of the United States, according to the provisions of this act, to any other depositary constituted by the same, at his discretion, and as the safety of the public moneys and the convenience of the public service shall seem to him to require; which authority to transfer the moneys belonging to the Post-Office Department is also hereby conferred upon the Postmaster-General so far as its exercise by him may be consistent with the provisions of existing laws, and every depositary constituted by this act shall keep his account of the money paid to or deposited with him, belonging to the Post-Office Department, separate and distinct from the account kept by him of other public moneys so paid or deposited. And for the purpose of payments on the public account, it shall be lawful for the Treasurer of the United States to draw upon any of the said depositaries, as he may think most conducive to the public interests, or the convenience of the public creditors, or both; and each depositary so drawn upon shall make returns to the Treasury and Post-Office Department of all moneys received and paid by him at such times and in such form as shall be directed by the Secretary of the Treasury or the Postmaster-General.

SEC. 11. *And be it further enacted*, That the Secretary of the Treasury shall be, and he is hereby, authorized to cause examinations to be made of the books, accounts, and money on hand of the several depositaries constituted by this act; and for that purpose to appoint special agents, as occasion may require, with such compensation, not exceeding six dollars per day and traveling expenses, as he may think reasonable, to be fixed and declared at the time of each appointment. The agents selected to make these examinations shall be instructed to examine as well the books, accounts, and returns of the officer, as the money on hand, and the manner of its being kept, to the end that uniformity and accuracy in the accounts, as well as safety to the public moneys, may be secured thereby.

SEC. 12. *And be it further enacted*, That in addition to the examinations provided for in the last preceding section, and as a further guard over the public moneys, it shall be the duty of each naval officer and surveyor, as a check upon the assistant treasurers, or the collectors of the customs, of their respective districts; of each register of a land office, as a check upon the receiver of his land office; and of the director and superintendent of each mint and branch mint, when separate officers, as a check upon the treasurers, respectively, of the said mints, or the persons acting as such, at the close of each quarter of the year, and as much more frequently as they shall be directed by the Secretary of the Treasury to do so; to examine the books, accounts, returns, and money on hand of the assistant treasurers, collectors, receivers of land offices, treasurers of the mint, and each branch mint, and persons acting as such; and to make a full, accurate, and faithful return to the Treasury Department of their condition.

SEC. 13. *And be it further enacted*, That the said officers, respectively, whose duty it is made by this act to receive, keep, and disburse the public moneys, as the fiscal agents of the Government, may be allowed any necessary additional expense for clerks, fireproof chests or vaults, or other necessary expenses of safe-keeping, transferring, and disbursing said moneys; all such expense of every character to be first expressly authorized by the Secretary of the

Treasury, whose directions upon all the above subjects, by way of regulation and otherwise, so far as authorized by law, are to be strictly followed by all the said officers: *Provided*, That the whole number of clerks to be appointed by virtue of this section of this act shall not exceed ten; and that the aggregate compensations of the whole number shall not exceed eight thousand dollars; nor shall the compensation of any one clerk so appointed exceed eight hundred dollars per annum.

SEC. 14. *And be it further enacted*, That the Secretary of the Treasury may, at his discretion, transfer the balances remaining with any of the present depositaries, to any other of the present depositaries, as he may deem the safety of the public money or the public convenience may require· *Provided*, That nothing in this act shall be so construed as to authorize the Secretary of the Treasury to transfer the balances remaining with any of the present depositaries to the depositaries constituted by this act before the first day of January next: *And provided*, That for the purpose of payments on public account, out of balances remaining with the present depositaries, it shall be lawful for the Treasurer of the United States to draw upon any of the said depositaries, as he may think most conducive to the public interests, or to the convenience of public creditors, or both.

SEC. 15. *And be it further enacted*, That all marshals, district attorneys, and others having public money to pay to the United States, and all patentees wishing to make payment for patents to be issued, may pay all such moneys to the Treasurer of the United States, to the treasurer of either of the mints in Philadelphia or New Orleans, to either of the other assistant treasurers, or to such other depositary constituted by this act as shall be designated by the Secretary of the Treasury in other parts of the United States, to receive such payments and give receipts or certificates of deposit therefor.

Sec. 16. *And be it further enacted*, That all officers and other persons charged by this act, or any other act, with the safe-keeping, transfer, and disbursement of the public moneys, other than those connected with the Post-Office Department, are hereby required to keep an accurate entry of each sum received, and each payment or transfer; and that if any one of the said officers or those connected with the Post-Office Department shall convert to his own use in any way whatever, or shall use, by way of invest-ment in any kind of property or merchandise, or shall loan, with or without interest, or shall deposit in any bank, or shall exchange for other funds except as allowed by this act, any portion of the public moneys intrusted to him for safe-keeping, disbursement, transfer, or for any other pur-pose, every such act shall be deemed and adjudged to be an embezzlement of so much of the said moneys as shall be thus taken, converted, invested, used, loaned, depos-ited, or exchanged, which is hereby declared to be a felony; and any failure to pay over or to produce the public moneys intrusted to such person shall be held and taken to be prima facie evidence of such embezzlement, and if any officer charged with the disbursements of public money shall accept or receive, or transmit to the Treasury Depart-ment to be allowed in his favor, any receipt or voucher from a creditor of the United States without having paid to such creditor in such funds as the said officer may have received for disbursement, or such funds as he may be authorized by this act to take in exchange, the full amount specified in this receipt or voucher, every such act shall be deemed to be a conversion by such officer to his own use of the amount specified in such receipt or voucher; and any officer or agent of the United States, and all persons advising or participating in such act, being convicted thereof before any court of the United States of competent jurisdiction, shall be sentenced to imprisonment for a term of not less than six months nor more than ten years, and to a fine equal to the amount of the money embezzled. And upon the trial of any indictment against any person for embezzling public money under the provisions of this act, it shall be sufficient evidence, for the purpose of showing a balance against such person, to produce a transcript from the books and proceedings of the Treasury, as required in civil cases, under provisions of the act entitled "An act to provide more effectually for the settlement of accounts between the United States and receivers of public money," approved March third, seventeen hundred and ninety-seven; and the provisions of this act shall be so construed as to apply to all persons charged with the safe-keeping, transfer, or disbursement of the public money, whether such persons be indicted as receivers or depositaries of the same; and the refusal of such person, whether in or out of office, to pay any draft, order, or warrant, which may be drawn upon him by the proper officer of the Treasury Department, for any public money in his hands belonging to the United States, no matter in what capacity the same may have been received or may be held, or to transfer or disburse any such money promptly, upon the legal requirement of any authorized officer of the United States, shall be deemed and taken, upon the trial of any indictment against such person for embezzlement, as prima facie evidence of such embezzlement

SEC. 17. *And be it further enacted,* That until the rooms, offices, vaults, and safes, directed by the first four sections of this act to be constructed and prepared for the use of the Treasurer of the United States, the treasurers of the mints at Philadelphia and New Orleans, and the assistant treasurers at New York, Boston, Charleston, and St. Louis, can be constructed and prepared for use, it shall be the duty of the Secretary of the Treasury to procure suitable rooms for offices for those officers at their respective locations, and to contract for such use of vaults and safes as may be required for the safe-keeping of the public moneys in the charge and custody of those officers, respectively, the expenses to be paid by the United States.

And whereas by the thirteenth section of the act entitled, "An act to regulate the collection of duties imposed by law on the tonnage of ships or vessels, and on goods, wares, and merchandises imported into the United States," approved July thirty-one, seventeen hundred and eighty-nine, it was provided that all fees and dues collected by virtue of that act should be received in gold and silver coin only; and whereas, also, by the fifth section of the act approved May ten, eighteen hundred, entitled, "An act to amend the act entitled, 'An act providing for the sale of the lands of the United States in the territory northwest of the Ohio and above the mouth of Kentucky River,'" it was provided that payment for the said lands shall be made by all purchasers in specie, or in evidences of the public debt; and whereas experience has proved that said provisions ought to be revived and enforced, according to the true and wise intent of the Constitution of the United States:

SEC. 18. *Be it further enacted,* That on the first day of January, in the year one thousand eight hundred and forty-seven, and thereafter, all duties, taxes, sales of public lands, debts, and sums of money accruing or becoming due to the United States, and also all sums due for postages, or otherwise, to the General Post-Office Department, shall be paid in gold and silver coin only, or in treasury notes issued under the authority of the United States: *Provided,* That the Secretary of the Treasury shall publish monthly, in two newspapers at the city of Washington, the amount of specie at the several places of deposit, the amount of treasury notes or drafts issued, and the amount outstanding on the last day of each month.

SEC. 19. *And be it further enacted,* That on the first day of April, one thousand eight hundred and forty-seven, and thereafter, every officer or agent engaged in making disbursements on account of the United States, or of the General Post-Office, shall make all payments in gold and silver coin or in treasury notes, if the creditor agree to receive said notes in payment; and any receiving or disbursing officer or agent who shall neglect, evade, or violate, the provisions of this and the last preceding section of this act, shall, by the Secretary of the Treasury, be immediately reported to the President of the United States, with the facts of such neglect, evasion, or violation; and also to Congress, if in session, and if not in session, at the commencement of its session next after the violation takes place.

SEC. 20. *And be it further enacted,* That no exchange of funds shall be made by any disbursing officers or agents of the Government, of any grade or denomination whatsoever, or connected with any branch of the public service, other than an exchange for gold and silver; and every such disbursing officer, when the means for his disbursements are furnished to him in gold and silver, shall make his payments in the money so furnished; or when those means are furnished to him in drafts, shall cause those drafts to be presented at their place of payment, and properly paid, according to the law; and shall make his payments in the money so received for the drafts furnished, unless, in either case, he can exchange the means in his hands for gold and silver at par. And it shall be, and is hereby, made the duty of the head of the proper department immediately to suspend from duty any disbursing officer who shall violate the provisions of this section, and forthwith to report the name of the officer or agent to the President, with the fact of the violation, and all the circumstances accompanying the same and within the knowledge of the said Secretary, to the end that such officer or agent may be promptly removed from office or restored to his trust and the performance of his duties, as to the President may seem just and proper: *Provided, however,* That those disbursing officers having at present credits in the banks, shall, until the first day of January next, be allowed to check on the same, allowing the public creditors to receive their pay from the banks either in specie or bank notes.

SEC. 21. *And be it further enacted,* That it shall be the duty of the Secretary of the Treasury to issue and publish regulations to enforce the speedy presentation of all government drafts for payment at the place where payable, and to prescribe the time, according to the different distances of the depositaries from the seat of Government, within which all drafts upon them, respectively, shall be presented for payment; and in default of such presentation, to direct any other mode and place of payment which he may deem proper; but in all these regulations and directions it shall be the duty of the Secretary of the Treasury, to guard as far as may be, against those drafts being used or thrown into circulation as a paper currency, or medium of exchange. And no officer of the United States shall, either directly or indirectly, sell or dispose to any person or persons, or corporations, whatsoever, for a premium, any treasury note, draft, warrant, or other public security, not his private property, or sell or dispose of the avails or proceeds of such note, draft, warrant, or security, in his hands for disbursement, without making return of such premium, and accounting therefor by charging the same in his accounts to the credit of the United States; and any officer violating this section shall be forthwith dismissed from office.

SEC. 22. *And be it further enacted,* That the assistant treasurers directed by this act to be appointed shall receive, respectively, the following salaries per annum, to be paid quarter-yearly at the Treasury of the United States, to wit: The assistant treasurer at New York shall be paid a salary of four thousand dollars per annum; the assistant treasurer at Boston shall be paid a salary of two thousand five hundred dollars per annum; the assistant treasurer at Charleston shall be paid a salary of two thousand five hundred dollars per annum; the assistant treasurer at St. Louis shall be paid a salary of two thousand five hundred dollars per annum; the treasurer of the mint at Philadelphia shall, in addition to his present salary, receive five hundred dollars annually for the performance of the duties imposed by this act; the treasurer of the branch mint at New Orleans shall also receive five hundred dollars annually for the additional duties created by this act; and these salaries, respectively, shall be in full for the services of the respective officers, nor shall either of them be permitted to charge or receive any commission, pay, or perquisite for any official service of any character or description whatsoever; and the making of any such charge, or the receipt of any such compensation, is hereby declared to be a misdemeanor, for which the officer, convicted thereof before any court of the United States of competent jurisdiction, shall be subject to punishment by fine or imprisonment, or both, at the discretion of the court before which the offense shall be tried.

SEC. 23. *And be it further enacted*, That there shall be, and hereby is, appropriated, to be paid out of any money in the Treasury not otherwise appropriated, the sum of five thousand dollars, to be expended, under the direction of the Secretary of the Treasury, in such repairs or additions as may be necessary to put in good condition for use, with as little delay as may be consistent with the public interests, the offices, rooms, vaults, and safes herein mentioned, and in the purchase of any necessary additional furniture and fixtures, in the purchase of necessary books and stationery, and in defraying any other incidental expenses necessary to carry this act into effect.

SEC. 24. *And be it further enacted*, That all acts or parts of acts which come in conflict with the provisions of this act be, and the same are hereby, repealed.

Approved, August 6, 1846.

AMENDMENTS TO SUBTREASURY ACT.

(March 3, 1857.)

SECTION 1. *Be it enacted, etc.*, That the act to provide for the better organization of the Treasury, and for the collection, safe-keeping, transfer, and disbursement of the public revenu approved August sixth, eighteen hundred and forty-six, be, and the same is hereby so amended that each and every disbursing officer or agent of the United States, having any money of the United States intrusted to him for disbursement, shall be, and he is hereby required to deposit the same with the Treasurer of the United States, or with some one of the assistant treasurers or public depositaries, and draw for the same only in favor of the persons to whom payment is to be made in pursuance of law and instructions; except when payments are to be made in sums under twenty dollars, in which cases such disbursing agent may check in his own name, stating that it is to pay small claims.

SEC. 2. *And be it further enacted*, That the Treasurer of the United States, assistant treasurers, and public depositaries shall safely keep all moneys deposited by any disbursing officer or disbursing agent of the United States, as well as any moneys deposited by any receiver, collector, or other person which shall be the moneys of, or due, or owing to the United States, and for a failure so to do shall be held guilty of the crime of embezzlement of said moneys, and subject to the punishment provided for embezzlement in the act to which this is an amendment.

SEC. 3. *And be it further enacted,* That it shall be the duty of each and every person who shall have moneys of the United States in his hands or possession to pay the same to the Treasurer, the assistant treasurer, or a public depositary of the United States, and take his receipt for the same, in duplicate, and forward one of them forthwith to the Secretary of the Treasury, and for a failure to make such deposit, when required by the Secretary of the Treasury, or any other department, or the accounting officers of the Treasury, the person so failing shall be held guilty of the crime of embezzlement, and subject to the punishment for that offense provided in the act to which this is an amendment.

DEPOSITARIES.

(Section 3211 of the Revised Statutes.)

The Secretary of the Treasury is authorized to designate one or more depositaries in each State for the deposit and safe-keeping of the money collected by virtue of the internal-revenue laws; and the receipts of the proper officers of such depositary to a collector for the money deposited by him shall be a sufficient voucher for such collector in the settlement of his accounts at the Treasury Department.

DEPOSIT OF POSTMASTERS.

(Section 3847 of the Revised Statutes.)

Any postmaster, having public money belonging to the Government, at an office within a county where there are no designated depositaries, treasurers of mints, or Treasurer, or assistant treasurers of the United States, may deposit the same at his own risk and in his official capacity, in any national bank in the town, city, or county where the said postmaster resides, etc. [The remainder of the section forbids taking interest, etc.]

TRANSFERS OF POST-OFFICE MONEY.

(Section 3641 of the Revised Statutes.)

The Postmaster-General may transfer money belonging to the postal service between the Treasurer, assistant treasurers, and designated depositaries, at his discretion, and as the safety of the public money and the convenience of the service may require.

DISBURSING OFFICERS.

(Section 3620 of the Revised Statutes.)

It shall be the duty of every disbursing officer having any public money intrusted to him for disbursement, to deposit the same with the Treasurer or some one of the assistant treasurers of the United States, and to draw for the same only as it may be required for payments to be made by him in pursuance of law (and draw for the same only in favor of the persons to whom payment is made); and all transfers from the Treasurer of the United States to a disbursing officer shall be by draft or warrant on the Treasury or an assistant treasurer of the United

States. In places, however, where there is no treasurer or assistant treasurer, the Secretary of the Treasury may, when he deems it essential to the public interest, specially authorize in writing the deposit of such public money in any other public depositary, or, in writing, authorize the same to be kept in any other manner, and under such rules and regulations as he may deem most safe and effectual to facilitate the payments to public creditors.

ACCOUNTS.

(Section 3622 of the Revised Statutes.)

Every officer or agent of the United States who receives public money which he is not authorized to retain as salary, pay, or emolument, shall render his accounts monthly. Such accounts, with the vouchers necessary to the correct and prompt settlement thereof, shall be sent by mail, or otherwise, to the bureau to which they pertain, within ten days after the expiration of each successive month, and, after examination there, shall be passed to the proper accounting officer of the Treasury for settlement. Disbursing officers of the navy shall, however, render their accounts and vouchers direct to the proper accounting officer of the Treasury. In case of the nonreceipt at the Treasury, or proper bureau, of any accounts within a reasonable and proper time thereafter, the officer whose accounts are in default shall be required to furnish satisfactory evidence of having complied with the provisions of this section. The Secretary of the Treasury may, if in his opinion the circumstances of the case justify and require it, extend the time hereinbefore prescribed for the rendition of accounts. Nothing herein contained shall, however, be construed to restrain the heads of any of the departments from requiring such other returns or reports from the officer or agent, subject to the control of such heads of departments as the public interest may require.

NATIONAL BANK DEPOSITARIES.

(Section 5153 of the Revised Statutes, act June 3, 1864, as amended March 3, 1901, and March 4, 1907.)

All national banking associations, designated for that purpose by the Secretary of the Treasury, shall be depositaries of public money, under such regulations as may be prescribed by the Secretary; and they may also be employed as financial agents of the Government; and they shall perform all such reasonable duties, as depositaries of public money and financial agents of the Government, as may be required of them. The Secretary of the Treasury shall require the associations thus designated to give satisfactory security, by the deposit of United States bonds and otherwise, for the safe-keeping and prompt payment of the public money deposited with them, and for the faithful performance of their duties as financial agents of the Government: *Provided*, That the Secretary shall, on or before the first January of each year, make a public statement of the securities required during that year for such deposits. And every association so designated as receiver or depositary of the public money shall take and receive at par all of the national currency bills, by whatever association issued, which have been paid into the Government for internal revenue, or for loans or stocks: *Provided*, That the Secretary of the Treasury shall distribute the deposits herein provided for, as far as practicable, equitably between the different States and sections.

INTEREST ON PUBLIC DEPOSITS.

(Act May 30, 1908.)

That all national banking associations designated as regular depositaries of public money shall pay upon all special and additional deposits made by the Secretary of the Treasury in such depositaries, and all such associations designated as temporary depositaries of public money shall pay upon all sums of public money deposited in such associations interest at such rate as the Secretary of the Treasury may prescribe, not less, however, than one per centum per annum upon the average monthly amount of such deposits: *Provided, however,* That nothing contained in this act shall be construed to change or modify the obligation of any association or any of its officers for the safe-keeping of public money: *Provided further,* That the rate of interest charged upon such deposits shall be equal and uniform throughout the United States.

PENALTY FOR UNAUTHORIZED DEPOSIT OF PUBLIC MONEY.

(Act June 14, 1866, 14 Stat. L., 64.)

Every disbursing officer of the United States who deposits any public money intrusted to him in any place or in any manner except as authorized by law, or converts to his own use in any way whatever, or loans with or without interest, or for any purpose not prescribed by law withdraws from the Treasurer or any assistant treasurer, or any authorized depositary, or for any purpose not prescribed by law transfers or applies any portion of the public money intrusted to him, is, in every such act, deemed guilty of an embezzlement of the money so deposited, converted, loaned, withdrawn, transferred, or applied; and shall be punished by imprisonment with hard labor for a term not less than one year nor more than ten years, or by a fine of not more than the amount embezzled or less than one thousand dollars, or by both such fine and imprisonment.

PENALTY FOR UNAUTHORIZED RECEIPT OR USE OF PUBLIC MONEY.

(Act June 14, 1866, 14 Stat. L., 65, as amended February 3, 1879.)

Every banker, broker, or other person not an authorized depositary of public moneys, who knowingly receives from any disbursing officer, or collector of internal revenue, or other agent of the United States, any public money on deposit, or by way of loan or accommodation, with or without interest, or otherwise than in payment of a debt against the United States, or who uses, transfers, converts, appropriates, or applies any portion of the public money for any purpose not prescribed by law, and every president, cashier, teller, director, or other officer of any bank or banking association, who violates any of the provisions of this section, is guilty of an act of embezzlement of the public money so deposited, loaned, transferred, used, converted, appropriated, or applied, and shall be punished as prescribed in section fifty-four hundred and eighty-eight.

3.

Issue and Redemption of Currency.

Treasury Department,
Office Treasurer of the United States,

December 6, 1909.

Department Circular No. 66. }
Treasurer's Office, No. 79. }

The following regulations govern the issue and redemption of the paper currency and the gold, silver, and minor coin of the United States and the redemption of national-bank notes by the Treasurer of the United States:

I. Issue of United States paper currency.

1. New United States currency is sent in return for United States currency unfit for circulation, national-bank notes, subsidiary silver coin, or minor coin received for redemption.

2. Silver certificates are issued by the Treasurer or any assistant treasurer upon a deposit of standard silver dollars.

3. Gold certificates are issued by the Treasurer or any assistant treasurer upon a deposit of gold coin.

II. Issue of gold coin.

4. Gold coin is issued in redemption of gold certificates, United States notes, and Treasury notes of 1890, by the Treasurer or any assistant treasurer.

III. ISSUE OF STANDARD SILVER DOLLARS AND SUBSIDIARY SILVER COIN.

5. Standard silver dollars are issued by the Treasurer or any assistant treasurer in redemption of silver certificates or Treasury notes of 1890, and will be sent by express at the expense of the consignee.

6. Subsidiary silver coin is issued upon a deposit of United States currency or national-bank notes with the Treasurer or any assistant treasurer or national-bank depositary, and the coin will be sent by express from the nearest subtreasury at the expense of the Government for transportation, or by registered mail at the risk of the consignee, postage and registration free. Subsidiary silver coin is also issued for drafts sent to the Treasurer of the United States in Washington or the assistant treasurer in New York, payable in their respective cities to the order of the officer to whom sent. Drafts on New York must be collectible through the clearing house, and should be drawn to the order of the assistant treasurer of the United States, New York, and mailed directly to that officer.

4.

PUBLIC MONEYS AND OFFICIAL CHECKS OF UNITED
STATES DISBURSING OFFICERS.

TREASURY DEPARTMENT,
OFFICE OF THE SECRETARY,
December 7, 1906.

Department Circular No. 102. }
Division of Public Moneys. }

In accordance with the provisions of the above sections,
any public money advanced to disbursing officers of the
United States must be deposited immediately to their respective credits, with either the United States Treasurer,
some assistant treasurer, or by special direction of the
Secretary of the Treasury, with a national-bank depositary
nearest or most convenient, except—

1. Any disbursing officer of the War Department, specially authorized by the Secretary of War, when stationed
on the extreme frontier or at places far remote from such
depositaries, may keep, at his own risk, such moneys as
may be intrusted to him for disbursement.

2. Any officer receiving money remitted to him upon
specific estimates may disburse it accordingly, without
waiting to place it in a depositary, provided the payments
are due and he prefers this method to that of drawing
checks.

Any checks drawn by a disbursing officer upon moneys
thus deposited must be in favor of the party, by name, to
whom the payment is to be made, and payable to "order,"

with these exceptions: (1) To make payments of amounts not exceeding $20; (2) to make payments at a distance from a depositary; and (3) to make payments of fixed salaries due at a certain period; in either of which cases any disbursing officer may draw his check in favor of himself, or "order," for such amount as may be necessary for such payment, but in the first and last named cases the check must be drawn not more than two days before the payments become due.

Any disbursing officer or agent drawing checks on moneys deposited to his official credit must state on the face or back of each check the object or purpose to which the avails are to be applied, except upon checks issued in payment of individual pensions, the special form of such checks indicating sufficiently the character of disbursement. If the object or purpose for which any check of a public disbursing officer is drawn is not stated thereon, as required, or if any reason exists for suspecting fraud, the office or bank on which such check is drawn will refuse its payment.

Such statement may be made in brief form, but must clearly indicate the object of the expenditure, as, for instance, "pay," "pay roll," or "payment of troops," adding the fort or station, "purchase of subsistence," or other supplies; "on account of construction," mentioning the fortification or other public work for which the payment is made; "payments under $20," etc.

Any check drawn by a United States disbursing officer payable to himself, or "order," "to make payments of amounts not exceeding $20 each," under the provisions of this circular must bear indorsed thereon the names of the persons to whom the amount drawn is to be paid, or be accompanied by a list or schedule, made a part of the check, containing the same information.

The object or purpose to which the avails are to be applied in case of any check drawn by a disbursing officer of the army for an amount to be retained in his possession by authority of the Secretary of War, given under the provisions of this circular, or by any disbursing officer given such special authority by the Secretary of the Treasury, under the provisions of section 3620, Revised Statutes of the United States, must be clearly indicated by a statement on the check that it is to obtain cash to hold in personal possession, and date of authority given so to hold funds. Checks will not be returned to the drawer after their payment, but will be retained by the depositary, arranged separately by officers and consecutively by number and date convenient for ready reference, as they are liable to be called for by the department at any time as evidence of proper payment. The depositary will furnish each disbursing officer with a detailed monthly statement of his account.

All disbursing clerks and agents of the executive departments, independent offices, and commissions, and offices under and part of the executive departments located in the District of Columbia, to prevent carrying unnecessary balances of cash, are directed to deposit, on or before the 5th and 20th of each month, with the Treasurer of the United States, to their official credit subject to check, any and all balances of cash drawn to meet pay rolls and remaining in their hands; and thereafter, until the next regular pay day, to make payments appropriate to be made by check and not in cash.

Deposits to the credit of the Treasurer of the United States on account of repayment of disbursing funds must be made with the office or bank in which such funds are to the credit of the disbursing officer. Disbursing officers are not authorized to transfer funds standing to their credit with one depositary to their credit with another depositary; such transfers will be made by the Secretary of the Treasury upon the requests of the heads of the departments under which the officers are serving.

No allowance will be made to any disbursing officer for expenses charged for collecting money on checks.

Whenever any disbursing officer of the United States shall cease to act in that capacity he will at once inform the Secretary of the Treasury whether he has any public funds to his credit in any office or bank, and, if so, what checks, if any, he has drawn against the same, which are still outstanding and unpaid. Until satisfactory information of this character shall have been furnished, the whole amount of such moneys will be held to meet the payment of his checks properly payable therefrom.

In case of the death, resignation, or removal of any disbursing officer, checks previously drawn by him will be paid from the funds to his credit, unless such checks have been drawn more than four months before their presentation, or reasons exist for suspecting fraud. Any check previously drawn by him and not presented for payment within four months of its date will not be paid until its correctness shall have been attested by the Comptroller of the Treasury or his chief clerk.

Every disbursing officer, when opening his first account, before issuing any checks will furnish the depositary on whom checks are drawn with his official signature, duly verified by some officer whose signature is known to the depositary.

5.

The Assembling of Disbursing Officers' Checks and Vouchers and the Verification of their Balances in the Offices of the Auditors of the Treasury Department.

July 29, 1907.

1907, Department Circular No. 52.

To disbursing officers:

1. The practice of requiring public creditors to receipt for moneys in advance of actual payment will be discontinued after September 30, 1907. No payments after said date shall be evidenced by a receipt, except where receipts are required either by law or contract, unless such payments are made in cash, that is, currency.

2. After September 30, 1907, no receipt for moneys paid by disbursing officers' checks shall be required or taken by disbursing officers except where receipts are required either by law or contract. Disbursing officers will note on vouchers for check payments the date, number, name of payee, and amount of the check and the name of the depositary on whom drawn.

3. All vouchers for payment by disbursing officers, except those required by law to be verified by affidavit, and the expense accounts of the civilian officers, employees, and agents of the Government, which shall be verified by affidavit as heretofore, shall be certified by the claimant as correct and just, except that vouchers for personal compensation for services rendered under the personal supervision of some administrative officer and so certified by him, need not be certified by the claimant, provided

the voucher describes specifically the position, the rate of compensation, and the period covered.

4. Disbursing officers shall identify their official checks with the vouchers upon which they are issued in payment by noting on each check the number or other necessary description of the voucher. (See also paragraph 9.)

5. Disbursing officers shall make cash payments only in cases authorized by Treasury Department Circular No. 102, dated December 7, 1906, and then in only those cases where the payment is made by the disbursing officer in person, or by his deputy, and the exchange of money and the receipt therefor is simultaneous.

6. When payments are made in cash, that is, currency, they must be evidenced by a statement of such fact in the receipt and in substantially the following form (except upon pay rolls which shall embody instructions calculated to insure the receipt thereof only under the conditions laid down in the form given in this paragraph):

"Received from ...... in person, or by his deputy, and in cash, the sum of .... dollars and ...... cents, in full payment of voucher No. ...., account ...."

7. Unless required by law, vouchers shall not be taken in exact duplicate, triplicate, etc. Only one copy of a voucher, the original, shall contain signed certifications, approvals, and receipts. As many copies, in memorandum form, duly authenticated if desired, may be taken as administrative requirements demand.

Each officer or agent required by law to render accounts for public moneys and having such public moneys on deposit to his official credit shall, as soon after September 30, 1907, as practicable, forward to the Auditor of the

Treasury Department by whom his accounts are settled a certified statement of his checks, giving number, date, and amount of each, for each open depositary account outstanding and unpaid at the close of business September 30, 1907. Such statements will not thereafter be required.

9. On and after October 1, 1907, all disbursing officers who, for any reason (e. g., separate bonds, etc.), are required to render separate and distinct accounts to the Auditors of the Treasury Department, shall keep separate and distinct accounts of their funds in the Government depositaries, and shall unmistakably designate such *several depositary accounts* on their vouchers, requisitions, deposits, and accounts current.

10. Disbursing officers keeping and rendering to the Auditors of the Treasury Department separate and distinct accounts shall, as soon as practicable after the receipt of depositary statements for the month of September, 1907, designate to such depositaries the amounts of their balances, which shall be severally credited to the separate and distinct accounts herein provided for, and accompany such designation with a copy of each list of outstanding and unpaid checks required to be forwarded to the several Auditors of the Treasury Department by paragraph 8 of this circular.

11. When partial payments are made on account of salaries or wages and claim for credit for the same is deferred until completed payment for the period has been made, the amounts of such partial payments constitute a part of the acknowledged balance, and the total of such amounts, together with the facts, shall be set out in the analysis of balance provided by the standard form pre-

scribed by the Treasury Department Circular No. 46, dated May 24, 1906.

12. The balances acknowledged by disbursing officers and their analyses thereof must actually represent the state of their business at the close of the last day for which the accounts are rendered. They must so order their business that they may, when called upon so to do, close their accounts and analyze their acknowledged balances.

13. All transactions coming within the time covered by an account shall be reported therein. No payments or collections not actually made during the period of an account shall be included therein. The provisions of this paragraph do not apply to partial payments of salaries or wages which are provided for by paragraph 11 hereof.

14. If disbursing officers do not for any reason receive from their depositaries the monthly statements required to be rendered to them by paragraph 16 of this circular in time for them to analyze their balances in the manner contemplated by the standard form of account current prescribed by Treasury Department Circular No. 46 dated May 24, 1906, they shall not delay the rendition of their accounts so as to make them delinquent, but shall compute their net balances from their check stubs and state that such balances are so computed, together with a report of the cause of their failure to compute such balances in the prescribed manner.

15. Each officer disbursing in part by cash and drawing his official checks to obtain cash to make payments shall render with his account current a subsidiary cash account, the balance of which should agree to be reconciled with his cash as shown by his analysis of balance with his account current.

To the Treasurer and assistant treasurers of the United States and designated depositaries:

16. The Treasurer of the United States, each assistant treasurer of the United States, and each designated depositary (herein elsewhere collectively termed "depositaries") shall render monthly statements to officers having public funds on deposit to their official credit.

17. Depositaries shall also render statements to officers having public funds on deposit to their official credit upon request of said officers to enable them to close their accounts, and to inspecting and administrative officers upon their request when engaged in the duly authorized inspection of accounts.

18. Depositaries shall keep separate accounts with and render separate statements to officers, as required by paragraphs 16 and 17 hereof, corresponding to the accounts rendered by such officers to the several auditors of the Treasury Department. (See pars. 9 and 10.) Checks drawn prior to October 1, 1907, shall be charged to the account indicated by the list of outstanding checks required to be furnished depositaries by paragraph 10 of the circular. Checks so drawn, that is, prior to October 1, 1907, and paid after September 30, 1907, shall be included in current depositary statements, but the paid checks will be retained by depositaries as provided by Treasury Department Circular No. 102, dated December 7, 1906.

19. The statements provided for by paragraphs 16 and 17 hereof shall show a full and true account, including the date, number, and amount of each check paid, and the

date and amount of each item placed to the officers' official credit during the period of such statement.

20. The said statements shall always be rendered to officers in time for them to use the information contained therein in analyzing their balances in the manner provided by the standard account current form prescribed by Treasury Department Circular No. 46, dated May 24, 1906. Depositaries will so order their business that they will be enabled to comply with the provisions of this paragraph.

21. Depositaries will forward to the Secretary of the Treasury (Division of Public Moneys) a copy of each statement rendered to officers having public funds on deposit to their official credit.

22. Beginning with the month of October, 1907, the copies of statements herein required to be forwarded to the Secretary of the Treasury (Division of Public Moneys) *shall be accompanied by the paid checks scheduled therein*, except checks drawn prior to October 1, 1907, which will be retained by the depositary as provided in paragraph 18 hereof.

23. The copies of statements and paid checks shall be forwarded, as herein provided, to the Secretary of the Treasury (Division of Public Moneys), together with a list of balances standing to the official credit of disbursing and other officers of the United States.

24. To prevent fraud or the misuse of paid checks the depositaries will immediately, upon the payment of a check, mark, stamp, or otherwise plainly indicate thereon the fact of its payment.

To the Division of Public Moneys:

25. The Division of Public Moneys shall, upon receipt of the list of balances standing to the official credit of disbursing and other officers of the United States, accompanied by the individual monthly depositary statements and paid checks required to be forwarded by paragraphs 21, 22, and 23, check the individual balances shown by the individual monthly statements against the list of balances, and promptly transmit the individual monthly statements and the paid checks to the Auditor of the Treasury Department charged with the settlement of the account to which they pertain.